Transport for Suburbia

Transport for Suburbia

Beyond the Automobile Age

Paul Mees

publishing for a sustainable future

London • Washington, DC

First published by Earthscan in the UK and USA in 2010
Reprinted 2010 (twice)

ISBN: 978-1-84407-740-3

Typeset by JS Typesetting Ltd, Porthcawl, Mid Glamorgan
Cover design by Rogue Four Design www.roguefour.co.uk

Earthscan Ltd, Dunstan House, 14a St Cross Street, London EC1N 8XA, UK
Earthscan LLC, 1616 P Street, NW, Washington, DC 20036, USA
Earthscan publishes in association with the International Institute for Environment and
Development

For more information on Earthscan publications, see www.earthscan.co.uk or write to
earthinfo@earthscan.co.uk

A catalogue record for this book is available from the British Library

Library of Congress Cataloging-in-Publication Data
Mees, Paul, 1961–
    Transport for suburbia : beyond the automobile age / Paul Mees.
        p. cm.
    Includes bibliographical references and index.
    ISBN 978-1-84407-740-3 (hbk.)
 1. Urban transportation. 2. Suburbs. 3. Transportation–Planning. I. Title.
    HE305.M43 2009
    388.409173'3–dc22
                                    2009018984

At Earthscan we strive to minimize our environmental impacts and carbon footprint
through reducing waste, recycling and offsetting our CO_2 emissions, including those
created through publication of this book. For more details of our environmental policy,
see www.earthscan.co.uk.

This book was printed and bound,
in the UK by TJ International Ltd.
The paper used is FSC certified.

Mixed Sources
Product group from well-managed
forests and other controlled sources
www.fsc.org Cert no. SGS-COC-2482
© 1996 Forest Stewardship Council
FSC

To my parents, Roma and Tom Mees,
on their 50th wedding anniversary

Contents

List of Figures and Tables

FIGURES

TABLES

Preface

This book is for people concerned about the environmental and social costs of automobile-dominated cities. There are plenty of books that outline these costs, and the other reasons for moving beyond the automobile age, but few that offer practical suggestions about how the move can be made. We need alternatives to the car, and we need them now, because problems like climate change and insecure oil supplies are urgent.

Public transport is not the only alternative to the car – indeed, walking and cycling are the only truly sustainable transport modes – but it is a necessary ingredient in a post-automobile future. Unless public transport is so convenient that it offers real competition to the car, then schemes to promote walking and cycling, and restrain car use, will founder. But providing first-rate public transport seems too hard in most English-speaking countries: the Swiss and some other Europeans can manage it, but we can't. And the task seems impossible in the spread-out suburbs and ex-urbs where most population growth is taking place.

My central argument is that the public transport problem is easier to solve than people think. We don't need to demolish our suburbs and rebuild them at many times their current densities; nor do we need a fundamental transformation in human consciousness, however desirable that might be for other reasons. The high-quality public transport found in places like Switzerland has been adapted to serve the existing urban environment, and a population that shares our faults and failings.

The critical ingredients of first-class, 'European-style' public transport are planning and politics, the same factors behind public transport failures across much of the English-speaking world. The idea that compact cities, or consciousness-raising, or the free market can provide a substitute for getting policies and planning right has been widespread across the 'Anglosphere' for at least two decades. The results have not been promising. It's time for a new approach: this book outlines that approach and the grounds we have for believing it can work.

In putting these ideas together, I have had the assistance of a great many people, too many to name. But I do want to mention some.

First among them is Erica Cervini, who has supported me through the whole process that produced this book, dating back to my PhD and before.

I also want to thank my students, who have challenged and educated me, helping produce and test many of the ideas that appear in the following chapters. In particular, I acknowledge the contributions of five research students whose work I have used extensively: Sami Al-Dubikhi (Ottawa, Vancouver and Perth), Tim Petersen (Zurich and Graubunden), Eden Sorupia (Curitiba, Foz do Iguacu and Graubunden), John Stone (Vancouver and Perth) and Wei Wang (Singapore).

I was helped to write this book by part of the proceeds of an Australian Research Council grant (LP0455266). This enabled me to employ Rachel Funari, who provided invaluable research assistance. Thanks to Sami Al-Dubikhi for permission to use Figure 7.1, to the *Zürcher Verkehrsverbund* for Figure 8.1, and to Truls Lange of Civitas Consultants for Figure 9.1.

I was part way through writing this book when Melbourne University, where I had worked for ten years, charged me with academic misconduct for criticizing the officials responsible for the failed privatization of Melbourne's public transport. My observations, made at a public forum, were along similar lines to those in Chapter 6, although expressed in more robust language. The university podcast my talk; the Department of Transport complained and asked for the podcast to be removed.

The university complied with the request and, without consulting me, prosecuted me for 'bringing it into disrepute'. The university's 'investigator' rejected my defence, which was that I had reported the truth I'd uncovered in my academic research. He held that since my comments had offended the official who complained, it did not matter whether they were true or not. When this was reported in the press, in May 2008, I am relieved to record that the Melbourne community showed a much stronger interest in truth than the university.

As I have not had a chance to do so, I would like to thank those academic colleagues and members of the public who supported my right to speak my mind, including those who did so despite disagreeing with what I said. I also thank my new colleagues in the Environment and Planning Program at RMIT, for welcoming a political refugee from the other end of Swanston Street.

Good public transport requires good planning and policy, along with honest and competent public administration. These things do not come about by accident; they require an active, informed community that demands high standards from its politicians and bureaucrats, and insists that policies be based on evidence rather than spin. The truth really does matter, no matter how upsetting it is to the powers that be.

Paul Mees
Melbourne
August 2009

List of Abbreviations

ABS	Australian Bureau of Statistics
ALRT	Automated Light Rapid Transit
AMPO	Auckland Metropolitan Planning Organisation
ARA	Auckland Regional Authority
ARC	Auckland Regional Council
ARPA	Auckland Regional Planning Authority
ARTA	Auckland Regional Transport Authority
BCC	Brisbane City Council
BRT	Bus Rapid Transit
CABE	Commission on Architecture and the Built Environment
CATS	Chicago Area Transportation Study
CBD	central business district
CEC	Commission of the European Communities
COE	Certificate of Entitlement (Singapore)
CTA	Chicago Transit Authority
DfT	Department for Transport, UK
EEA	European Environment Agency
ECMT	European Conference of Ministers of Transport
ETH	*Eidgenössische Technische Hochschule*/Federal Institute of Technology (Zurich)
GM	General Motors
GVRD	Greater Vancouver Regional District
HOV	High Occupancy Vehicle
IEA	International Energy Agency
IPCC	Intergovernmental Panel on Climate Change
LTA	Land Transport Authority (Singapore)
MMBW	Melbourne & Metropolitan Board of Works
MMTB	Melbourne and Metropolitan Tramways Board
MTA	Metropolitan Transit Authority (Melbourne)
OECD	Organisation for Economic Co-operation and Development
ONS	Office for National Statistics, UK

OPEC   Organization of the Petroleum Exporting Countries
PE   Pacific Electric Railway (Los Angeles region)
PRT   personal rapid transit
PTC   Public Transport Corporation (Melbourne)
PWC   Public Works Committee, Queensland
RATP   *Régie Autonome des Transports Parisiens*/Paris public transport agency
RCEP   Royal Commission on Environmental Pollution (UK)
RhB   *Rhätische Bahn*/Rhaetian Railway (Graubunden)
RIT   *Rede Integrada de Transporte*/Integrated Transport Network (Curitiba)
S-Bahn *Schnellbahn*, or fast city train (Germany, Austria and Switzerland)
SBB   *Schweizerische Bundesbahnen*/Swiss Federal Railways
STA   State Transit Authority (NSW, Australia)
S-Tog   Copenhagen S-Bahn
SURS   Singapore Underground Road System
TfL   Transport for London
TTC   Toronto Transit Commission
UBC   University of British Columbia
UN   United Nations
URBS   *Urbanização de Curitiba*/Curitiba municipal transport department
VBSH   *Verkehrsbetriebe Schaffhausen*/Schaffhausen municipal public transport agency
VBZ   *Verkehrsbetriebe Zürich*/Zurich municipal public transport agency
ZVV   *Zürcher Verkehrsverbund*/Zurich regional public transport agency

Public Transport 101

MONASH UNIVERSITY

The second university of the Australian city of Melbourne celebrated its 50th anniversary in 2008. Since the passage of its enabling legislation in 1958, Monash University has educated over 200,000 students at its campus in suburban Clayton, granting degrees in disciplines ranging from medicine to literature. But regardless of their academic discipline, most Monash students over the half-century have been educated in one unofficial common subject. This subject could be called Public Transport 101, and it has been offered continuously since the Clayton campus opened on 11 March 1961.

Sir John Monash, the Australian engineer and general after whom the University is named, spent much of his early career building railways. In military and civilian life, Monash demanded the highest standards of planning, organization and delivery. He might not have been impressed had he tried to reach the university named after him by public transport. To do so, one takes a suburban train to Huntingdale Station, some 17km from the city centre. From there, the campus is just over 2km away by privately operated bus.

Let's visit Huntingdale Station in the first week of the academic year and join the students taking Public Transport 101.

The most popular train reaches Huntingdale at 8:40 am, which should leave plenty of time to reach campus for the first lectures at 9:00 am. The Clayton campus is home to 32,000 staff and students, and even though most drive, that still means around 200 alight from the train. They must queue to leave the station, as the single exit is a narrow ramp, leading to a cramped subway. Passengers emerge into the station car park, which must be crossed in the open. It's raining, so they cop the full force of the weather.

Past the car park is a busy road. On the other side are two bus stops, one for each route that travels to Monash. Each stop is in a different street, with a blind corner in between, so if a passenger waits at one and the first bus comes to the other, they will miss the bus. There is no such problem today: the 8:35 am bus is still waiting, as a long queue of passengers from the previous train boards, one by one, each required to insert a ticket into a validating machine. Eventually the bus departs, ten minutes late and packed to the gunwales, leaving dozens of passengers behind. They are joined by those from the 8:40 train. As the shelter at the stop only holds five people, everyone else waits in the rain; some take refuge among cars parked in the undercroft of a nearby factory. The 8:46 bus arrives and eventually leaves, full, at 9. The last passengers from the 8:40 train reach Monash University at half past nine.

At quieter times, the problem is the opposite of overcrowding. Some students stay back at night as the campus libraries are open late, while students living on campus often go out at night and come home through Huntingdale. Because the bus and train timetables are not co-ordinated, waits can be up to half an hour. The main bus stop is in a laneway between the blank concrete wall of a road overpass and the blank brick wall of a factory. Students are understandably afraid to wait there after dark.

A visiting Canadian academic colleague returned from a trip to Monash fuming. The squalid facilities, the long walk in the open and the lack of timetable coordination astonished her. The visitor was from York University in Toronto, which is of similar age and size to Monash, and also a few kilometres from the nearest station. Dedicated 'university rocket' express shuttles leave every two minutes (the frequency drops to every two minutes 15 seconds in the off-peak)[1] from the top of the escalators serving the station platform. As explained in Chapter 6, there are no delays from ticket checking as the bus terminal is inside the station fare gates. The Toronto Transit Commission is currently planning to extend the rail line to York University.

My colleague could not understand why things were so much worse at a place that in other respects was so similar. 'How long has this been going on?' she asked me. The answer is: since Monash opened in 1961. For many years, the main bus route and the train service both ran every half-hour during the evening: as the bus actually ran in the evening, it was regarded as good by Melbourne standards. Each bus reached the station two minutes after the corresponding train left, ensuring a 28-minute wait for the next train – which was even helpfully shown on the timetable. This continued until 1990, when the bus company, citing low demand, scrapped most evening services.

I told the story of the bus missing the train in my 2000 book *A Very Public Solution*, but apparently nobody in Melbourne noticed, because in 2006 the saga was repeated. A second bus route, called 'Smart Bus', was introduced between Huntingdale Station and the university, as part of a government response to complaints about Melbourne's privatized, but state-subsidized, public transport. Smart Buses provide the very best Melbourne has to offer: they even run seven days a week – which is handy because the Monash library is open every day, including Sunday. The new Smart Bus ran every half hour on Sunday mornings, just like the train, with buses departing Huntingdale at 4 and 34 minutes past the hour. As trains reached the station at 7 and 37 past the hour, each bus missed the nearest train by three minutes. After 7 pm, trains arrived three minutes earlier – at exactly the time the buses left. Since even an Olympic sprinter would take two minutes to reach the bus stop from the station, all this ensured was that passengers could view the departing bus from the station platform, before waiting half an hour for the next one.

This story does have a happier ending. I incorporated the printed Smart Bus timetable, which actually showed the buses and trains missing each other, into a presentation for the Australian Government's Garnaut Climate Change Review. My presentation was placed on the review's website, where it embarrassed the bus company into changing the timetable. Smart Buses now connect with trains at Huntingdale on Sunday mornings and evenings, although not during the day or most of the rest of the week. The interchange facilities remain as appalling as ever.

So what have 200,000 Monash graduates learned in Public Transport 101? Before the end of first semester, the crowding problems at Huntingdale ease as students begin to desert public transport and drive cars. By graduation, nearly all of them are driving to campus. The student environment office helps them by organizing car pooling: even it has given up on public transport. The Monash Clayton campus is surrounded by a sea of parked cars, and parking shortages are a constant subject of on-campus discussion.

These same students are among the most environmentally aware section of the community, concerned about issues like pollution and global warming. They are avid followers of the Garnaut Review's warnings about the need to reduce carbon emissions, including those from transport.[2] Monash students take courses on climate change, insecure oil supplies and other constraints on a car-dominated future. They learn that a sudden interruption to supplies of affordable oil, or a serious attempt to reduce carbon emissions from transport, would cripple the university and the metropolis of Melbourne. Some of the more curious ask why their city and campus are not better prepared for the future. Why has public transport to campus been so hopeless for so many years, and why is nothing being done about it?

The answer students at Monash and other Australian universities most commonly receive is that their parents' housing preferences are to blame. Urban density is the major cause of automobile dependence, so public transport problems can't be fixed until Melburnians abandon their separate houses and backyards, and begin living in apartments like Europeans.

STERNENBERG

Nobody in Sternenberg lives in an apartment. The 349 residents of the highest and remotest municipality in the Canton, or State, of Zurich prize their rural lifestyle. Sternenberg's rustic charms were celebrated by its most famous resident, the poet Jakob Stutz, who lived there from 1841 to 1857 after being convicted on a 'morals charge' in his previous home town. In Stutz's time, the municipality had 1400 residents, but rural depopulation reduced this to a low-point of 297 by the 1980 census. People live on farms or in tiny hamlets of three or four dwellings scattered across the municipality's 9km². The village centre is a few houses grouped around the picturesque 1706 church. Farming is still important, but so is tourism, particularly summer hiking along the Jakob Stutz Way and other trails.[3]

In recent years, the population has begun growing again, thanks to commuters with jobs in the City of Zurich and its suburbs. The majority of workers are still employed locally, mainly in rural industries, but nearly half now travel to jobs outside the municipality. This reflects a pattern seen across the Canton of Zurich and indeed across Europe: the City of Zurich, which houses a third of the canton's 1.3 million residents, has been losing people since the 1960s, while suburban and rural populations are booming.[4]

The church at Sternenberg is 42km from the centre of Zurich, but because of the mountainous terrain, the route by road or rail is longer. It takes an hour by train to reach the village of Bauma from Zurich's main railway station, and then another 15 minutes by bus up the hairpin bends of the Sternenberg-Strasse.

Of the 171 municipalities making up Canton Zurich, Sternenberg has the worst public transport service – because it's the only one without an urbanized population of 300, the minimum required for regular-interval, all-day public transport (see Chapter 8).[5] Bauma, with just over 1000 residents, has two trains an hour every day of the year, from 6:00 am to midnight, with an hourly all-night bus service on Fridays and Saturdays. Of course, if Sternenberg was in Australia or the UK it would have no public transport at all, and Bauma would be lucky to see a bus a day.

There are seven buses to Sternenberg each weekday, five on normal weekends and seven on summer Sundays and holidays. Each Sunday bus leaves from outside Bauma station at 24 minutes past the hour, connecting with trains arriving at 20 past the hour. The bus calls at the church, dropping off hikers, then does a circuit of the main hamlets collecting locals before returning to Bauma to connect with an outward train. Once they board the bus, residents of Sternenberg don't need to worry about timetables. Each bus meets the train at Bauma, which in turn connects at the regional hub of Winterthur with another train to Zurich, as well as departures to Zurich Airport and major centres across the canton. Each of these trains is met by connecting bus services at stations en route, providing access to every place with more than 300 residents or jobs.

Sternenberg is about as car-dependent as it gets in Canton Zurich. Only 19 per cent of workers used public transport on census day in 2000; 10 per cent more walked or cycled. These figures are, however, much higher than the mode shares of 13 and 3 per cent respectively recorded for metropolitan Melbourne at the following year's Australian census.[6] They are also higher than every US metropolitan area except New York, and higher even than most British urban regions. Public transport is only the second-most popular mode for travel to work in Sternenberg, but its share of travel is increasing: Zurich is the only Swiss canton in which public transport's share of travel is growing, and the increase is occurring mainly in suburban and rural areas. Only 14 per cent of Sternenbergers took public transport to work in 1990. The shift away from the car that Zurich City achieved in the 1980s is now being repeated, admittedly on a more modest scale, in the rest of the canton.

So if the oil supply was suddenly interrupted, or carbon emissions from transport rationed, even rural areas of Canton Zurich could cope. Sternenberg has not yet moved beyond the automobile age, but it is ready if it needs to. And the hikers could keep coming.

DENSITY AS DESTINY

Nobody in Sternenberg thinks the population density is too low to justify an integrated, albeit basic, public transport service designed to make travel by car a choice instead of a necessity. But the dominant view in the much larger, denser metropolis of Melbourne is that suburban densities cannot support viable public transport. It's a local truism that transport policies that work in European cities could not possibly hold lessons for Australia.

Urban planners across Australia, the UK, the US, Canada and New Zealand insist that transport patterns are outcomes of urban form. The way to improve public transport is through compact cities, new urbanism, smart growth and transit-oriented design. In the words of one prominent New Urbanist, 'we have to earn our transit through urbanism.' There is much less interest in directly tackling transport policy, reflecting a mindset among planners that goes back decades. Transport planning is boring and mathematical; design is artistic and creative. Planners 'own' city design; transport means working with engineers and economists, who are much better at maths than us. Urban design is what we do; transport planning is what other people do.

Many transport planners are happy to agree with these arguments. Even Switzerland has powerful highway agencies that specialize in building new and expanded roads. The professionals who staff these agencies are intelligent enough to realize that, as communities become more concerned about the environment, questions will increasingly be asked about the wisdom of continued large-scale road-building. The notion that urban form, rather than transport policy, determines transport outcomes is convenient for these bodies. It can also suit those responsible for providing public transport, because it pins the blame for poor services on suburban residents rather than public transport providers.

For two decades, the Australian capital, Canberra, was racked by controversy about a proposal to build a freeway through the Canberra Nature Park. Hardly surprisingly, environmentalists and concerned citizens were horrified. They argued that the funds would be better spent tackling Canberra's woeful public transport. In 2001, a parliamentary inquiry was called to resolve the controversy. It conceded that the freeway was environmentally disastrous, but argued that there was no alternative:

> *The committee is struck by [the] major differences between the transport studies with a car-oriented approach and those making public transport pre-eminent ... the car-oriented strategy is associated with a dispersed city of mostly low rise buildings; whereas the public transport approach is associated with fairly dense 'urban villages'... The committee is not convinced that the [Canberra] community is ready, or would understand the need, for town planning changes of the kind associated with the public transport strategy... These town planning considerations lead the committee to conclude that the car-oriented strategy ... continues to be appropriate.[7]*

The freeway went ahead in the face of legal challenges and protests, opening in 2008. Escalating construction costs helped create a financial crisis that led to closure of a fifth of Canberra's government schools. Within weeks of opening, the freeway was jammed with traffic, and the government announced that it would be doubled in width.

While the results of the committee's decision to give the green light to the freeway were disastrous, it is difficult to argue with the logic. If suburban densities in cities like Canberra really are too low for viable alternatives to the car, then we are in serious trouble, because large increases to the density of big cities take many decades, and may be politically impossible in a democratic society.

Suburbanization is now a global phenomenon. It may have been invented in the US – although Chapter 6 argues that Australians were the true pioneers – but it has been successfully exported. Europe's suburbs house the majority of the populations of their metropolitan regions, and account for most or all population growth. Suburban sprawl can be found across the continent, as the European Environment Agency notes in a 2006 report suggestively titled *Urban Sprawl in Europe: The ignored challenge.*[8] Employment is also decentralizing, and urban Europe is becoming increasingly poly-centric. Even if we wanted to see The End of Suburbia, as the title of a popular documentary suggests, this would require the rebuilding of entire urban regions – a task that might take a century even if it were affordable or politically possible.

The difficulty of the task can be seen in the glacial rate of progress in the two decades since ideas like new urbanism and the compact city became dominant among planners. The amount of new housing that has been built in accordance with these ideas is vanishingly small, but more importantly, there is little reliable evidence that it has produced any appreciable reduction in automobile use. The slide shows look great, but where are the data on mode share? The new urbanist solution risks becoming like the new religion lampooned by G. K. Chesterton back in the 1920s: 'it only manages to remain as the New Religion by always coming to-morrow and never to-day.'[9]

Meanwhile, most transport analysts argue that the task of providing effective public transport in spacious suburbs is impossible, and should be given up as hopeless; few have even contemplated attempting the task in the still more difficult terrain of rural towns and villages like Bauma and Sternenberg.

SOLUTIONS FOR SUBURBIA

The central argument of this book is that density is not destiny. Transport policy itself has a bigger impact on transport patterns than urban planners have realized, and suburbs don't have to be totally reliant on the car. Planners who insist that car dominance can only be addressed by impossibly large increases in density may actually be entrenching the problem they are trying to solve.

In recent years, problems like climate change and precarious oil supplies have led an increasing number of people to ask whether the end of the automobile age is at hand. As explained in Chapters 2 and 3, there are many good reasons to change course on urban transport. But problems like global warming and volatile oil prices are real and urgent: they can't wait decades for solutions – especially when those solutions are not backed by solid evidence of effectiveness.

There is an alternative, and Zurich is not the only example of it. In parts of Europe and some other places, the high-quality public transport previously found only in dense city centres is being extended to suburbs and even rural areas. Public transport networks which once catered only for peak-hour commuters have been reconfigured to serve cross-city, off-peak and – as we saw with the hikers of Sternenberg – even recreational trips. By providing a complete substitute for the car, high quality public transport networks also promote increased walking and, in some cases, cycling. A model of successful public transport network planning for low-density urban areas is emerging, with evidence of effectiveness to back it. This is a genuine success story which should be welcomed by urban planners and environmentalists.

But the story remains a secret. Most of the work building effective suburban public transport has been done by practising public transport planners, who don't have time to write books or travel the world showing PowerPoint slides. Transport academics have largely ignored the real-world success stories; prestigious journals are instead filled with endless reports on new technologies and the intricacies of mathematical modelling. Urban planners, as Chapter 4 explains, can't see the gains achieved because there is no accompanying development in the desirable new urbanist form. The dominant school of economists dislikes these success stories because they have not relied on the free market (see Chapter 5). Some environmentalists are so certain that cycling is the answer to the urban transport problem that they are not interested in hearing about public transport – or in many cases, walking (see Chapter 11). And for some critics, fixing public transport may be unattractive precisely because it is easier than demolishing suburbia: for these people, hating the suburbs has become a kind of moral crusade.

The main purpose of this book is to share the secret of successful suburban public transport. Chapters 6 to 8 examine a range of very different urban regions that have managed to provide effective public transport in low-density areas. All the successful cities have discovered what I call the 'network effect'. As Chapter 9 explains, this occurs when public transport imitates the flexibility of the car by knitting different routes and modes into a single, multi-modal network. Making transfers between the different routes near effortless enables the public transport network to mimic the 'go anywhere, anytime' flexibility of a road system. I argue that this is a genuinely new model of public transport planning that can be applied in most suburban environments, and in Chapters 10 and 11 discuss the policies required to bring it about.

Interestingly, the different cities discovered the network effect independently of one another. There have been no books or journals in which public transport planners can read about transfer-based networks. When the Norwegian transport planner Gustav Nielsen produced the HiTrans guides to providing high-quality public transport in smaller cities and regions, he reported that 'the literature search has not revealed any comprehensive studies or reports that have their main focus on the topic of public transport network design.'[10] Nielsen's HiTrans manuals are excellent resources, but something more comprehensive and widely available is also required; hence this book.

The book is intended for planners, but also for citizens. One of the most encouraging lessons from the success stories discussed here is the critical role played by citizens and their elected representatives in bringing about transport policy change. Technical expertise is very important, but technicians can become set in their ways and resistant to change, as the story of Auckland in the next chapter illustrates. Real innovation requires a creative tension between experts and the public.

This is not the first study to have used a comparative cities approach to shed light on transport policy questions. The tradition was pioneered in 1977 with J. Michael Thomson's *Great Cities and Their Traffic*, which examined road, public transport and land-use policies in cities across five continents. Thomson's book remains a classic, and his observations are as relevant today as three decades ago. Robert Cervero's *The Transit Metropolis* (1998) is a contemporary take on the comparative study, with a focus on innovative approaches to public transport. This book revisits some of the cities studied by Cervero and Thomson, with a direct focus on the question of creating public transport networks. Some of my conclusions back theirs, but as will be seen, there are also some key differences.

What follows is not a critique of new urbanism or the compact city. I am arguing that urban form has been used as an excuse for not directly tackling public transport service quality, but I am not suggesting that urban form has no influence. I am certainly not advocating deregulated land-use planning, or urban sprawl – in the original sense of scattered, unplanned fringe growth that is 'neither town nor country'. There are things land-use planners can do to encourage public transport and walking, and others that will discourage them, although not all of them are about population density. Many books have been written about these issues and I am not seeking to add to that literature. My argument is that these policies should be part of an integrated package of measures that include direct changes to transport, and will fail if they are pursued on their own.

My own attitudes to suburbs and transport have been shaped by my background. I grew up in suburban Melbourne, a long stone's-throw from Pinoak Court, Vermont South, better known to *Neighbours* viewers as Ramsay Street (apologies to North American readers, to whom this will mean nothing). This quintessential piece of post-World War II suburbia originated as a transit-oriented development: it grew up around the Glen Waverley rail line, and all the major shopping centres were adjacent to railway stations. When I was young, many of the fathers in our street could be seen each day making the long walk to and from the station, but over time the numbers doing so declined. In fact, it was fiendishly difficult to get around without a car, except to destinations along the train line, and even that required a long walk to the station. Monash was my local university, but was actually more difficult to reach than the older, more distant University of Melbourne in the city centre.

Most of my peers reacted rationally to these problems by buying cars as soon as they were legally able to drive. I was more stubborn, particularly once I became involved in debates over freeways in Melbourne. These debates were heated because the reservations set aside for the roads usually passed through parklands and river valleys, just like in Canberra. I read Thomson's *Great Cities*, which was particularly harsh in its judgement of both the quality and honesty of Melbourne's freeway planning, and wondered why we could not do better. Why was Melbourne not learning from the European cities that were moving away from the car towards first-rate public transport? The answer, I kept hearing, was density: because most Australians live in places like Ramsay Street, the car will be king forever.

This led me to ask whether there were any places where effective public transport and lower-density housing coexisted. My PhD compared Melbourne with Toronto and showed that similar densities had not prevented very different results. Since publishing this study in 2000 as *A Very Public Solution*, I have had the opportunity to study other cities that allow people to enjoy both backyards and quality public transport. Much of this work was carried out with postgraduate students, so what you will read is as much the result of their work as mine.

The public transport success stories outlined in this book are a very diverse group of cities, but they have striking elements in common. They suggest that there is a general model that can be used to provide effective public transport in suburban environments, a model that will help us move beyond the automobile age.

NOTES

1   TTC (2008, p67).
2   Garnaut (2008, ch. 21).
3   www.sternenberg.ch (accessed 30 August 2009).
4   www.statistik.zh.ch (accessed 30 August 2009).
5   Sternenberg has the second-smallest population of the canton's 171 municipalities. The smallest is Volken, with 268 residents at the 2000 census. It receives a regular service because it is on the road to the neighbouring village of Flaach, which has more than the designated minimum population.
6   Swiss Federal Statistical Office, 2000 Census, 'pendler' table A2A, Gemeinde Sternenberg (171); excluding those who did not travel to work ('kein arbeitsweg'). Melbourne figures from P. Mees et al (2007).
7   Standing Committee on Planning & Urban Services (2001, pp101–102).
8   EEA (2006).
9   Chesterton (1929, p69).
10 Nielsen (2005, p168).

2

The Automobile Age

HAPPY BIRTHDAY

The centenary of the automobile age should have been commemorated in 2008. The first Model T Ford went on sale on 1 October 1908, a fortnight after the General Motors Company was formed.[1] At this time, barely one US family in 40 owned an automobile: the car was essentially a plaything for the rich. Only 18 years later, in 1926, 'a staggering 19,000,000 of 23,400,000 families owned cars'[2] – at least half of them Model T Fords. Henry Ford used mass production to create an affordable, reliable car that could serve both urban and rural markets, and steadily reduced the selling price after introducing the assembly line in 1913. He became America's richest man.

Ford's assembly line led to other innovations that made him a national figure. While the new manufacturing techniques greatly increased productivity, they also made the work boring, contributing to high rates of staff turnover. Ford responded in 1914 by introducing a minimum wage of $5 a day, and cutting daily working hours to eight. This announcement was accompanied by an orchestrated flurry of publicity. It solved the labour problem, and made Ford a national and international celebrity. His advice was sought and offered on problems ranging from world peace to city planning.[3]

The automobile, along with the truck and the tractor, dramatically transformed rural life. The Model T had been specifically designed to operate on rough rural roads, and sold strongly among farmers. The trusty farm horse was rapidly displaced across the US, and isolation was reduced. Contemporary observers confidently predicted an end to the long-standing drift of population from rural to urban areas, but the mechanization of agriculture actually accelerated rural depopulation.[4]

The motor vehicle was also expected to transform urban life. Perhaps surprisingly, in light of subsequent history, improvements in the urban environment were the main benefits predicted. While horses posed few environmental problems in the countryside, in the confined spaces of cities the excreta from thousands of horses was an irritant and a health hazard. The electric tram had reduced the demand for horse-powered urban transport, but the car, the bus and the truck eliminated it, a measure that met with the universal approval of urban reformers. But the motor vehicle held out the prospect of more dramatic urban change: 'We shall solve the city problem by leaving the city', Ford declared.[5]

Affordable cars, higher wages and shorter working hours are the prerequisites for the model of urban development that came to characterize suburbs across the US. Higher-paid workers could aspire to own houses as well as cars, while shorter working hours allowed more time for commuting. Workers could trade off cramped inner city tenements for detached suburban homes, linked to workplaces and shops by the car. The new world pioneered by Ford made car-based suburbia possible, but was it inevitable? The connections are now so obvious that most observers think that the car and the car-based suburb displaced public transport and the high-density city as naturally as the motor vehicle displaced the farm horse. The mileage travelled by car across the US was only a quarter of that by rail in 1922; by 1925 it was twice as high, and by 1929 the ratio was four to one. Public transport patronage in the US declined continuously for many decades, apart from a brief recovery during World War II.[6] And as wages and car ownership rose in other countries, it looked as if the American transport trends would become universal.

Many urban planners thought the car-based city was not just inevitable but desirable. Bad housing in congested and crowded cities were the very problems that town planning had arisen to tackle, at least in the English-speaking world. Ebenezer Howard, the father of British town planning, had proposed a marriage of town and country in his 1902 book *Garden Cities of Tomorrow*. The 'correct principle of a city's growth' was a kind of federation of self-contained towns separated by countryside and connected by electric trams and a high-speed 'inter-municipal railway'. The car was not part of Howard's plan: the towns would be kept small enough to be walking-scale, while the inter-municipal railway would provide 'rapid communication between off-shoots'.[7]

Howard's city would require meticulous planning of transport and land use. The automobile, many American reformers decided, would enable similar results to be achieved with less effort – and importantly, less collective effort. As James Flink points out, this was an important reason for the popularity of the automobile.

> *[T]he adoption of the automobile seemed ... to afford a simple solution to some of the more formidable problems of American life associated with the emergence of an urban-industrial society. The motorcar seemed to be a panacea for the social ills of the day, one that necessitated minimal collective action or governmental expenditure. Best of all, perhaps, the individual did not need to wait for others to act; by buying a car, he could immediately improve his own life appreciably.*[8]

This perspective suggests that automobile dominance in cities may not have been a natural, inevitable process. Much has been written in praise of the freedom conferred by the car – the liberty, in the words of the Australian historian Graeme Davison, 'to travel where, when and as often as we like'.[9] In rural and remote areas with little or no public transport, the car certainly did provide this freedom, but the situation is more complicated in cities. Had Ebenezer Howard's Garden City ever been built, its residents would travel as they chose on foot or by rail, and the car would provide little additional freedom. What the car really offered urban residents was freedom from reliance on public transport; the extent of the gain depended on the quality of the public transport system.

The car also offered urban planners freedom from having to solve the problem of providing effective public transport, a problem that was particularly fraught in American cities for reasons that will be discussed shortly. With car use rising and public transport declining, the easiest option for city planners was to go with the flow. In such an environment, it was easy to treat the rise of the car as unstoppable, but was it? Or were there alternatives that, rather than failing, were simply left untried?

By the 1960s, the collapse of public transport in US cities was creating concern from city halls to the White House. On taking office in 1961, President Kennedy set up a series of inquiries into the problem, which asked whether anything could be done. Again, the questions of inevitability and desirability were conflated: the experts who advocated a continuation of car-based policies argued that the trends were irreversible; those who advocated change took the opposite view.

The majority of analysts presented the dominance of the car in US cities as a natural process. One influential study of the period, *The Urban Transportation Problem* by John Meyer, John Kain and Martin Wohl, encapsulates the argument:

> An array of technological, economic and social forces has altered the structure and character of American cities in recent decades… American cities have been decentralizing … there is considerable evidence that consumers may prefer an 'automobile' solution to their urban transportation needs, even if it is a very costly solution.[10]

Note the use of the word 'forces', which implies that the process was natural, even inevitable, and discounts the possibility that different policies may have changed the outcome. The arguments made by Meyer, Kain and Wohl have not been significantly improved on since: they remain the arguments of contemporary advocates of the automobile solution.

The experts who advocated change were less clear about the causes, but agreed that the dominance of cars in US cities did not simply happen by itself. Many pointed to the different results achieved in European and even Canadian cities, but critics countered that these places were following the American trend, having simply started later. The most popular explanation for public transport's decline was insufficient investment in new rolling stock and rail lines, suggesting that the solution lay in increased capital funding. In the 1970s, an alternative explanation emerged, which focused much more on politics and policy: the demise of public transport in US cities was the result of a conspiracy by the automobile industry.

WHO FRAMED GENERAL MOTORS?
THE LOS ANGELES 'CONSPIRACY'

Los Angeles provides the most popular image of car-dominated suburbia. Although its freeway system is actually less extensive than New York's,[11] when travel patterns are considered, LA really is a great big freeway, as Dionne Warwick sang back in 1968.

But Los Angeles once had an extensive network of tramways, made up of the 'urban' service provided within city boundaries by the 'yellow cars' of the Los Angeles Railway, and the 'interurban' service run by the 'big red cars' of the Pacific Electric Railway to suburban communities such as Long Beach and Orange County. At its peak in the 1920s, the Pacific Electric network extended over 1873 route kilometres, the largest system of its kind in the world.[12] Urban historians agree that this network, rather than the automobile, created the dispersed, poly-centric layout of the Los Angeles region. So what happened to it, and why did the car take over?

The most popular answer is that the Pacific Electric system was purchased and closed down by a holding company set up by General Motors as part of a conspiracy to destroy the tram systems of the US. The story is recounted by award-winning investigative journalist Edwin Black in his 2006 book *Internal Combustion*, suggestively subtitled 'How corporations and governments addicted the world to oil and derailed the alternatives'. The trams of Los Angeles and other US cities are covered in a chapter entitled 'The GM Conspiracy'.[13] The conspiracy was the subject of *Taken For a Ride*, a documentary which aired on US public television in 1996, and even featured as a sub-plot in Steven Spielberg's 1988 movie *Who Framed Roger Rabbit?*

The General Motors conspiracy story would, if correct, offer a dramatic refutation of the claim that automobile dominance was inevitable. As the economist Glenn Yago pointed out in his 1984 book *The Decline of Transit*, 'researchers from fields as diverse as geography, sociology, economics, political science, and urban planning [had] argued for decades that the population, income and spatial characteristics of cities impossibly constrained mass transit services'. In doing so, these researchers had discounted the role played by public and corporate policy, 'thereby promoting motorization by federal, state, and local planners'.[14] Yago recounts the General Motors conspiracy, suggesting that it dated from the 1920s, when sales of cars began to stagnate as the market became saturated. The auto industry responded with a strategy to replace trams with buses, knowing that the latter 'would be ineffective in counteracting the lure of the automobile.'[15]

The starting point for Yago and the other critics of GM is *American Ground Transport*, a 1974 report by Bradford Snell, a staff attorney with the US Senate Judiciary Committee. The report is a general indictment of General Motors, accusing the car giant not just of destroying tram systems but even of collaborating with the Nazis during World War II (a claim that may have piqued the interest of Edwin Black, who has written books about American links to the Holocaust). Snell argues that GM joined with oil and tyre companies in 1936 to establish National City Lines, a holding company that purchased tram companies across the US, replaced tram services with GM-built buses, then sold the resulting business and moved on to the next city. This campaign 'had a devastating impact on the quality of urban transportation and urban living in America. Nowhere was the ruin more apparent than in the Greater Los Angeles metropolitan area.'[16] Snell says the 'quiet, pollution free electric trains' of Pacific Electric served the region well – his report even includes a map showing the network at its peak – until National City Lines obtained control of the company in 1940. National scrapped the big red cars, then acquired the yellow cars of the Los Angeles Railway in 1944 and closed them as well. Los Angeles was transformed into 'an ecological wasteland'.

Snell's thesis has attracted many critics, beginning with General Motors itself, which produced a lengthy rebuttal which it successfully demanded the Senate append to Snell's report. According to GM, the company and its allies 'helped give mass transportation a new lease of life which lasted into the postwar years', until public transport was laid low by 'rising incomes and further dispersion into the suburbs.'[17] Other critics agree. Cliff Slater, a businessman and adviser to the Reason Foundation (a free-market think-tank), rebutted the Snell thesis in a 1997 paper for *Transportation Quarterly*. The bus was simply 'a superior technology', and 'by 1950 it was obvious that the streetcar was obsolete.'[18] Scott Bottles' 1987 study *Los Angeles and the Automobile* argues that 'nobody imposed the automobile on the public. Americans adopted the automobile willingly, for they saw it as a liberating and democratic technology.'[19]

The Snell report impressed many readers with its 500 footnotes that meticulously reference every statement made in the main text. Even more powerful support came from the fact that National City Lines and its backers – including General Motors, Standard Oil and Firestone Tire – were indeed convicted of conspiracy in 1949, and the conviction was upheld on appeal two years later.

Snell says the plotters were convicted of 'having criminally conspired … to replace electric transportation with gas- or diesel-powered buses and to monopolize the sale of buses and related products … throughout the country.'[20] This is not quite correct: Snell overstated his case. The appeal court's decision, which Snell cites as his source, states that the defendants were convicted of conspiring to 'monopolize … the sale of busses, petroleum products, tires and tubes used by local transportation systems'. They were acquitted of the additional charge of conspiring to 'secure control of a substantial number of the companies which provide public transportation service in various cities … and to eliminate and exclude all competition in the sale of motor busses, petroleum products, tires and tubes to such transportation companies'.[22] Both charges alleged a conspiracy to monopolize the bus market, not to replace trams with buses – to exploit the trend for buses to replace trams, not to initiate it. In the words of the appeal court: 'In

1938, National conceived the idea of purchasing transportation systems in cities where street cars were no longer viable and supplanting the latter with passenger busses.'[22]

So why had trams become non-viable in so many American cities? As early as 1919, six years before General Motors started building buses,[23] President Woodrow Wilson appointed a Federal Electric Railway Commission to enquire into a crisis in the industry: '50 or more urban systems ... are in the hands of receivers [and] the industry as a whole is virtually bankrupt.'[24]

The Commission's 1920 report blamed the crisis on problems stemming from the origin of the industry. Tram systems in the US began as private undertakings operating under municipal franchises, which conferred monopoly rights in return for control over fares and other aspects of service. The Commission said the companies 'were not conservatively financed in their early years', a polite way of saying that promoters had fleeced investors by extracting excess profits then decamping, leaving behind debt-ridden, under-capitalized businesses. Tram systems were then bought up by bank-backed 'holding companies', which by the time of the report controlled three-quarters of the industry. These companies 'issued shares upon an inflated basis', creating a further incentive to maximize short-term dividends at the expense of long-term planning and investment. Meanwhile, franchise agreements prohibited raising fares in line with increasing costs and made it difficult to reduce or withdraw service on unprofitable routes. Finally, World War I led to a credit squeeze, and near-bankrupt tram companies could not 'compete in the money market with prosperous and unregulated enterprises.'[25] They were unable even to re-finance their debts, let alone invest in modernization and expansion.

The problems of the tramway industry in 1920 were not primarily due to cars, although the Commission did point to competition from automobiles and 'jitneys' (cars and small vans offering an unregulated micro-bus service). It argued that jitney competition was unfair and should be restricted by regulation, but was surprisingly sanguine about the private car. 'In spite of the immense development of the automobile industry the demand for electric railway transportation has increased at a rapid rate.'[26] American public transport operators failed to appreciate the seriousness of the threat posed by the car, but even if they had, they were struggling to survive from day to day and lacked any capacity to respond.

Problems with privately operated, government-franchised urban public transport had arisen by this time all over the developed world. The solution virtually everywhere except the US was a public takeover upon the expiry of the franchise, or even earlier. The City of Zurich 'nationalized' its tram system following a referendum in 1894; Frankfurt did so in 1897 when local elites became dissatisfied with the private operator;[27] Auckland bought out its private tram firm when it sought to raise fares in 1919;[28] Melbourne and Toronto took public control in 1919 and 1921 respectively, following the expiry of their franchise contracts. London had a mixture of private tram services and public routes operated by the

London County Council, but all were merged in 1933 into a public undertaking controlled by the London Passenger Transport Board.

Nationalization was too much for the men of the Federal Electric Railway Commission, which included representatives of the Electric Railway Association and even the Investment Bankers' Association.[29] Public ownership was impractical because of 'constitutional and statutory prohibitions, financial and legal obstacles … and the state of public opinion'. While it might be possible in the distant future, 'there is nothing in the experience thus far obtained in this country that will justify the assertion that it will result in better or cheaper service than privately operated utilities could afford if properly regulated.'[30]

This prediction proved to be disastrously wrong, and tram systems began shutting down in the 1920s. Nowhere were the consequences more serious than in Los Angeles.

FROM BIG RED CARS TO GREAT BIG FREEWAY

The City of the Angels had been built around the red and yellow cars of the tram operators, particularly the Pacific Electric system. Pacific Electric was created by Henry E. Huntingdon, in parallel with his Huntington Land Improvement and San Gabriel Water companies. The interurbans were 'loss-leaders' financed by profits from the housing developments Huntington constructed along each route, having first organized the supply of essential water and transportation. The result was the characteristic low-rise form of the region, with mile upon mile of 'California bungalows' spreading along the tentacles of the Pacific Electric network. This extensive urban spread gave Los Angeles a reputation, which has lasted to this day, as the very model of urban sprawl.

This reputation may not have been entirely deserved. While single-family homes produce lower urban densities than the multi-family units that dominated older US cities, they were not the main reason the LA region extended over such great distances. Land beyond walking distance of the big red cars was not developed, so even within the boundaries of the City of Los Angeles, the great majority of land was rural or simply vacant. This latter factor is the main reason for the very low gross density recorded for the city at this time: only 6 residents per hectare in 1930, compared with 17 in New York and 15 in Chicago.[31] The gross density of the Canton of Zurich at the census of 2000 was only 7 residents per hectare[32] because its urban form resembles Los Angeles prior to the automobile: urban settlements dispersed through open countryside, mainly along rail lines. As Los Angeles' population grew, the vacant areas were converted to residential use, particularly once widespread car ownership removed the need to live near rail lines. The filling in of these areas dramatically increased gross densities, with the City of Los Angeles recording 32 residents per hectare at the 2000 census.

Urban growth also magnified the problems of the Los Angeles region's tram companies. Even before automobiles became widespread, the city centre suffered from congestion, as the red and yellow tram cars clogged narrow streets that had not been planned with trams in mind. This problem increased dramatically once moving and parked automobiles flooded the city. In suburban areas, Pacific Electric tracks were often segregated from motor traffic, but conflicts still arose at level crossings. A spate of collisions led to calls for a reduction in tram operating speeds. As suburban demand grew, lines that had initially been built with only a single track were unable to cope (these are shown on the map in the Snell report). Services became progressively slower, less reliable and more crowded, and attempts by Pacific Electric to raise fares were greeted with outrage.

By the 1920s, it was clear that the Pacific Electric system would need substantial investment to modernize equipment, segregate services from traffic congestion, improve level crossing safety and duplicate single-track sections. Cross-suburban routes to complement the mainly radial network, and extensions to new growth areas, would also be needed to compete with the car. But Pacific Electric lost money in all but one of the years from 1912 to 1941,[33] and had stopped expanding the system by the time of World War I. What was to be done?

The city and county administrations engaged engineering consultants Kelker, De Leuw & Company to investigate the problem.[34] Interestingly, the consultants were hired in 1924, the year both the Pacific Electric and LA Railway systems reached their inter-war patronage peak.[35] The consultants' 1925 report advised that the region required an integrated, multi-modal public transport system comprised of high-speed rapid transit trains running on segregated rights of way, fed and linked by urban and interurban trams, with buses serving sparsely settled and recently developed areas. A single organization would need to control these services to ensure integration and eliminate wasteful duplication, and substantial public funding would be required for the capital works.

The plan foundered on the rocks of politics and was never implemented. The consultants recommended that the rapid trains run mainly on elevated tracks like the famous Loop in their home of Chicago; the public preferred subways, even though these were more expensive. Concern increased when the steam railroads proposed to run their long-distance trains over the elevated tracks, as an alternative to replacing their three separate depots with a single Union Station (which Bottles argues would have opened the system up to competition from rival railroad companies). A Taxpayers' Anti-Elevated League was formed, and capitalized on public suspicion of the privately owned steam and electric railway companies. The elevated plan was resoundingly defeated in a 1926 referendum, and the Los Angeles Union Station finally opened in 1939.

Once separated from the Union Station issue, the rapid transit plans became mired in years of controversy. The new system would cost some $130 million, which would have to come from public sources, but the private railways would be the beneficiaries. 'What has the Pacific Electric and Los Angeles Railways ever done for the people of Los Angeles that the property owners should have to contribute over a hundred million dollars in the building of subways?' one critic asked in 1930. 'We believe that the people of Los Angeles do not owe a single dollar to the Pacific Electric or Los Angeles Railway Corporations.'[36] By this time, the Depression was cutting the tramway companies' revenues even further: despite rapid population growth, patronage on the Pacific Electric system fell from 101 million in 1924 to 97 million in 1929, then to only 60 million by 1933.[37] Desperate to cut costs, the company began to replace trams with buses, and in some cases to abandon services altogether. Lightly patronized lines were cut, along with long-distance routes operating on single-track lines that would otherwise have required expensive duplication. The decline was well underway long before National City Lines entered the Los Angeles transport market.

In 1937, the Automobile Club of Southern California proposed an alternative solution to the region's transport problems: a network of limited-access 'express highways' financed and owned by the public sector. Public transport could be provided by express buses on the new highways. The report argued that the widely dispersed trip pattern and low urban density of the region made successful rapid transit problematic – an argument that has been repeated faithfully by freeway advocates ever since – but the freeway network proposed in the report was mainly radial, with most routes following existing rail corridors and converging on the central business district (CBD).[38] The most attractive aspect of the plan was that it could be carried out entirely by the public sector, without involving private transit operators.

The city's mayor responded by appointing a Transportation Engineering Board made up of engineers from the city and country governments, and private consulting firms. The Board reported in 1939 and endorsed the Automobile Club's proposals. While the long-term answer was rail rapid transit, difficulties in arranging finance and the region's dispersed population suggested freeways as the immediate priority. The problem of funding was solved by lobbying the California government to make state petrol tax revenue available for urban roads, a precedent set in the 1930s with California's first freeway, the Arroyo Seco Parkway. In 1947, the state government made $300 million available towards the Los Angeles freeway plan.[39] Even allowing for inflation, this would have more than covered the cost of the rapid transit system proposed by Kelker, De Leuw & Co.

Los Angeles became the archetype of what Reyner Banham christened 'autopia' and a model for transport planners in other places. In 1956, the US government inaugurated the Interstate Highway system, offering to fund 90 per cent of the cost of a national network, with almost half the total expenditure committed to urban freeways. Freeways proved unsuitable as bus routes because they bypassed the destinations travellers wanted to reach, and public transport in Los Angeles continued to decline. Eventually the State established a Metropolitan Transit Authority, which acquired the near-bankrupt Pacific Electric and Los Angeles Railway networks in 1958. The Authority's first priority was to restore public transport to regions which had been abandoned by the private firms, and newly-developed areas that never had any. It did this with buses, moving quickly to close the remaining tram lines. The last of the interurban big red cars ran in 1961; the last urban tram lines were closed in 1963.

So the victory of the freeway over the railway in Los Angeles was not the result of a conspiracy by General Motors. There was indeed a conspiracy, but it seems to have been one to corner the market opened up by the demise of the US tram industry, a demise which was already underway at the beginning of the 1920s. GM and its allies may have sped the process in some cities, but not in LA, where the die was cast in the 1920s and 1930s. Bottles was correct to reject Snell's conspiracy-based explanation for the dominance of the automobile in Los Angeles, but not when he claimed that the outcome 'largely reflects choices made by the public itself.'[40] It is true that 'urban dwellers saw the automobile as a democratic alternative to the seemingly corrupt railway companies and the inefficient streetcars',[41] but this is because attempts to reform privately operated public transport failed.

As Peter Hall says, 'Los Angeles allowed its … light rail systems to be built by buccaneer capitalists chiefly interested not in supplying transportation but in massive land speculation; then, it abandoned this system to its fate'.[42] Robert Fogelson argues that 'municipal authorities were at least partly responsible. Their unwillingness to acquire the Los Angeles [tram] system and to implement the Kelker, de Leuw rapid transit plan removed what little hope remained for the electric railways.'[43]

This does not mean that there have never been conspiracies to replace public transport with the automobile. In fact, across the Pacific Ocean from Los Angeles there was such a conspiracy, and it was successful. This conspiracy was not the work of greedy car and oil executives, but transport planners working for public authorities – led by the Professors of Geography and Architecture at the local university.

'ESSENTIALLY A TECHNICAL PROBLEM':
AUCKLAND REJECTS RAIL

Since 1999, New Zealand's tourism board has marketed the country as '100% Pure New Zealand'. The campaign draws on the country's scenic beauty, displayed to the world in the *Lord of the Rings* movies, and a reputation for environmental activism dating back to 1970s campaigns against nuclear weapons testing in the Pacific. International visitors lured by the marketing campaign arrive in Auckland, home to the country's major airport. Many proceed directly to eco-tourism destinations in the rest of the country, but others stay to explore New Zealand's biggest city. Auckland is built around Waitemata Harbour, which provides a scenic setting to rival Sydney, San Francisco or Vancouver. The CBD slopes down to ferry wharves and moorings for yachts; Auckland calls itself the 'City of Sails'.

Auckland is also a city of cars. Its transport system is untouched by the environmental activism for which New Zealanders are renowned. The CBD is bounded to the north by the harbour, but on all other sides by a gigantic spaghetti junction, the largest in Australasia. The three motorways which feed into the junction debouch into the city centre, jamming it with cars and buses for most of the day. This is quite an achievement in a metropolis with only 1.3 million residents and a relatively weak CBD in terms of employment and retailing. Auckland's centre is different from its Australasian neighbours: the absence of large stores is reminiscent of an American downtown. Whole streets of shops have closed down and the multi-storey Farmers department store shut nearly 20 years ago, when the firm moved its business to suburban malls.

Only 6 per cent of Aucklanders travelled to work by public transport at the 2001 census. Although this just beats the 5 per cent recorded in 2000 for the Los Angeles census area (which includes LA and neighbouring counties such as Orange and Ventura), use of public transport for non-work trips in Auckland is negligible. The average resident of greater Los Angeles made 49 annual public transport trips for all purposes in the mid-1990s, while the average Aucklander managed only 41.[44] If attracting people to public transport was a boat race, the City of Sails would reach the finish line behind the City of the Angels.

Public transport in Auckland has not always been this marginal. In 1954, when the city began work on its first master transportation plan, the average resident made 290 trips. Public transport accounted for 58 per cent of trips by motorized modes, private transport only 42 per cent. When walking and cycling, which were not surveyed, are taken into account, it is likely that fewer than a third of daily trips were by car.[45] By contrast, the car accounted for 62 per cent of trips to the Los Angeles CBD, and an even greater share of city-wide travel, as early as 1930.[46]

The collapse of public transport in Auckland in the following four decades may have been the greatest such decline recorded anywhere in the world, but General Motors had nothing to do with it. New Zealand has never had a significant automobile industry: it imports its cars. Nor can privately owned public transport be blamed, except possibly for the last few years, because trams, trains and most buses were run by public authorities until 1990.

Public transport collapsed in Auckland because the city's transport planners made a conscious decision to abandon it and make roads the priority, even though this was the more expensive alternative. Los Angeles opted for freeways only after attempts to rescue public transport foundered; Auckland made the choice at a time when upgrading public transport was the more practical option. The city's transport planners deliberately adopted a transport policy that only evolved by historical accident in Los Angeles. Because this policy was unpopular with the public, the planners and their allies conspired to prevent the community having a say.

Public transport was initially provided by the Auckland Electric Tramway Company, which was granted a 30-year franchise in 1901. Years of conflict between the city council and the company over fares and service quality led to a municipal takeover in 1919, followed by significant upgrading and extension of the network including, from 1924, the use of buses as feeder services.[47] 1924 also saw the emergence of private buses, which competed with council trams for passengers. The council reacted with a by-law banning buses from Queen Street, the main shopping and tram artery. The following year, the New Zealand government gave councils the power to regulate bus services, and the private competitors were bought out. This created a series of operating deficits (even though trams remained profitable), which eventually led to the transfer of all street-based public transport to a metropolitan agency called the Auckland Transport Board.[48] The Great Depression and World War II limited opportunities for major improvements to the system and, after the war, the board's major capital works project was scrapping the now ageing trams and replacing them with cheaper, modern buses.[49]

Street-based public transport had served Auckland well, as shown by the high usage rates maintained until the mid-1950s, but by this time, the future of public transport seemed to be trains, not trams. Auckland had a small suburban rail system, operated by steam trains out of a terminal some distance from the city centre by the New Zealand Railways Department. As early as 1924 the Railways Department proposed that the network be electrified and extended into the city centre through a tunnel. The project was expensive, and was postponed while the Railways electrified the suburban network of the capital, Wellington, between 1937 and 1950. As the Wellington scheme neared completion, attention returned to Auckland, and the national government engaged British consultants William Halcrow & Partners to provide advice.[50]

The Halcrow report of 1950 recommended electrification, construction of the central city tunnel and the reorganization of bus services to act as feeders to the rail system, on a similar model to that suggested for Los Angeles by the 1925 Kelker, De Leuw report. Coordination between modes would be ensured by creating a new multi-modal public transport agency, or alternatively by extending the Auckland Transport Board's jurisdiction to include heavy rail and privately-operated buses. Finally, since urban roads would compete with the rail–bus system for both passengers and government funds, Halcrow advised that 'expenditure on arterial streets in the Auckland Metropolitan Area be restricted until the results of the recommended schemes are seen.'[51]

The Halcrow recommendations were supported by both Auckland's major newspapers, and by both parties in the 1951 national elections, but beneath the apparent unanimity dissent was stirring. Auckland's City Engineer was a fierce opponent of the plan, especially the recommendation to restrict spending on roads. He argued that motorways should take priority. Enthusiasm for motorways increased in 1953 when the National Roads Board, responsible for rural roads, opened New Zealand's first section of motorway in Auckland's outer suburbs. At the ceremony, the national Transport Minister, W. S. Goosman – responsible for both road and rail – told a journalist who had the temerity to ask about rail: 'my boy, the future of Auckland is with the motor car.'[52] Goosman may have also been influenced by opposition from public and private bus interests, who opposed the establishment of a new public transport authority and demanded compensation if one was established.[53] Public expressions of dissent remained muted, however, since as the *Auckland Star* editorialized in 1954, abandoning the rail scheme 'could be politically explosive and dangerous'.[54] A national election was due at the end of the year, and 20 per cent of voters lived in the Auckland region.

The first open opposition came from Professor Kenneth Cumberland, head of Geography at Auckland University from 1946 to 1980, and the Chairman of Auckland City Council's Town Planning Committee. In an op-ed piece for the *Star*, Cumberland called the railway scheme a 'white elephant' that 'may well prejudice any chances of getting material improvement of our highway system'. Those pointing to successful rail systems overseas 'must remember that Auckland, with its low population densities and sprawling area, is not to be compared with a city of 1,000,000 people and more in a smaller area'.

Cumberland concluded: 'A full-scale expert inquiry seems to be the first necessity.'[55] A week later, the city council established a special transport committee to consider the issue. Following advice from the City Engineer and a meeting with Goosman, the committee recommended that the Technical Committee of the Auckland Regional Planning Authority, an advisory body established in 1946, be asked to prepare a Master Transportation Plan to settle the rail-versus-motorways question. Professor Cumberland was a member of the Authority's executive, and the City Engineer chaired its Technical Committee.

The council adopted the committee's recommendation on 28 October 1954; the regional authority agreed the following day. Why the hurry? The national election was due on 13 November, and the *Star* (which appears to have been 'in' on the deal) reported: 'the Government does not want the underground to become an election issue, on the ground that this would lead to confusion over what is essentially a technical problem.'[56] The rival *New Zealand Herald*, which had not been privy to the arrangement, called the decision 'a curiously perverse move to postpone discussion and lift all pressure from the Minister', adding that the council had 'walked blithely into the trap prepared by the "no-men" of Wellington'. Councillors had apparently decided to 'accept the city engineer as an authority on rail transport' and 'accept the "master transportation plan" from a group of individuals largely preoccupied already with elaborate schemes for arterial highways.'[57]

Both newspapers accepted that referring the issue to the technical committee doomed the rail scheme. The committee included road engineers from municipalities and public authorities across the region, plus one from the National Roads Board. The other members were a solitary representative from the Railways Department, and Cumberland's colleague Cyril Knight, the Dean of Architecture at Auckland University.

The Master Transportation Plan for Metropolitan Auckland was released in 1955 and reversed the recommendations of the Halcrow Report. Funding for the rail scheme should be diverted to fund a motorway network, with public transport delivered by buses operating on the motorways. Even the recommendation for a single public transport authority was cursorily rejected: 'There is no evidence before the Committee which would indicate any radical change being necessary in the present system of [public] transport service control, or which would justify the setting up of any other authority, although some minor changes may be found beneficial.'[58] The city council and national government rapidly endorsed the report, and agreed to share the costs of the motorway network. Goosman (who was also Minister of Works) promised that the Public Works Department would take charge of construction.

LIES, DAMN LIES AND POPULATION DENSITY

Although the ruse of declaring the rail–motorway issue a 'technical problem' had prevented it becoming an issue at the 1954 election, motorway supporters remained concerned about public opposition. After all, the great majority of Auckland's population were public transport users, while motorists remained in the minority. The Master Plan was published in 1956 as a glossy public relations document, replete with breathless endorsements and high-quality photography. Five full-page photos of traffic congestion in Auckland contrasted with eight of free-flowing American roadways, such as the Arroyo Seco and Santa Ana Freeways in Los Angeles. The contrast is accentuated by the fact that the Auckland photos appear to have been taken during overcast weather, while the Los Angeles freeways are bathed in Californian sunlight.

Given the low rate of car use in Auckland at the time, the report's authors struggled to find convincing examples of congestion. One photograph shows Queen Street, with two double-parked cars delaying through traffic and a turning truck holding up a tram: an argument for better traffic policing, perhaps, but not quite gridlock. The most convincing photo shows another arterial road in peak hour. The roadway is jammed, but mainly with public transport vehicles: there are six trams, seven buses, nine cars and a taxi.[59] Assuming that the trams and buses were full but not overcrowded, they would have carried 300–400 passengers, compared with fewer than 20 in the cars.

Streets jammed with full trams and buses might have led readers of the report to wonder why the option of an underground railway had been rejected, so what were the technical arguments on which the decision was based? They were those Cumberland had offered in his op-ed piece, the same reasons that had been used in 1937 by the Automobile Club of Southern California:

> *The form and structure of Metropolitan Auckland through the years has been largely determined by developments in ... transportation. During the last 25 years, the overall effect of motor transportation*

has so radically changed the pattern that Auckland is now one of the
most dispersed cities in the World. The individual has been freed from
absolute dependence on tramways and railways with their inflexible
fixed routes... The pattern of travel has become more diffused and
traffic cannot now be channelled along a few fixed routes with the same
destination.[60]

In support of these claims, particularly that of world-beating urban dispersal, the report set out in a table the population densities of a range of cities, showing Auckland with the lowest figure of all, 4 people per acre (10 per hectare), below even Brisbane and Los Angeles (both 5 per acre or 12 per hectare).[61] The source for the table is stated to be a book called *X-Ray the City!* by Dr Ernest Fooks. Nobody apparently noticed at the time, but the use of these figures was a complete misrepresentation of the point Fooks was making in his book, and apparently a deliberate one.

I own a copy of *X-Ray the City!*, a present from Ernest's widow Mrs Noemi Fooks, who arrived in Australia with him in 1939 as part of the exodus of Viennese Jews that has enriched so many countries. Ernst Fuchs – 'we changed the spelling', Mrs Fooks told me: 'you can imagine how people pronounced it' – was the first person in Australia to hold a doctorate in town planning, which he had obtained in Vienna with an investigation of linear cities. He was the first lecturer in town planning in Melbourne, but ultimately ended up working as an architect.[62] Fooks wanted to place Australian town planning on a more intellectually rigorous footing, and wrote the book to show how this might be done.

The central argument of *X-Ray the City!* is one that still needs to be made in the 21st century. Most reported measurements of urban density, such as the figures cited earlier in this chapter in the discussion of Los Angeles, are calculated by dividing the population of a municipality or other administrative region by its gross area. 'It is of the utmost importance,' Fooks says, 'to stress the major defect of such figures: THE ARBITRARY NATURE OF URBAN BOUNDARIES.'[63] Municipal and administrative boundaries rarely correspond to actual urbanized areas. Some cities (such as Los Angeles in 1930) contain large areas of vacant land within their boundaries, while others (almost every central municipality in the world in the 21st century) occupy only the inner part of the urbanized area. Therefore, more accurate density measures are needed: Fooks proposed a series of them, linked to form a 'density diagram' that could be used to 'X-Ray the city' (more on this issue in Chapter 4).

Fooks provided examples to illustrate his main point:

The artificial character of legal and administrative urban boundaries
makes overall density figures meaningless. A study of the two accompany-
ing tables makes this clear.[64]

The two tables show self-evidently absurd results, such as Vienna's density being lower than Melbourne's and about the same as Los Angeles', and Detroit having double the density of Zurich. But they are the source from which the Auckland Technical Committee derived its comparative density figures.

The Technical Committee knew what it was doing: Professor Knight, who was a town planner as well as an architect, chaired the sub-committee responsible for the 'general information' in the Master Plan.[65] The Committee carefully sifted the Fooks table, deleting all the anomalous cities, such as Vienna and Zurich, that might have alerted readers to its real purpose. The Committee then added its own density estimate for Auckland, calculated using the very methodology Fooks wrote his book to debunk, namely dividing the population of the region by the gross area under the jurisdiction of the Auckland Regional Planning Authority. This was not an inadvertent error either, as the same Technical Committee (with much the same membership) had only four years earlier estimated the urbanized area of the region at 30,000 acres, instead of the 113,000 used for the Master Plan's calculations.[66] This gave a density of 15 residents per acre not 4 (37 per hectare not 10), double the figures for Australian cities cited in the Master Plan and triple the figure given for Los Angeles.

Ernest Fooks opened *X-Ray the City!* with the old aphorism 'there are three kinds of lies: lies, damned lies and statistics.'[67] The authors of Auckland's Master Transportation Plan shamelessly distorted his work to tell a damn lie, or in the elegant expression of the Danish planner Bent Flyvbjerg, a 'strategic misrepresentation'.[68]

100 PER CENT PURE AUTOPIA

The Auckland Technical Committee's cost estimates proved to be no more robust than its density calculations. It had claimed that the rail scheme would cost £11 million, almost as much as the £15 million price tag for the motorways. In 1962, an engineer named Joseph Wright claimed that both figures had been distorted to favour motorways. Motorway costs had been underestimated, with the true figure closer to £40 million, while rail costs had been inexplicably inflated from the Halcrow estimate of £7.25 million. 'Where did the figure of £11 million come from?' he asked. 'I understand that the committee which produced the Master Transport Plan had 26 members, only three of whom had any experience of handling public transport... The whole Master Transport Plan has a motor car complex'. The Halcrow report had been correct: the new rail system should have been built before the motorways, and a central authority was needed to coordinate all forms of public transport.[69] Wright was no car-hating train-spotter: he was the Ministry of Works engineer in charge of the Auckland motorway project.

By this time, traffic had grown much more rapidly than the Master Plan predicted, thanks mainly to a collapse in public transport patronage following closure of the tram network in 1956. By 1963, public transport's share of motorized trips had fallen to only 22 per cent, less than half the figure only nine years earlier. The city council made a large contribution to the decline by following the City Engineer's advice to retain the ban on buses in the central artery of Queen Street, which dated from the 1920s. This forced services into confusing, inconvenient routes: 'bus services have seemed to many to be going around in circles'. The council had hoped that giving priority to parking and traffic would help central city retailing, but by 1967 even retailers were pleading for the return of the buses.[70] The problem was not resolved until the 1970s, two decades after the departure of the trams, by which time the city's retail core had declined in line with public transport, presenting an increasing contrast to other Australasian cities. In 1966, the council asked the British transport planner Colin Buchanan for advice. Buchanan reported that traffic made the city centre 'unpleasant to the point of being uncivilised', and that completion of the motorways 'far from easing the position in the central streets, would make them worse.'[71]

A new Auckland Regional Authority (subsequently Regional Council) replaced the Planning Authority in 1963, but inherited many of its staff. It immediately engaged the firm of De Leuw Cather, responsible for the 1925 Los Angeles rapid transit plan, to update the motorway plan in light of higher traffic levels. The consultants produced an interim report arguing that the most urgent need was actually for improved public transport, and that this should receive higher priority than completion of the motorway network.[72] The Regional Authority agreed to allow the consultants to look at rail, but it is noteworthy that the initiative came from the Americans, not local transport planners. In two reports released in 1966, the consultants recommended an expanded motorway network and a rapid transit system similar to the Halcrow proposals of 1950.

The rail proposals were energetically championed in a long campaign by Sir Dove-Myer Robinson, the first chair of the Authority and Auckland's Lord Mayor for most of the period from 1959 to 1980. He may have been seeking to make amends: as a junior councillor, he had moved the fateful 1954 motion that led to the 1955 Master Plan.[73] 'Robbie's rapid rail' campaign was undermined by his own staff, pilloried by Cumberland and other academics from Auckland University and opposed by the New Zealand Town Planning Institute. The national government finally rejected it in 1976, in line with the conclusions of a review of the De Leuw Cather reports conducted by a Regional Authority technical committee with strikingly similar composition to that which produced the 1955 plan. The way to manage traffic problems, the committee argued, was to limit employment growth in the city centre.[74] By 1983, the Regional Authority proposed closing the Auckland rail system altogether, but was defeated by public opposition.[75]

The motorway network from the Master Plan was completed with the opening of the central spaghetti junction in the late 1970s – with the exception of an elevated link along the waterfront that would have walled the City of Sails off from its harbour. After a few years the roads were clogged again, and the network is constantly being expanded and extended. Central area employment stagnated and retailing collapsed, but without producing the anticipated traffic reductions. The share of CBD workers arriving by public transport fell from an already-low 42 per cent in 1973 to 24 per cent in 1994, ensuring that more cars were required to transport the reduced workforce.[76] Congestion has spread to suburban areas, as it did in American cities. The final blow came in 1989, when the New Zealand government adopted the bus deregulation policy implemented in Britain (see Chapter 5). Just as in the UK, patronage dropped sharply, and Auckland's tripmaking rate finally fell below that of Los Angeles.

General Motors and its fellow conspirators did not aim to turn Los Angeles into autopia, and neither did the city's policy makers of the 1920s and 1930s. The Auckland conspirators of the 1950s consciously aimed to create a city based on the car, although unlike GM, their motives were not financial. The conspirators believed autopia was in the best interests of the Auckland public, even if the public were insufficiently enlightened to understand where their interests lay. As Professor Cumberland explained in 1971:

> *A far-flung fringe of low-density suburban development – so long scorned by planners, popular press and public alike – will, in this pollution-conscious age, become increasingly preferable ... all within an hour's run, say 50 or 60 miles, of almost any part of the metropolitan complex and its daily congested and nightly dull and depressing core of otherwise unrelieved urban pressures and neuroses.*[77]

The Auckland public remain as ungrateful to the promoters of autopia as their parents and grandparents. Very few Aucklanders actually use public transport, but most would like to be given the opportunity, as shown by their decades-long record of electing local representatives who support rail upgrades and voting out those who do not.[78] At the time of writing, the region's elected leaders have endorsed a 21st-century version of the Halcrow rail plan, but without biting the bullet and accepting that motorway construction must be curtailed if the upgrade is to be funded. And to get even this far, politicians and citizens have had to fight their transport planners every inch of the way.

The planners remain committed not just to the old policy directions, but also to the old rationale. The Auckland Regional Council's latest regional transport plan, published in 2005, allocates two-thirds of the budget to roads. The justification echoes almost word-for-word the argument of the 1955 Master Plan:

> *The region has developed as a relatively low density, decentralised region. Travel in the region is characterised by large numbers of dispersed journeys... Cars will remain the most predominate [sic] travel mode... Cars give Aucklanders a wide choice of living and work locations.*[79]

History does not support Glenn Yago's version of the General Motors conspiracy theory, but the experience of Los Angeles and Auckland does vindicate his claim that policy helps produce autopia – and that arguments attributing car dominance to impersonal forces like density are convenient for policy makers seeking to foist it on an unwilling public.

Chicago: scientific planning proves
that density is destiny

The Los Angeles solution to urban transport was exported by example, as we saw in Auckland, and through funding programmes, notably the US Interstate Highway program. It was also spread through scientific, computer-based transport planning.

The attempt to make transport planning scientific can be traced to a pioneering post-war study of Philadelphia by two academics at the University of Pennsylvania, Robert Mitchell and Chester Rapkin. The study was published in 1954 as *Urban Traffic: A Function of Land Use*, and the title summarizes the key findings. Land use patterns cause transport outcomes and can be related to them as mathematical functions, leading to a new methodology for estimating future needs for roads and public transport. Mitchell and Rapkin did not set out to promote autopia: indeed, Rapkin later played a prominent role in saving New York's SoHo district from a planned freeway. But the techniques they pioneered soon became an important ingredient in the export of the Los Angeles model.

The new techniques were first applied by Dr J. Douglas Carroll Jr, of the University of Michigan, beginning in the Detroit Metropolitan Area Traffic Study of 1953–1955, but culminating in the Chicago Area Transportation Study (CATS). CATS was established by the city, county and state governments – apparently as a result of a proposal from Carroll[80] – and ran from 1955 to 1962. It attracted such widespread interest that CATS was made a permanent agency that still exists today.[81] Here, it seemed, was the scientific method rationally attacking what had been thought of as an intractable urban problem. As the German planning historian Karl Fischer says, CATS 'introduced the precision of objectively determined measurement into one aspect of town planning. Since scarcely any other field of town planning possessed such precision … traffic engineering soon gained absolute superiority in town planning, almost replacing [it] in the 1950s and 1960s in a march of victory through countless motorized nations.'[82] An army of transport planning consultants set forth from Chicago, armed with the new study techniques, but also with the mantra that density is destiny.

CATS began with an 'inventory', or survey, of land use and transport in the greater Chicago region in 1956. The analysis of urban form would have satisfied Ernest Fooks, as it distinguishes between different ways of measuring density, from 'gross' through to 'net residential' (see Chapter 4). Both gross and net densities declined with increasing distance from the city centre. The analysis of travel revealed that a quarter of regional trips were by public transport and three-quarters by car (the study did not count walking or cycling), with public transport's share of the market also declining with distance from the CBD. 'This evidence', the study team concluded, 'partially destroys the idea that people choose their mode of travel.'[83] Public transport mode share could be predicted using an equation in which the variables were density and car ownership.[84]

Having established the equations relating traffic to land use for 1956, the study used them to predict travel patterns for the design year of 1980. The starting point was a prediction of future land-use patterns. CATS assumed that the historical trend towards a more spacious city would continue, leading to a continued decline in density. The consequence, according to the CATS equations, would be a further reduction in public transport's share of the market, from 24 per cent of trips in 1956 to 14 per cent in 1980. Given these trends, CATS recommended that 92 per cent of investment should go to highways and the remaining 8 per cent to public transport (half of this was for car parking at stations). Anticipating criticism that planning for public transport decline would be a self-fulfilling prophecy, the study team responded: 'The conditions of land use and density ... are the major determinants of the travel market. If demand is constrained by these factors, it is unlikely that changes in supply will have any great effect on the number of users.'[85]

In fact, CATS claimed, regular public transport could not operate at all at the densities found in Chicago's suburbs in the 1950s, densities that were predicted to become the norm by 1980. The inventory had established that most bus trips occurred within the boundaries of the city of Chicago or adjacent inner suburbs. 'The explanation', according to the study team, 'lies in the density of land use, and car ownership. Bus service can be provided only where there are enough passengers to pay operating costs... There are enough passengers only in districts which have a certain minimum density [which] appears to be about 25,000 persons per net residential square mile'. Below this figure, which is equivalent to 96.5 per hectare, 'buses apparently cannot operate economically'.[86]

This finding was picked up by other writers and so widely disseminated that it has become a truism. The British economist Colin Clark took the CATS figure, halved it to allow for non-residential uses, and concluded that 'a population density of 12,500 per gross sq. mile (48 persons/hectare) in a predominantly residential area is likely to be the limit below which 'bus services will be unremunerative without a subsidy'. This suggested public transport did not have a long-term future, since '[r]esidential densities in modern cities ... are tending to stabilize well below this limit.'[87] The Australian transport planners Peter Newman and Jeff Kenworthy took Clark's figure, reduced it again on the basis that most public transport systems now receive some subsidy, and arrived at a minimum density of 30 persons per hectare below which public transport cannot be provided.[88] Contemporary British planners use even higher figures, as we shall see in Chapter 4.

Nobody seems to have taken the trouble to examine the original CATS figures to see if they really prove that bus services could not have been provided in Chicago's suburbs. In fact, the lack of a suburban bus service in Chicago was as much a result of politics as the collapse of the Los Angeles tram systems.[89] Despite strong support for public ownership, demonstrated in a series of plebiscites beginning in 1902, Chicago's private transit franchisees held onto their properties until they went bankrupt during the Depression. More than a decade of indecision and decline followed before the banks, acting as receivers, sold operations to the Chicago Transit Authority (CTA), a body created by state legislation in 1947. The CTA was financially hamstrung by the need to rehabilitate the dilapidated systems it inherited, and cut costs by replacing ageing trams with buses (the changeover was completed by 1958, five years before Los Angeles). An attempt in 1956 – the very year CATS officially commenced – to use state fuel tax funds to finance modernization and an extension of CTA services was defeated by vigorous lobbying by a coalition of highway interests.

Suburban municipalities could choose whether to join the CTA, and given its parlous state most did not: they were served by private commuter railroads and may not have seen a great need for buses. A few closer-in suburbs did join the CTA, and were provided with a bus service. These were the suburbs CATS observed as having bus passengers. Density had nothing to do with it, as the density map in the CATS report shows they were all well below the supposed minimum.[90]

So the Chicago density threshold was a pseudo-scientific rationalization for a state of affairs that had arisen through public policy failures. Even Carroll's assistant Roger Creighton later acknowledged that the treatment of public transport had been the weakest part of the Study: 'the answer was never considered satisfactory… In retrospect, one looks at these arguments with mixed emotions… But this was the fault of the times'.[91] Nobody apparently noticed, however, and the Chicago density threshold has been used ever since. The techniques developed by CATS became part of a juggernaut of scientifically planned autopia that marched across the world in the following decades.

AND THE WINNER IS … DENSITY

The first serious proposal for building cities around the car came from the French architect Le Corbusier. In his 1924 book *Urbanisme* (published in English as *The City of To-morrow and Its Planning*), Le Corbusier offered a more radical approach than that which emerged in the US:

> *In Paris … the combined superficial area of the vehicles using the roads is actually greater than that of the roads themselves… And where do all these motors go? To the centre. But there is no proper superficial area available for traffic in the centre. It will have to be created. The existing centres must come down.*[92]

Cities must be demolished and rebuilt at higher densities, to make room for cars. Otherwise, things would become as bad as New York, where 'the congestion is so complete that business men have to leave their cars on the outskirts of town and take the tube to their offices.'[93] *Quelle horreur!*

Skyscrapers would be built on stilts so the ground could be covered with car parking, served by elevated roads or 'machines for traffic'. Le Corbusier invented the urban freeway: 'Running north and south, and east and west ... there would be great arterial roads for fast one-way traffic built on immense reinforced concrete bridges 120 to 180 yards in width and approached every half-mile or so by subsidiary roads from ground level.'[94] Underneath the roads and parking, railways would run in tunnels, but trams would be abolished. 'The tramway has no right to exist in the heart of the modern city.'[95]

Le Corbusier's version of autopia contradicted Ebenezer Howard's garden city in every way: it was authoritarian whereas the garden city was cooperative; high-rise instead of village-like; and based on cars (albeit supplemented by underground railways) rather than walking, trams and trains. But as the 20th century unfolded, the position gradually changed. The low-rise city came to be seen as intimately linked with the car, and public transport with high densities, and by the 21st century, the Le Corbusian skyscrapers invented to make room for cars were routinely presented as the antidote to car dependence.

Cars and suburbs seemed to have developed together in the US, while public transport held its own mainly in European cities, which remained much denser. The contributions made by different urban transport histories and policies, including the European tradition of public ownership of public transport, have been largely forgotten. Even critics of automobile dominance accepted the overwhelming importance of urban form, with the result that the 'compact city' has emerged as the most popular pathway for moving beyond the automobile age.

NOTES

1   Flink (1988, chs 4 and 5).
2   Batchelor (1994, p55).
3   Batchelor (1994); Merz (1929); Hall (1998, ch. 13).
4   Flink (1988, pp139–140, 153).
5   Flink (1988, p139).
6   Flink (1988, p360); Yago (1984, p11).
7   Howard (1966, p143).
8   Flink (1970, p112).
9   Davison (2004, pxii).
10 Meyer et al (1966, pp360–361).
11 Hall (1998, p838).
12 Hall (1988, p812); Snell (1974, pA-31). The following account draws on those of Flink, Hall, Snell, Black, Yago, Bottles and Fogelson.

13 Black (2006, ch. 10).
14 Yago (1984, p1).
15 Yago (1984, p58).
16 Snell (1974, pA-31).
17 GM reply, in Snell (1974, pA-124).
18 Slater (1997, p61).
19 Bottles (1987, p249).
20 Snell (1974, pA-32, fn 210).
21 *United States v National City Lines Inc, et al.* 186 Federal Reporter, 2d Series, 562–574, at p564.
22 Ibid., p565.
23 Snell (1974, pA-28).
24 *Report of the Federal Electric Railway Commission 1920*, in Smerk (1968, p10).
25 Smerk (1968, p24).
26 Smerk (1968, p16).
27 Yago (1984, p90).
28 Bush (1971, pp227–228).
29 Smerk (1968, p11).
30 Smerk (1968, p15).
31 Figures given in Hall (1998, p815).
32 736/km^2 at 2000 census; from Swiss Federal Statistical Office 'Regional Portrait: Zurich' www.statistics.admin.ch (accessed 30 August 2009).
33 Bottles (1987, p264, fig. 8); Fogelson (1993, tables 18–22).
34 This section based on Bottles (1987, ch. 5), Hall (1998, pp818–824) and Fogelson (1993, ch. 8).
35 Fogelson (1993, tables 18–22).
36 Cited in Bottles (1987, pp166 & 168).
37 Fogelson (1993).
38 Hall (1998, p827); the freeway plan is reproduced at Bottles (1987, p217).
39 See Bottles (1987, ch. 8); Hall (1998, pp824–831).
40 Bottles (1987, p249).
41 Bottles (1987, p247).
42 Hall (1998, p838).
43 Fogelson (1993, p185).
44 Census figures from US and NZ statistical agencies; tripmaking from J. Kenworthy and F. Laube (2001).
45 ARPA (1956, p117). Walking rates estimated by comparison with other Australasian cities that surveyed walking in the 1950s.
46 Hall (1998, p816).
47 Bush (1971, pp154–158, 229–233).
48 Bush (1971, pp234–241).
49 Bush (1971, p338). Trolleybuses were installed on busier routes, but were replaced with diesels in the 1970s.
50 The following account is based on Bush (1971, pp419–428); Harris (2005); Mees and Dodson (2002); Mees and Dodson (2007).
51 Quoted in ARPA (1956, p129).

52   Quoted in Harris (2005, p52, note 13).
53   ARPA (1956, pp130–132).
54   Quoted in Harris (2005, p45).
55   *Auckland Star*, 26 August 1954; see also Harris (2005, p45).
56   *Auckland Star*, 21 October 1954, quoted at Harris (2005, p45).
57   *New Zealand Herald*, 28 October and 1 November 1954, quoted at Harris (2005, p46).
58   ARPA (1956, p50).
59   ARPA (1956, p22).
60   ARPA (1956, p5).
61   ARPA (1956, p31).
62   Townsend (1998).
63   Fooks (1946, p43, capitalization in original).
64   Fooks (1946, p48).
65   ARPA (1956, p17).
66   AMPO (1951, p34). The AMPO became the ARPA in 1953.
67   Fooks (1946, p7).
68   Flyvbjerg et al (2002).
69   'Motorways "Ill-timed And Major Blunder"', *New Zealand Herald*, 7 July 1962; 'We should be aworking on the railroads', *Auckland Star*, 7 July 1962.
70   Bush (1971, pp371–373).
71   Quoted in Bush (1971, p390).
72   Bush (1971, pp426–427).
73   Bush (1971, p422).
74   ARA (1976).
75   ARA (1983).
76   Mees and Dodson (2002, p284).
77   Cumberland (1971, p10).
78   See Mees and Dodson (2007).
79   ARC (2005, pp45–46).
80   See 'Guide to the J. Douglas Carroll, Jr. Papers, 1938-1985', Cornell University Library, Coll. No. 4178, box 1, folder 10.
81   In 2005, CATS merged with the local planning commission to form the Chicago Metropolitan Agency for Planning. See www.catsmpo.com (accessed 30 August 2009).
82   Fischer (1984, p68).
83   CATS (1959, vol. 1, p74).
84   CATS (1959, p119, table 37).
85   CATS (1960, vol. 2, p53).
86   CATS (1959, vol. 1, pp43–44).
87   Clark (1967, p366). Clark's assumption that half of developed land was residential was incorrect: CATS actually found that only a third was, so Clark's density threshold should have been 32 per hectare, not 48.
88   Newman and Kenworthy (1989, p131).
89   See Yago (1984, ch. 6); Flink (1988, pp362–364).
90   CATS (1959, vol. 1, p21).

91 Creighton (1970, pp303–304).
92 Le Corbusier (1971, pp116–117).
93 Le Corbusier (1971, p118).
94 Le Corbusier (1971, p164).
95 Le Corbusier (1971, p165).

3

Beyond the Automobile Age

BEYOND BALANCED TRANSPORT

At its opening, the automobile age was expected to produce an improved urban environment. Looking back a century later, it is hard to believe that people could ever have thought this way. The current situation is encapsulated by the title of David Banister's 2005 book *Unsustainable Transport*, which catalogues the environmental problems created by autopia, including air pollution, traffic noise, accidents, degradation of landscapes by transport facilities, wastage of space and global warming from the burning of fossil fuels.[1]

These problems are all serious, and many have been recognized for decades. Local air pollution and the destruction caused by freeway building triggered the 'freeway revolts' that began in US cities in the 1960s and spread across the developed world. The policy conflicts of the time were also triggered by concerns about equity: as a pioneering study of the 1970s explained, the car can never provide access for all, because even in a wealthy community substantial numbers of people are prevented from driving by youth, age, disability, income, recent immigration or simply personal preference. These groups combine to form a large share of the population even in car-dominated cities and households with cars.[2]

The conflicts of the 1970s settled down to an uneasy truce in most places. Freeway construction was scaled back, the cuts falling heavily on inner city projects that threatened homes; some freeways went underground, the vast increase in costs itself acting as a brake on construction. Public transport received more attention, even in the US, where a modest amount of federal funding was made available following the inquiries initiated by President Kennedy (see Chapter 2). Kennedy's 1962 transport statement spoke of the need for 'balanced urban transportation',[3] and this became the slogan of the time. Public transport was the appropriate mode for commuting trips to congested city centres and travel within densely populated areas, but the car dominated all other trip types. Construction of freeways continued unabated in suburban and rural areas.

The result of the compromise was that automobile dependence continued to grow, albeit more slowly than before. The trip types assigned to public transport under the 'balanced' model have reduced in relative importance virtually everywhere in the world: inner city populations are declining as a percentage of metropolitan totals and are falling absolutely in many cities; work trips have fallen as a share of overall travel; the share of metropolitan employment in city centres is tending downwards.

The balanced transport model might be an improvement on unfettered autopia, but it is still unsustainable, particularly on a global scale. As incomes rise in developing nations like India and China, their urban middle classes aspire to western lifestyles and western travel opportunities. If per capita car usage in China alone reached current US levels, it would double the worldwide total. The rise of India and China comes just as scientists are pointing to the devastating consequences of global climate change. But how can Western nations credibly demand that developing countries adopt sustainable travel patterns if we are making no progress ourselves?

TRANSPORT AND CLIMATE CHANGE

The US presidential election of 2008 marked the end of official climate change scepticism, with both John McCain and Barack Obama committing to emission reductions targets. The other leader to resist binding targets had been Australia's John Howard, but Howard lost office (and his seat) at the national election of 2007. Now the challenge is to actually do something about greenhouse emissions.

The urgency of tackling climate change has been stressed in sources ranging from Al Gore's movie *An Inconvenient Truth* to the reports of the Intergovernmental Panel on Climate Change. The scale and seriousness of the problem has also been chronicled by national studies such as the 2007 Stern Report in the UK and the 2008 Garnaut Review in Australia. Transport is a critical element of the climate challenge, since it is the second-largest source of energy-related greenhouse emissions after electricity generation, accounting for around a quarter of the world total. Transport is also the fastest-growing source of emissions, the rate of increase having overtaken that for electricity generation in the last decade. Three-quarters of transport-related emissions come from road vehicles. OECD countries currently account for two-thirds of global transport emissions, but developing nations are fast catching up.[4]

Walking and cycling produce no greenhouse emissions and are the only truly sustainable travel modes. Public transport generally produces lower emissions per passenger than cars, but the difference depends on two factors. The first is the energy source used to power it: coal-fired power stations are actually less efficient energy sources than petrol- or diesel-powered engines, while hydro-electricity hardly produces any emissions. The second factor is vehicle occupancy rates: a bus with half a dozen passengers will be no more efficient, in greenhouse terms, than if the passengers travelled in cars at average occupancies. The Transport Working

Group of the Intergovernmental Panel on Climate Change (IPCC) reported that this is actually the case in the US, with emissions per bus passenger-kilometre being similar to those for car trips, 'mostly because buses have low load factors.'[5]

So a mode shift to walking and cycling will reduce greenhouse emissions, but shifts to public transport will only do so if low occupancy rates can be avoided. The challenge of shifting travel without unduly lowering occupancies has daunted many policy makers, with the result that key reports on climate change are rather subdued in their discussion of transport.

The IPCC's fourth Climate Change Assessment Report was released in 2007. The Synthesis Report focuses on regulatory reforms such as carbon trading schemes and financial incentives, and contains few direct mentions of transport. This reflects the cautious tone of the report from the Transport Working Group, which expressly excluded changes in mode share from its estimate of potential emissions reductions. The omission is the result of a lack of agreement about the potential for mode shift: 'Providing public transport systems ... and promoting non-motorised transport can contribute to GHG mitigation. However, local conditions determine how much transport can be shifted to less energy intensive modes.'[6] The problem is our old friend density. The potential for mode shift is 'strongly influenced by the density and spatial structure of the built environment', but 'densities are decreasing everywhere'.

The Stern Review has a similar focus on financial and regulatory instruments, and suggests that transport will be a particularly difficult sector in which to reduce emissions. Urban transport is discussed briefly, with Stern commenting: 'Higher energy prices [resulting from carbon pricing] and rising congestion require ... mass transit systems... Such systems lead to large gains in energy efficiency and reduced emissions as passengers transfer from private cars to public transport.'[7] The most positive assessment of the potential for mode shift comes, perhaps surprisingly, from Australia. The Garnaut Review argues that '[t]ransport emissions could be reduced faster and at lower cost if governments plan for more compact cities and invest in a shift from high-emissions modes to rail, public transport, walking and cycling'.[8]

The pessimism arises partly from the fact that demand for urban transport appears relatively price inelastic, meaning that large changes in prices are required to significantly influence demand. This creates a problem for carbon reduction strategies that rely mainly on increasing the price of high-carbon modes of transport. Of course, the price of petrol may well increase anyway, if the advocates of peak oil theory prove correct.

WHERE WILL THE OIL COME FROM?

As oil and petrol prices climbed to record highs in 2007 and 2008, 'peak oil' theory suddenly became mainstream, after decades of being the private obsession of a small group of researchers and enthusiasts. The basic principle is simple enough: there is only a finite amount of oil and eventually it will run out. Before it does so, production will peak and then decline. This has already occurred in the US, where local oil supplies peaked in the 1970s, and Australia, where the peak occurred at the turn of the millennium. Current world reserves of 'proven oil' are claimed to be sufficient to last for decades, even allowing for the rapid growth in consumption, but peak oil commentators argue that these reserves have been overstated (OPEC allocates production quotas on the basis of declared reserves, giving its members an incentive to overestimate).

The peak oil debate has not been helped by extravagant predictions that civilization is in imminent danger of collapse. These have something of the quality of the 1990s hysteria over the 'Y2K millennium bug', which in the end did little more than give bus travellers in Adelaide and Hobart unscheduled free rides on New Year's Day 2000. Peak oil does not mean that there will be no oil left; rather, if true, it means the end of cheap oil.

If conventional oil runs out or becomes prohibitively expensive there are substitutes available, but these are neither cheap nor environmentally friendly. Canada and Venezuela have vast fields of shale and sand oil, while coal can be converted to oil-like fuels through industrial processes. In each case, more energy is used to produce the oil than it actually provides, so extensive use of these substitutes would dramatically increase greenhouse emissions. Biofuels are a partial substitute for oil-based fuels, but are also fraught with problems. Biofuels are either made from food, in which case they drive up prices and increase hunger among the world's poor, or from specially grown crops planted on land created by clearing rainforests in places like Brazil and Indonesia.[9]

The idea that dependence on uncertain oil supplies is a problem, especially in concert with global warming, is gaining increasing acceptance. The Swedish government appointed a Commission on Oil Independence in 2005. The following year, the Commission reported that climate change and the risk of peak oil provide 'strong reasons for phasing out Sweden's dependency on oil … and in the long term replacing fossil fuel energy sources with renewable energy.'[10] Among the measures recommended were increasing the attractiveness of public transport for urban and interurban travel. In 2008, a consortium of British companies calling itself the UK Industry Taskforce on Peak Oil & Energy Security released a report entitled *The Oil Crunch: Securing the UK's energy future*. The taskforce commissioned two assessments of peak oil, one from Shell and the other from the consulting editor of *Petroleum Review*. Both reports concluded that supplies of 'easy oil' will peak, either in the period 2011–2013 or (Shell's view) a decade later. The taskforce recommended urgent action to prepare for an environment of constrained oil and constrained carbon emissions.

Even the International Energy Agency (IEA), which until recently scoffed at talk of peak oil, has modified its stance. The Agency's *World Energy Outlook 2008* report warns: 'The era of cheap oil is over'. Although the world is not about to run out of oil just yet, oil will be much more expensive than the agency had previously predicted. Very large increases in investment will be required to keep oil flowing, while dependence on the politically unstable Middle East will increase as production peaks in other countries. And oil appears headed for a plateau, even if not a peak: 'Although global oil production in total is not expected to peak before 2030, production of conventional oil is projected to level off towards the end of [this] period ... as almost all the additional capacity from new oilfields is offset by declines in output at existing fields.'[11] The difference is expected to be made up with natural gas and Canadian sand oils.

Perhaps there is a vast supply of easy, cheap oil about to be discovered. Perhaps, as peak oil sceptics claim, human ingenuity will provide an effortless solution to the problem. Alternatively, perhaps the peak oil pessimists are right and we will experience severe shortages in the next few years. Prudent governments should not be content to simply wait and hope something comes up, especially when the challenge posed by the possibility of peak oil is so similar to that presented by the probability of climate change. As the IEA says, current trends are unsustainable. 'It is not an exaggeration to claim that the future of human prosperity depends on how successfully we tackle the two central energy challenges facing us today: securing the supply of efficient and affordable energy; and effecting a rapid transformation to a low-carbon, efficient and environmentally benign system of energy supply.'[12]

SUSTAINABLE AUTOPIA? THE TECHNICAL FIX

The urgency of dealing with climate change and the uncertainty of global oil supplies provide ample reason for reconsidering the desirability of continued automobile dominance. Older problems like urban pollution and transport equity have not gone away either; they have been joined by new concerns, including the health effects of sedentary lifestyles involving little or no walking. Little wonder, then, that the United Nations' *Agenda 21* 'programme of action for sustainable development' adopted at the 1992 Rio Earth Summit and reaffirmed at the Johannesburg summit of 2002 calls for a mode shift away from the car. It urges countries to 'encourage development patterns that reduce transport demand', favour 'high-occupancy public transport' and 'encourage non-motorised modes of transport'.[13]

Agenda 21 was adopted by most of the world's countries, but has been honoured more in the breach than in the observance. The dominant approach to the environmental problems of automobile dominance has been to seek salvation in technology, rather than mode shift. The clean car becomes the preferred solution, thus absolving policy makers of the need to make substantive changes to transport policy.

Support for the technical fix is not confined to lazy governments. As we have seen, even the Transport Working Group of the IPCC emphasizes technical solutions while being reluctant to commit on mode shift. This reflects the composition of the working group itself: the coordinating authors were a Brazilian engineer specializing in biofuels and a Japanese researcher working at the Toyota R&D laboratory on 'clean energy vehicles'; the other 15 contributors to the report had similar backgrounds. Apparently, nobody was appointed with expertise in multi-modal transport planning, despite the ample evidence of the potential for mode shift available just outside the front door of the IPCC offices in Geneva.

The difficulty with a purely technical approach to vehicle efficiency is that cars are purchased and driven by human beings. Improvements that can be demonstrated in laboratories are rarely sustained in real cities. After all, as many as half of the trips even in the most auto-dependent cities are short enough to be made on foot or by bicycle, cutting emissions to zero. And small, light cars that use very little fuel have been available for many decades. The Fiat 500 launched in 1936, nicknamed Topolino (Mickey Mouse), managed fuel economy rates comparable to modern hybrids; the original 1948 model Morris Minor was almost as economical. Critics of public transport often point out that people will not use transit services just because they exist; the same applies to more efficient cars.

The gains in fuel efficiency that have been reported in recent decades should be treated with scepticism. They reflect improvements achieved in particular engines under laboratory conditions, not the on-road efficiency of the car fleet as a whole. If engine efficiency improves, it becomes more affordable to drive a larger vehicle, like a sports utility vehicle (SUV, or four-wheel drive, as they are called in Australia), and to add accessories like air conditioning. Cars can be made heavier and more powerful; this process explains why later Fiats and Morris Minors had lower fuel economy than the original models. And as urban areas expand, a larger share of driving takes place under congested city conditions rather than on open rural roads. So what is happening in the laboratories is not necessarily reflected on city roads.

What is required are data on the actual fuel efficiency of the on-road car fleet, something that is rarely provided in discussions of technical solutions (the IPCC's 2007 transport chapter offers only a graph of fuel economy standards set by governments). An excellent set of real-world data is available for Australia, thanks to the Survey of Motor Vehicle Use conducted by the Australian Bureau of Statistics (ABS) every few years since 1963. The results, which have been studiously ignored in discussions of greenhouse gas mitigation in that country, are set out in Table 3.1.

The average fuel economy of the Australian car fleet was the same in the last survey as in the first: there was no progress at all in more than four decades. The detailed data from the survey even show that cars manufactured since 2000 use more fuel than those built in the 1990s, mainly because the newer vehicles are more likely to be four-wheel drives.[14] The trend is not confined to Australia. The British Royal Commission on Environmental Pollution noted back in 1994 that increases in the size and weight of vehicles had negated the effect of improved

Table 3.1 *Fuel efficiency of the Australian car fleet, 1963–2006*

Year	Litres/100km
1963	11.4
1971	12.3
1976	12.6
1979	12.5
1982	12.5
1985	12.1
1988	11.9
1991	12.3
1995	11.5
1998	11.7
1999	11.6
2002	11.3
2004	11.5
2006	11.4

Source: ABS (1963–2007) *Survey of Motor Vehicle Usage*

engine efficiency in the UK and Europe.[15] More recently, the Stern Report notes that 'incremental improvements to existing [car engine] technologies … have been more than offset by the growth in demand and shift towards more powerful and heavier vehicles.'[16]

If electrically powered cars ever become viable, they will largely eliminate emissions from the tailpipe – by transferring them to the power station. The Royal Commission on Environmental Pollution concluded that there would be 'no overall benefit for the environment in the widespread use in the UK of electrically powered cars.'[17] The Australian Garnaut Review estimated that electric cars would increase emissions in the State of Victoria (where most electricity comes from dirty brown coal) by 60 per cent, but cut them by 85 per cent in the small island state of Tasmania where most power comes from hydro-electric schemes (built in former wilderness areas: everything comes at a cost).[18] The global effect of a large shift to electric cars would be to increase greenhouse emissions, since coal is still the main source of power.

This is not a reason to abandon the search for cleaner and more efficient engine technology, but it is a reason why technological change is unlikely to be enough. If the car fleet really became more fuel efficient, this would reduce the cost of travel, and would produce a similar effect to a drop in the fuel price: travel would increase and so would emissions. The same human and social complexity that makes the task of providing viable public transport so challenging makes it unlikely that technology will solve the problems created by automobile dependence.

ECONOMISTS TO THE RESCUE: CHARGING FOR CONGESTION

Gavin Newsom was sworn in for a second term as Mayor of San Francisco in January 2008. His inaugural address covered the full gamut of municipal issues, but singled out one: 'a sensible congestion-pricing plan is the single greatest step we can take to protect our environment and improve our quality of life.'[19] This is a big claim, but as the mayor said, it is one 'national and international experts agree on'. Congestion pricing has come a long way since 1992, when Anthony Downs called it 'a theoretically interesting device invented by academics but implemented only in their imaginations.'[20]

The academics, economists and engineers who invented congestion charging did not have the environment in mind, and had never heard of global warming. These concerns were not mentioned at all in the Smeed Committee's 1964 report on road pricing to the UK Department of Transport, which is generally accepted as the starting-point for the idea. Road pricing was directed at reducing congestion, not environmental damage, and was designed to expand overall road capacity by encouraging people who could do so to travel at times when spare capacity was available. An electronic system would levy city-wide tolls, with higher rates at busy times and in congested areas, and lower tolls for quiet times and places.

Since cars use less fuel per kilometre in uncongested conditions, some have argued that congestion pricing can reduce greenhouse emissions and other environmental 'externalities'. The same argument has been made by advocates of new and expanded freeways, and the same objection applies in both cases. Uncongested driving will reduce emissions per kilometre travelled, but increase the amount of travel, as people respond rationally to the reduced time cost of travel. In theory, road pricing offers a way out of this dilemma, if the charges are set to redistribute travel from the car to other modes, rather than from congested to uncongested roads. It is on this basis that environmentalists have swung their support behind the concept.

Environmentalists had nothing to do with the 1971 Concept Plan for Singapore, which led to the city-state becoming the testing-ground for congestion charging. The plan was developed by Australian consultants who were strongly influenced by the planning of their country's capital.[21] The Canberra plan had one overriding objective, to eliminate traffic congestion. This was to be achieved by restricting employment in the city centre and providing an extensive network of freeways. Canberra was laid out as a Y-shaped 'linear city', a popular concept in planning circles at the time, and one intended to allow a 'balanced' transport system incorporating a bus rapid transit connection between major centres. The proposed busway was never built, but most of the freeways were, and Canberra has become a paradigm of autopia, albeit one with an urban form that would make it feasible to retro-fit a public transport system.

It is ironic that Singapore has been presented as a paradigm of sustainable transport, because the model for its 1971 Concept Plan was the Canberra Y-

Plan. The consultants had to adapt the concepts developed for Canberra to the constrained site and higher population. They twisted the linear city into a circle, and the Y-Plan morphed into a Ring-Plan. Bus rapid transit was replaced by a Mass Rapid Transit (MRT) rail system (and in contrast with Canberra, the MRT was actually built). Major freeways were proposed, and built, for new growth areas, but '[i]n the present urban area, however, and particularly in the densely populated and valuable areas in and near the central city, problems of land acquisition pose enormous difficulties'. Therefore, other measures would be needed, such as 'Central Area licensing, road pricing or parking controls'.[22]

The Singapore government diligently implemented the plan, including the world's first central area licensing scheme, which commenced in 1975. Cars entering the central business district (CBD) in peak hour paid a fee at toll gates, which were later replaced by electronic gantries. The system has since been expanded to provide road pricing on major expressways. Singapore also restricts car ownership through a quota system: new vehicles must have a Certificate of Entitlement (COE), and only a limited number of certificates are issued.

Singapore's recent transport policies are no more based on environmental concerns than was the 1971 Concept Plan. The 1996 White Paper *A World Class Land Transport System* makes no mention of climate change. Its objective is 'providing commuters with a wide spectrum of transport choices'. The White Paper acknowledges that '[t]he attractiveness of car travel will increase still further when we expand future road capacity', through projects such as the Singapore Underground Road System (SURS), which 'promises the equivalent of 40 per cent more road capacity within the [central] city. With SURS, motorists can enjoy the same average travel speed with 40 per cent more traffic.' Road pricing supplements the new roads; it 'will keep the key roads and expressways free-flowing' and allow a relaxation of restrictions on car ownership through the issuing of more COEs.[23]

Hardly surprisingly, then, car use in Singapore is growing rapidly. Mileage per vehicle is very high: the average car in Singapore travelled 21,100km in 2006, double the figure for 1980 and virtually identical to the 21,317km reported for Los Angeles. This is fully 58 per cent higher than the 2006 Australian average of 13,900km, quite an achievement considering that Australia is 10,000 times as large as Singapore.[24] Total car travel is being kept in check not by congestion pricing, but by the COE system, and even this is under pressure. The number of Singapore residents rose by 6 per cent in the five years to 2007, but the number of cars jumped 19 per cent, traffic entering Singapore's CBD grew by 14 per cent and CBD traffic speeds fell by up to 30 per cent. Public transport's share of peak hour travel in 2004 was a very high 63 per cent, but still lower than the 67 per cent recorded in 1997. Car ownership is only 126 vehicles for every 1000 residents, but this is double the 1980 rate of 64, and continues to grow as incomes rise.[25] And why wouldn't it? Singapore has made cars very expensive, but also very attractive.

While car use remains lower than in most high-income cities, Singapore risks becoming a smaller, denser version of Los Angeles – a model of 'balanced transport' perhaps, but not of sustainability. The city-state's latest Land Transport Strategy, released in 2008, expresses concern about this trend, noting the rapid growth in car travel and the decline in public transport's share of the market. The proposed solutions are yet more road-building, upgraded public transport and increased electronic road pricing charges. The key measure, however, is a reduction in the number of COEs issued, intended to reduce growth in vehicle numbers from 3 per cent per annum to 1.5 per cent.[26]

This is not the story that is generally told about Singapore. Economists have been joined by environmentalists and public transport activists in a chorus of praise that ignores the steady growth of car use and the key role of the COE rationing system.

Road pricing may have been implemented first in Singapore, but the notion was developed and refined in Britain. So it is appropriate that London was the first major city to follow Singapore's example (apologies to Bergen, Norway, which adopted a similar scheme in 1986), and the British government the first to seriously entertain a national road pricing scheme. The London congestion charge introduced by Mayor Ken Livingstone in February 2003 drew on four decades of dogged work by British transport planners and economists. This helps account for the rapturous reception it received from planners, one of whom called it 'the most radical transport policy to be introduced in any major European city centre since the centre of Rome was closed off to chariots … 2000 years ago.'[27]

This was something of an overstatement, as a closer look at the results shows. Transport for London (TfL), the agency responsible for the scheme, conducted careful before and after surveys that enable changes to be tracked. Between October 2002 and October 2003, the number of cars entering the central charging zone each day fell by 63,000 or 33 per cent, and the number of people entering by bus rose by 71,000 or 37 per cent. Similar results were recorded for outbound trips, and the project was hailed a stunning success.

Most reports neglected to mention that before the charge only 12 per cent of people travelling to central London did so in cars and 7 per cent in buses; the overwhelming majority, 77 per cent, travelled by train.[28] So what happened to train numbers? They fell by 5 per cent or 90,000, a figure that received considerably less publicity than the others. This suggests that many of the additional bus passengers were former train users, and that overall travel to central London had declined. Livingstone optimistically interpreted the results as showing that 'improvements to bus operations appear to be providing some breathing space by attracting passengers … who would otherwise have been on highly congested trains'. David Banister points out that other surveys showed a 7 per cent fall in the number of visitors to central London and concludes that the charge probably depressed retail sales by 1–2 per cent.[29] Much of the decline in rail patronage was due to the closure of the Underground's Central Line for repairs, however, and rail numbers rebounded in 2005 while car traffic remained at the 2004 levels.

Those hailing the success of congestion charging also omitted to mention that peak-period car trips to central London had been declining for a long time, with a 13 per cent fall recorded between 1990 and 2000 despite a small rise in travel by all modes.[30] Overall, it seems reasonable to conclude that the London congestion charge and associated bus improvements accelerated this trend, and transferred up to 100,000 car trips per day, plus some rail trips, to bus. The reduction in car trips deserves to be counted as a success, but a modest one. There were 11 million daily car trips across Greater London in 2001,[31] so the result was a reduction of under 1 per cent. Given that Livingstone cited survey evidence pointing to a 4 per cent mode shift from the car to public transport by 2004,[32] perhaps more attention should be given to the measures that produced the other three-quarters of this change. Congestion charging may have a role to play in building sustainable urban transport systems, but it is unlikely to be a major one. It also offers one way of raising funds for public transport improvements; this was an important motivation in London.

AN INCONVENIENT TRUTH

The real problem with road pricing, as Singapore has demonstrated, is that it makes car travel more attractive, especially for those who can afford to pay the charge. Travel time has a greater influence on demand than price, unless prices are kept at punishing levels, so as incomes rise over time road pricing will increase demand in the same way as any other speeding-up measure. Congestion, on the other hand, gives even wealthy motorists an incentive to consider alternatives, as long as public transport is able to avoid the worst congestion through priority measures. That's why European cities with relatively low car use have slow traffic speeds, while most US cities combine fast traffic with high car use. As the transport component of Vancouver's Livable Region Strategic Plan says:

> Congestion is usually considered an evil; however, allowing congestion to deteriorate for single-occupant vehicles is a practical method of promoting transit and carpools... For instance, buses/carpools in HOV [high occupancy vehicle] lanes will gain an edge since the relative time saved by escaping lineups will be greater.[33]

The Livable Region Plan came into effect in 1993, and used congestion as part of a package of policies designed to promote self-containment and mode shift away from the car. In 2006 and 2008, Statistics Canada released the results from the 2005 Canadian Social Survey and the 2006 census. These received little attention from planners, which is a shame, because they show that the 1993 plan has worked. Despite rapid population growth, Vancouver was the only Canadian urban region where the average time taken for the journey to work had declined, from 70 minutes in 1992 to 67 in 2005. By contrast times in Montreal jumped from 62 to 76 minutes. The Vancouver result was due to a decrease in average journey lengths, combined with improvements in the speed of public transport.

Vancouver reduced journey times by promoting congestion, while the other Canadian cities increased them by planning for higher speeds! The share of trips made by car drivers dropped from 70.6 per cent to 67.3 between 1996 and 2006, as walking and public transport use both rose.[34] And as if to reassure those afraid that promoting congestion would damage the economy, Vancouver was awarded the title of 'world's most livable city' two years running – not by Friends of the Earth, but by the Economist Intelligence Unit.

Vancouver has squared the circle, albeit on a modest scale, making progress towards Ebenezer Howard's vision of a self-contained city based on walking and public transport. Given that other attempts to combine self-containment and mode shift away from the car have apparently failed, one might have expected planners to be shouting these results from the rooftops.

Vancouver and Singapore both confirm that car use cannot be reduced by making it more attractive. Vukan Vuchic makes the point with a simplified discussion of incentives and disincentives.[35] Imagine there are only two travel modes, called auto and transit. Demand for these modes is determined by the differences between them in overall costs to users: out-of-pocket expenses and travel time. These costs can be changed through incentives and disincentives. A policy package combining auto incentives and transit disincentives, as seen in past decades in Los Angeles and Auckland (see Chapter 2), will naturally shift travel from transit to auto. A 'balanced' package providing incentives for both modes will probably increase travel overall, but is unlikely to shift many trips to transit. The only way to produce mode shift is to combine transit incentives with auto disincentives: Vuchic cites Munich as an example, because it upgraded public transport while pedestrianizing and narrowing inner city streets. The logic of this position is difficult to avoid, although transport policy makers in most cities remain determined to do so.

Neither technology nor congestion charging provides the magic wand that will enable us to reduce emissions from cars while using them more. If our planet and our cities are to remain habitable, the time has come to move beyond the automobile age. This does not mean abolishing the car, any more than the end of the age of horse-drawn transport meant that people were no longer able to ride or race horses. But it does mean that cities and suburbs can no longer be planned with the car as the dominant mode. The solution is neither autopia nor balanced transport, but for walking, cycling and public transport to collectively become the majority mode, in suburbs as well as city centres.

Some idea of what the future needs to look like can be seen in the City of Zurich, where one of the wealthiest communities in the world has been happy for the car to become a minority mode. In 1990, Zurich had the lowest car use of ten sustainable transport 'success stories' studied by Stefan Bratzel of the Free University of Berlin, with 37 per cent of total trips made by public transport, 35 per cent on foot or cycle and 28 per cent by car.[36] Since then, public transport use has gained further ground: more city residents now own public transport passes than cars. Unfortunately, general travel surveys are difficult to compare, because different cities conduct them at different times and with different methodologies: there are particular problems with recording walking trips, as Chapter 11 explains. Census figures usually only cover trips to and from work (and sometimes school), but are much more useful for comparative purposes. At the Swiss census of 2000, 63 per cent of work trips by residents of Zurich City were by public transport, 12 per cent on foot or cycle and 25 per cent by 'motorized individual transport' (mainly car), the car share having fallen from 26 per cent in 1990. The equivalent figures from 2000 for the Canton as a whole are 41, 12 and 47 per cent respectively.[37] The whole Zurich region has not yet moved beyond the automobile age, but the prospect is not as daunting there as in most other places.

It is no coincidence that Zurich is renowned for the high degree of public involvement in political decision-making as well as for its transport patterns (see Chapter 8). In many cities, citizens have a keener understanding of the need for change than transport planners, with environmental awareness particularly strong among younger residents. Critics respond that this enthusiasm is not necessarily reflected in transport choices, but in places where viable alternatives exist, younger urban residents are beginning to practise what they preach. There was a modest increase in the share of 'sustainable modes' (walking, cycling and public transport) across Canada's cities between the 2001 and 2006 censuses; the change was driven by a large shift away from the car by workers in the 25–34 age bracket and a smaller shift by workers aged 35–44.[38]

Citizens are voting with their ballot papers, and occasionally their feet, for the alternatives to autopia. However, the same citizens who are most concerned about sustainable transport are often the fiercest defenders of leafy, low-rise neighbourhoods. Policy makers face a dilemma: is it possible to provide public transport solutions for suburbia, or must all sustainable cities look like Hong Kong?

Notes

1   Banister (2005, chs 2 and 3); see also Gilbert and Perl (2008, chs 3 and 4).
2   Schaeffer and Sclar (1975).
3   In Smerk (1968, pp304–310 at p306).
4   Figures taken from Kahn-Ribeiro and Kobayashi (2007).
5   Kahn-Ribeiro and Kobayashi (2007, p348).
6   Kahn-Ribeiro and Kobayashi (2007, pp326, 367).
7   Stern (2007, p436).
8   Garnaut (2008, p525).

9   See Giampetro and Mayumi (2009).
10 Commission on Oil Independence (2006, p24).
11 IEA (2008, pp3, 40).
12 IEA (2008, p37).
13 UN (1993, 7.52).
14 SMVU 2005 data cubes, ABS Cat. 9210.0.55.001, table 10 (this information was not available for the 2006 survey at the time of writing). Another factor may be that people in rural areas tend to drive older cars.
15 RCEP (1994, pp130, 135).
16 Stern (2007, p404).
17 RCEP (1994, p143).
18 Garnaut (2008, p519).
19 Inaugural Address 8 January 2008, p9; available at www.sfgov.org/site/mayor_index.asp?id=22016 (accessed 30 August 2009).
20 Downs (1992, p60).
21 The following is based on Cervero (1998, ch. 6); Thomson (1977, pp290–294); Wang (2005) and a special edition of the *Royal Australian Planning Institute Journal* dealing with the Singapore Concept Plan: vol. 9, no. 2, April 1971.
22 Olszewski and Skeates (1971, pp67, 68).
23 LTA (1995, pp3, 10, 22, 12, 35).
24 LTA (2008b); 1980 figure from Kenworthy and Laube (1999, p501); LA figure is for 1990, from Kenworthy and Laube (1999, p467); Australian figure from ABS (2007, p9, table 1). The average figure for Australia's capital cities in 2006 was 11,800km (2007, p14, table 6).
25 From LTA *Land Transport Statistics*, 2008 and 2004 editions, Kenworthy and Laube (1999) and LTA (2008, pp20, 54).
26 LTA (2008).
27 Banister (2004, p499).
28 TfL (2004, pp26 (car)); TfL (2005, pp45 (bus) and 52–53 (rail)); mode shares from Downs (2004, p172) (these figures may understate the number who walked or cycled).
29 Livingstone (2004, p495); Banister (2004, p500).
30 TfL (2001, p8).
31 Mayor of London (2001, p40, figure 2.12).
32 Livingstone (2004, p495).
33 GVRD (1993, p26).
34 Travel times from Statistics Canada (2006, p15, table 1); mode shares from Statistics Canada (2008b).
35 Vuchic (1999, pp238–244).
36 Bratzel (1999, p183, table 1).
37 Swiss Federal Statistical Office, 'pendler' table A2A, Gemeinde Zurich (261); Kanton Zurich (1). Figures are for all resident workers, including those employed outside the city or canton.
38 Statistics Canada (2008b, table 12).

4

The Compact City

WHY NOT CONTROL LAND USE?

If urban traffic is a function of land use, then it follows that land-use planning is the key to sustainable transport. If low population densities cause autopia, then high densities will reverse the trend. This is the reasoning behind the idea of the compact city.

The proposal is not new. The Chicago Area Transportation Study (CATS) canvassed it half a century ago, citing unnamed writers who 'argue that the suburban dweller should be prevented from stretching out into quarter acre lots because a high density, compact city would be more efficient'. So 'why not control land use and density so as to control the level of mass transportation usage?' The study team's answer was that people prefer dispersed living and would be unlikely to accept measures to restrain densities. 'A more reasonable position is that people, acting in their own interests in a relatively free society, are gradually evolving their desired environment'.[1]

As concern about the environmental and other problems of autopia grew, the reasonableness of this position was increasingly questioned. Contemporary advocates of the compact city have the opposite view of car dominance to the Chicago transport planners of the 1950s, but their recipe for undoing autopia accepts the same logic, namely that unless densities are substantially increased, alternatives to the car are impossible. Environmentalists who argue in this manner can unintentionally provide support for the continuation of unsustainable transport policies, in the same way that we saw the density argument being used in Los Angeles, Auckland and Chicago in Chapter 2.

This problem can be seen in the UK today. Outside London, urban public transport is extremely unattractive and offers no serious competition to the car, for reasons discussed in the next chapter. But many British advocates of sustainable transport seem more interested in higher-density housing than in fixing public transport. The dominant view is presented in *Building the 21st Century Home*, a widely used guidebook published in 1999:

> *We may lament the decline in public transport and the effects of deregula-*
> *tion and reducing subsidy. However it must be recognised that the dis-*
> *persal of development and the reduction of housing densities has also*
> *played its part. The Local Government Management Board estimates*
> *that densities of 100 persons per hectare are required to support a viable*
> *bus service and 240 persons per hectare for a tram service, whereas*
> *the average density of new housing development is just 22 units to the*
> *hectare [or] around 50 people.*[2]

So deregulation and lack of funding are not the main barriers to improved public transport; density is the problem. Apparently, development densities need to double just to make bus services possible, and to increase five-fold before Britons can think about trams. Quite simply, this is never going to happen. No metropolitan areas in Europe should have trams on this basis, although the City (but not the suburbs) of Paris just squeaks in with around 250 residents per gross hectare. This an argument for giving up on alternatives to the car.

So where do the density figures come from? The report cited as the source, published by the Local Government Board but written by academics from the University of the West of England in Bristol, does specify 100 residents per hectare as the minimum density for buses, but I could find no reference in it to a minimum for trams.[3] The report did not 'estimate' the bus figure, however; it simply cited Peter White's 1976 book *Planning for Public Transport* as the source. White's only mention of a specific density threshold comes in a sceptical discussion of the then-new concept of 'dial-a-bus', which refers to un-named American consultants who believe it requires 'about twenty to forty persons per acre' (50 to 100 per hectare). White omitted the figure from later editions of the book, noting that dial-a-ride was a high-cost mode and most services have been withdrawn.[4] So the supposed density requirement for buses is not the result of estimation or calculation at all, while the higher figure for trams seems to have emerged from thin air.

The CATS did develop a density threshold for bus services of 100 persons per net residential hectare, which Clark translated to a 'neighbourhood' density of 48 per hectare. As we saw in Chapter 2, these figures didn't really prove anything, and were subsequently disowned by the study's deputy director. In the process of migrating to the UK, the CATS/Clark figure has mysteriously doubled for buses and increased five-fold for trams. It has also become gospel and is now cited in almost any discussion of sustainable cities in the UK. For example, the Commission for Architecture and the Built Environment endorsed the 100 for bus and 240 for tram figures in its 2005 Better Neighbourhoods report. The Commission even endorsed 275 people per hectare as a 'sustainable urban density' – bad news for the City of Paris, with only 250.[5]

Britain is not the only place where low densities are said to create insuperable problems for public transport. The American architectural historian Robert Bruegmann writes in his 2005 book *Sprawl*: 'It appears that 10,000 people per square mile [39 per hectare] is a threshold for the extensive use of public transportation systems'. Although Bruegmann never mentions CATS in his book, he derives his threshold from the gross density of the City of Chicago, on the basis that it and New York are the only US cities where public transport is used extensively.[6] Alan Moran, from the Australian free-market think-tank the Institute of Public Affairs, offers the highest figures of all. 'A rule of thumb is that rail-based systems require 40,000 people per square kilometre [400 per hectare] to be viable… Express bus systems need 26,000 per square kilometre [260/ha].' No source is cited for these figures.[7]

As we saw in the previous chapter, the Transport Working Group of the Intergovernmental Panel on Climate Change also sees low and declining densities as a major barrier to mode shift. The Working Group even argues that expanding bus services in US cities would make global warming worse, since it means adding extra services, 'targetting less dense corridors',[8] resulting in lower occupancies. This argument echoes CATS, which observed: 'Suggesting that buses should serve lower densities immediately implies the chance of financial loss.'[9]

If densities of 400, 240 or even 100 per hectare are really required to make transport sustainable, then we had better begin searching for a new planet to live on. Built form changes very slowly in aggregate – most of the houses New Yorkers or Melburnians will inhabit in 2050 already exist – but climate change requires urgent action, and the other problems of automobile dependence cannot be put off for decades either.

Arguments that densities many times current levels are needed before transport trends can change are really arguments for continuing with automobile dependence. Bruegmann and Moran intend us to draw this conclusion, and while other commentators seek to encourage higher-density development, the main effect of their arguments is to provide support for the advocates of autopia. We need to find a way of reducing automobile dependence without impossibly large changes to urban densities. Fortunately, a closer look at the evidence suggests that this task might be achievable, and that density is no more a barrier to transport change now than it was in Los Angeles in the 1920s or Auckland in the 1950s.

THE DENSITY DEBATE

Murdoch University is a most unlikely place to have spawned the compact city movement. The campus opened in 1973 in a paddock adjacent to a freeway in the suburbs of Perth, a low-density city even by Australian standards. Murdoch was the base from which Peter Newman and Jeff Kenworthy conducted their pioneering study of cities and transport, beginning after the oil shock of the 1970s and culminating in 1989 with publication of *Cities and Automobile Dependence* and supporting papers in planning journals. *Cities* and its 1999 update *Sustainability and Cities* set the terms for the debate over density in the last two decades, coining the term 'automobile dependence', reviving the idea of the compact city as the response, and establishing the multi-city comparison of transport and urban form as the methodology for investigating the issue.

Compared with Alan Moran and the British density enthusiasts, Newman and Kenworthy are moderates, suggesting the critical threshold is around 30 per hectare, rather than 100 or more. This figure was, as we saw in Chapter 2, derived from CATS via Colin Clark, but Newman and Kenworthy corroborated it with their comparison of densities and automobile use across a range of cities and countries. The comparison was expressed as a much-reproduced graph showing a hyperbolic relationship in which car use increases exponentially once densities drop below about 30 per hectare. Hong Kong had the highest density and lowest energy use; Houston the lowest density and highest energy use. Interestingly, an almost identically shaped graph, comparing car trip-making and density in different parts of Chicago, appears in the first volume of the CATS report.[10]

The compact city thesis has been debated for more than two decades, and the debate may have produced more heat than light. David Banister offers a comprehensive review of the literature, observing that much of the analysis has been 'very simplistic in its approach', and concluding that 'the situation is very much more complex than is often argued'.[11]

Some compact city sceptics have criticized the quality of Newman and Kenworthy's data, generally without offering anything better to replace it – the principal exception here is the American transport and planning critic Wendell Cox.[12] With each successive edition of the database, now in its third iteration, Newman and Kenworthy have corrected errors and omissions as well as expanding the range of cities reported. Interestingly, over time their figures have converged with those of their rival Cox.

Other critics, mainly American opponents of compact cities and rail transit, have claimed that the problem of automobile dependence is being resolved by the spread of cities. In *Sprawl*, Robert Bruegmann argues that the Newman and Kenworthy thesis is disproved by research showing that flexible land markets allow firms and workers to co-locate, producing trips that take fewer minutes, even if not fewer miles. This work, by Peter Gordon and Harry Richardson – based appropriately enough at the University of Southern California in Los Angeles – shows that autopia is sustainable.[13] Unfortunately, by the time *Sprawl* was published, the theory had been resoundingly debunked by results from the US Census, which includes a question on the time taken to travel to work. The national average rose from 21.7 minutes in 1980 to 22.4 minutes in 1990, then jumped to 25.5 minutes in 2000.[14] The increase in urban areas was even greater. Gordon and Richardson now concede that trips are not getting shorter, and rather unconvincingly suggest that rapid income growth during the 1990s might explain the result.[15] They do not address the question why similar income growth in Vancouver over the same period was accompanied by reduced travel times.

Not all critics of the compact city are advocates of autopia. Professor Ian Lowe is President of the Australian Conservation Foundation, and author of dozens of papers and monographs on environmental issues, including *Living in the Hothouse* (2005), a plea for serious action to combat climate change. But Lowe also understands the attractiveness of leafy suburbs, and the equity issues involved:

> *This comparatively uncrowded urban form is one of the aspects of Australian urban lifestyle which appeals to those of us who have lived in the northern hemisphere. I live in a Brisbane suburb, ten minutes bicycle ride from Griffith University and near an express bus route which takes twelve minutes to the city centre, but in a quiet street backing onto bush. I am more likely to be awakened by rainbow lorikeets than traffic. Few of the world's cities offer such a lifestyle to any but the very rich.*[16]

Lowe acknowledges that the current transport pattern in Australia 'fails on all three criteria of sustainability'. Change is needed, but Lowe would like it to happen without depriving ordinary Australians of quiet streets backing onto bush. He seems unsure about how this might be accomplished.

Other Australian urbanists share Lowe's concerns. Pat Troy of the Australian National University penned *The Perils of Urban Consolidation* (1996), a swingeing rebuttal which indicts the compact city on efficiency, equity, environmental and democratic grounds. The economic historian Hugh Stretton shares these concerns and adds a political argument. 'Australians would rather lose their cars than lose their cars and their houses. However hard it may be to get them to trade their big cars for little ones … or to give them up altogether, it would be harder still to get them to do it by first giving up their houses and gardens and neighbourhood parks and playing fields.'[17]

Stretton lives in Adelaide, the plan for which provided much of the inspiration for Ebenezer Howard's 'correct principles of city growth'. He advocates a modern version of the garden city – 'poly-centred conurbations in which land is used generously for housing but more densely for many public and commercial uses'[18] with efficient public transport connecting the centres. This alternative version of the sustainable city is championed as an antidote to global warming by Brendan Gleeson, director of the Urban Research Program at Ian Lowe's home base, Griffith University in Brisbane.[19] Howard might well have approved of this alternative road away from the automobile age, but it appears to be a minority taste among 21st-century urban planners.

LET'S LOOK AT THAT AGAIN

Troy's most telling criticism of compact city advocacy is that correlation is not the same as causation. Walking and public transport use tend to be higher the closer one comes to the city centre, for a variety of reasons: the share of trips made to the centre (the best-served destination by public transport and the hardest to reach by car) increases; municipally provided public transport is usually better in the central municipality (as we saw in 1950s Chicago in Chapter 2); and radial public transport routes converge, reducing walking distances to stops and stations. Car use rises with distance from the centre even in cities with uniform densities, such as Canberra. Since density also declines with distance from the centre in most cities, there will appear to be a relationship between density and car use. But this correlation does not prove causation: the number of fire engines sent to a fire correlates strongly with the amount of damage done by the fire, but sending fewer crews will not reduce the damage bill.

There is no doubt that very large differences in density do affect transport patterns. It would be impossible for the car to dominate travel in Hong Kong or Manhattan, no matter how much effort was devoted to the task (and in the case of New York, considerable effort was employed by transport supremo Robert Moses, until public opinion finally turned against him[20]). Conversely, in spacious cities like Houston and Canberra, it is possible to plan on the basis that cars will dominate. So the general relationship shown in Newman and Kenworthy's famous graph is undoubtedly correct. But Houston is never going to become Hong Kong or anything like it: that would require demolition and rebuilding on a Corbusian scale. The question is whether achievable changes in density are likely to make a significant difference, and here the evidence is less compelling.

In 2004, a team of Israeli researchers re-examined the Australian and US cities in the original *Cities and Automobile Dependence* dataset. Their analysis, replete with a reproduction of the famous hyperbola, found no correlation between density and energy consumption: the US cities had similar densities to the Australian cities, but much higher car and energy use.[21] The Newman and Kenworthy graph actually shows that Australian cities' car use rates are closer to those of the European cities than to the US cities, despite the large differences in density.

These results suggest the need for a closer look at the whole question. It is time to open up Dr Ernest Fooks' six-decades-old toolkit and X-ray some cities. The key point Fooks made in *X-Ray the City!* was that useful measures of density should be based on the area of urbanized land, not on arbitrary administrative boundaries. The whole urban area should be counted, not just that portion lying with the boundaries of a central municipality: urbanized New York extends far beyond the five boroughs of New York City, into Long Island and even the neighbouring states of Connecticut and New Jersey. Conversely, only urbanized land should be counted when measuring density, so the density given in Chapter 2 for Los Angeles in 1930 is too low, because it includes non-urban land that happened to lie within city boundaries.

Density can be X-rayed in more detail by distinguishing between residential and non-residential land. *Net residential density* is calculated by considering only the residential blocks on which houses are built. *Gross residential density* includes non-residential uses found within residential neighbourhoods, such as local schools and open space. *Overall urban density* includes all other urban uses, such as industrial areas, transport terminals and regional open space.[22] Different definitions of density will naturally produce different figures. For example, CATS found that less than half the study area was urbanized, and only a third of this urbanized area was residential. So while the Chicago region's net residential density was 110.5 per hectare, its overall urban density was 34.5 per hectare. Simply dividing the population into the total study area would have produced a 'density' of only 16.1 per hectare.[23]

When comparing the densities of different cities, or parts of cities, it is important to use consistent definitions, count only urbanized land and count all the urbanized land. Most discussions of density by urban planners have failed this test. Countless discussions of metropolitan areas have compared 'densities' of inner and outer municipalities based on the whole area within municipal borders. Since outer municipalities often incorporate large areas of non-urban land, the result always appears to be a steep decline in density with distance from the centre. But this decline is likely to be exaggerated or even completely illusory: a careful analysis of the Australian city of Adelaide found that the apparent decline in density was a statistical artefact, with residential densities actually highest on the urban fringe, and overall urban densities roughly constant throughout the metropolis.[24]

Newman and Kenworthy expressly attempted to avoid problems of this kind in their multi-city comparison, by using a definition that corresponds to overall urban density in the above discussion. They were successful in most cases, but not all. In some cities, especially in Europe, land-use data for complete urbanized areas proved difficult to obtain, and only the central municipality was studied. Because the central municipality is the most densely populated part of the region, this means the density figures are too high for all such cities. In the case of the 1999 *International Sourcebook*, this means Amsterdam, Brussels, Frankfurt, Hamburg, Munich, Stockholm and Vienna – most of the European cities shown on the famous hyperbola.[25]

A similar problem affected Newman and Kenworthy's density data for Toronto, which was confined to the City of Toronto (formerly the Municipality of Metropolitan Toronto). The resulting overstatement of density was magnified by the fact that the gross residential area was inadvertently used as the basis for calculating density, instead of the overall urban area. This can be seen clearly from the map of urbanized Toronto in the *International Sourcebook*, which shows Toronto and York Universities, two large cemeteries, the main racecourse and numerous parks as non-urban.[26] These deficiencies were corrected for the third edition of the dataset, the 2001 *Millennium Database*, resulting in a large decline in the density figure reported for Toronto. Unfortunately, in the meantime the erroneous figure had been widely cited, particularly in Australia, as proof that huge density increases were needed to compete with the car.

Newman and Kenworthy had little difficulty specifying the densities of American cities, because the US Census Bureau has been calculating overall urban density figures for some time. An 'urbanized area' is defined for each metropolitan region, made up by combining adjacent 'census blocks' (the smallest units for which data are collected) with more than 1000 residents per square mile, or 386 per square kilometre, regardless of how many municipal or even state boundaries are crossed. This generally contains most of the population of the equivalent 'metropolitan statistical area', which covers non-urban as well as urban land.[27] The main exception is free-standing suburbs and ex-urbs within the boundaries of the census area, which are counted as separate urbanized areas if sufficiently distant from the main area.

Newman and Kenworthy used the urbanized area density figures for US cities, but did not use their equivalents for Australian and Canadian cities, possibly because these were hard to locate until recently. Statistics Canada defines 'urban areas' on an almost identical basis to the US, using a density threshold of 400 per square kilometre. The Australian Bureau of Statistics does the same for 'urban centres', although with a threshold of 200 per square kilometre, which means that Australian urban densities will be slightly understated relative to the other two countries.

Each country's statistical agency also asks a question in the census about the method of travel to work, in a manner that enables the answers to be compared. While work trips only account for a minority of urban travel, they are the only kind for which this type of consistent information is available across such a range of cities. Surveys of overall travel are usually conducted locally, in different years and often with inconsistent methodologies.

Despite the limitations of this census data, it enables a more rigorous comparison of urban densities and transport patterns across the three countries than has been made previously – partly because not all the information was available at the time Newman and Kenworthy collected their data (the Canadian census has only included a question on the method of travel to work since 1996). The results are set out in Table 4.1, using figures from the most recent census in each country: 2006 in Australia and Canada, 2000 in the US. Because there are so many urban areas in the US, only the largest have been included.

SOME SURPRISING X-RAY RESULTS

The results are surprising, to say the least. Los Angeles is the most densely-populated urban area in the US, well ahead of New York, which actually comes fourth after San Francisco and San Jose. Los Angeles is more densely populated than any Canadian city, just edging out Toronto, and considerably denser than any city in Australia, even allowing for the understatement of the Australian figures. The metropolis that Australian, Canadian and American planners like to think of as the paradigm of urban sprawl actually has the highest density of all, while Portland Oregon, the national poster-city for 'smart growth', has less than half the density of the City of the Angels. Boston's density is lower than that of Detroit or Dallas, although higher than Atlanta's.

Canadian cities turn out to have similar densities to their US and Australian counterparts. The higher Canadian densities reported by Newman and Kenworthy were a result of inconsistent density definitions, as seen above in the case of Toronto.

These results call for some explanation. New York City does have a high urban density, but its 8 million residents are surrounded by 13 million suburbanites, many of whom live at very low densities. Schaeffer and Sclar identified a similar phenomenon in Boston in the 1970s. Bruegmann also notes the extremely low densities of many East Coast suburban areas, pointing out that the dependence of West Coast cities on piped water limits the potential for very low density development.[28] In each case the suburbs, where the majority of the population lives, have the greatest influence on overall results. The City of Los Angeles is less dense than New York City, but its suburbs are denser than those that surround New York, resulting in a higher overall figure. These results are consistent with those reported by Newman and Kenworthy, who also found that Los Angeles was denser than New York. High-rise city centres might stand out in slide-shows, but they are not good predictors of overall urban densities.

Not only are urban densities quite different from what was expected, but they bear no relation to public transport use. Brisbane has only a third the density of Los Angeles, but public transport's share of work trips is three times as high. Ottawa's density is a third lower than LA's, but public transport use is four times as high, walking three times as high and cycling four times as high. New York's density is about 30 per cent lower than San Francisco's, but the share of work trips by public transport is more than twice as great.

Despite similar densities across the three nations, the US cities, apart from New York, have the lowest use of public transport, with the Australians coming next and the Canadians having the highest mode share. The same national pattern is apparent for walking rates, which are generally highest where public transport is most extensively used. Again, there appears to be no relationship with density, although there is some connection with city size: smaller cities tend to have more walking.

Cycling is of negligible importance in all three countries, although again rates are lowest in the USA and highest in Canada – a surprising result given the inclement northern weather (Canada's census is taken in late autumn). The exception is Victoria, capital of the Province of British Columbia, which combines a low urban density of only 11 per hectare with high rates of walking and cycling, and respectable public transport use. Victoria presents an interesting contrast to Canberra, also a capital city and with similar size and density, but much lower usage of 'sustainable' modes, despite having Australia's best network of cycle paths.[29]

Rates of car use are, naturally, the mirror image of the other modes, highest in US cities other than New York, lowest in Canadian cities, and largely uninfluenced

Table 4.1 *Density and method of travel to work in US, Canadian and Australian cities, 2000–2006*

City	Country	Population	Density (per hectare)	Car (%)	Public transport (%)	Walking (%)	Cycling (%)	Other (%)
Los Angeles	US	16,373,645	27.3	91.1	4.7	2.7	0.6	1.1
Toronto	CA	5,113,149	27.2	71.1	22.2	4.8	1.0	0.9
San Francisco	US	4,123,740	27.0	84.2	9.7	3.4	1.1	1.4
San Jose	US	1,682,585	22.8	Included in San Francisco data: see notes.				
New York	US	21,199,865	20.5	67.6	24.8	5.7	0.3	1.6
Sydney	AU	4,119,189	20.4	71.2	21.2	4.9	0.7	2.0
Montreal	CA	3,635,571	19.8	70.4	21.4	5.7	1.6	0.9
New Orleans	US	1,337,726	19.7	89.3	5.4	2.7	0.6	1.4
Las Vegas	US	1,563,282	17.7	91.2	4.1	2.4	0.5	1.4
Ottawa	CA	846,802	17.2	68.1	21.2	7.6	2.2	0.9
Vancouver	CA	2,116,581	17.2	74.4	16.5	6.3	1.7	1.1
Miami	US	3,876,380	17.0	92.7	3.9	1.8	0.5	1.1
Melbourne	AU	3,592,592	15.7	79.3	13.9	3.6	1.3	1.9
Denver	US	2,581,506	15.4	91.4	4.4	2.5	0.7	0.8
Chicago	US	9,157,540	15.1	83.9	11.5	3.2	0.3	1.0
Sacramento	US	1,796,857	14.6	92.3	2.7	2.3	1.4	1.0
Winnipeg	CA	694,668	14.3	78.7	13.0	5.8	1.6	0.9
Calgary	CA	1,079,310	14.0	76.6	15.6	5.4	1.3	1.0
Phoenix	US	3,251,876	14.0	93.4	1.9	2.1	0.9	1.4
Adelaide	AU	1,105,839	13.8	83.1	9.9	3.2	1.5	2.3
San Diego	US	2,813,833	13.2	91.2	3.4	3.5	0.6	1.4
Washington DC	US	4,923,153	13.1	86.5	9.4	3.0	0.3	1.0
Portland	US	2,265,223	12.9	89.4	6.0	3.1	0.8	0.7
San Antonio	US	1,592,383	12.6	93.6	2.8	2.4	0.1	1.2
Perth	AU	1,445,073	12.1	83.3	10.4	2.7	1.2	2.4
Detroit	US	5,456,428	11.9	95.3	1.7	1.8	0.2	0.5
Baltimore	US	2,552,994	11.7	Included in Washington DC data: see notes.				

City	Country	Population		%				
Houston	US	4,669,571	11.4	93.9	3.3	1.6	0.3	1.1
Dallas	US	5,221,801	11.3	95.5	1.7	1.5	0.1	1.0
Victoria	CA	330,088	11.1	71.7	10.2	10.4	5.7	2.0
Philadelphia	US	6,188,463	11.0	86.1	8.8	4.0	0.3	0.8
Columbus	US	1,540,157	11.0	94.3	2.2	2.5	0.2	0.5
Seattle	US	3,554,760	10.9	87.7	7.0	3.3	0.6	1.4
Canberra	AU	368,129	10.8	82.0	7.9	4.9	2.5	2.7
Cleveland	US	2,495,831	10.7	93.7	3.4	2.1	0.2	0.6
Milwaukee	US	1,689,572	10.4	92.7	4.0	2.8	0.2	0.6
Hobart	AU	200,524	10.3	82.6	6.4	7.6	1.1	2.3
Minneapolis	US	2,968,806	10.3	91.8	4.5	2.5	0.4	0.6
Virginia Beach	US	1,569,541	10.2	93.7	1.8	2.7	0.3	1.6
Edmonton	CA	1,034,945	10.1	82.8	9.7	5.1	1.1	1.2
Orlando	US	1,644,561	9.9	95.4	1.6	1.3	0.4	1.1
Tampa	US	2,395,997	9.9	94.9	1.3	1.7	0.6	1.1
St. Louis	US	2,603,607	9.7	95.2	2.3	1.6	0.1	0.7
Brisbane	AU	1,763,129	9.2	78.6	13.8	3.7	1.1	2.8
Providence	US	1,188,613	9.0	93.1	2.4	3.3	0.2	0.7
Boston	US	5,819,100	8.9	85.1	9.0	4.2	0.4	0.9
Kansas City	US	1,776,062	8.9	96.0	1.2	1.4	0.1	0.8
Cincinnati	US	1,979,202	8.6	94.1	2.6	2.3	0.1	0.7
Indianapolis	US	1,607,486	8.5	96.0	1.2	1.7	0.2	0.8
Pittsburgh	US	2,358,695	7.9	88.8	6.2	3.7	0.1	0.6
Atlanta	US	4,112,198	6.9	94.2	3.6	1.3	0.1	1.1
Charlotte	US	1,499,293	6.7	96.6	1.3	1.2	0.1	0.8

Sources: Australian and Canadian Census 2006, US Census 2000

Notes: Population and mode share figures are for the entire census area, except for the following US regions: San Francisco Consolidated Metropolitan Statistical Area includes San Jose urban area, and Washington CMSA includes Baltimore, so Metropolitan Statistical Area figures have been used for population (unfortunately, mode share figures were only available for the larger CMSAs).

'Car' includes car passenger and truck; 'other' includes motorcycle and taxi (counted as public transport in some US studies).

by density. Even in Canada, the car remains the majority mode for trips to work, but Statistics Canada reports a small but significant decline in car mode share in the decade since the 1996 census, when the mode question was first asked. Unfortunately, differences in census questions prevent comparisons of car-pooling across the three countries, but the Australian and Canadian figures, which are compiled on a comparable basis, are similar.

Los Angeles' density is similar to the figure of 28.5 per hectare reported for Copenhagen in Kenworthy and Laube's *Millennium Database*, and higher than Oslo's reported density of 24.0 per hectare. Although comparisons should be made cautiously, as the European figures have been compiled differently, the difference between North America and Europe may not be as great as is generally believed. There is a larger distance between LA and the higher-density European cities in the *Sourcebook* and *Database*, but it should be recalled that nearly all of these are over-statements, as they cover only the central municipality not the entire urban area.

Like their North American counterparts, European central cities are surrounded by lower-density suburbs, as the European Environment Agency (EEA) confirms in its *Urban Sprawl in Europe* report (2006). The same difficulties of regional government that prevented Newman and Kenworthy extracting region-wide density figures have also made it difficult to control land use beyond central city boundaries. 'European cities have become much less compact' thanks to '[n]ew transport investment, in particular motorway construction'. The report cites Helsinki, Copenhagen and Brussels among its examples of 'sprawled' cities, while Munich, Milan and Bilbao are listed as compact.[30] The proposed solutions are improved regional planning and governance, with greater Munich cited as a model. European cities might be grappling with the problem of urban sprawl, but this has not prevented many of them establishing effective, region-wide public transport systems that carry much higher shares of travel than in most US, Canadian and Australian cities.

European cities have been less successful at controlling suburban sprawl than their counterparts across the English Channel, where green belts and strong national policies have worked against extremely low-density scattered growth. As a result, English urban areas probably have higher overall urban densities than most of their continental counterparts, despite having less dense city centres: the English cities are more like Los Angeles, while European cities are more like New York or Boston.

The UK Office for National Statistics (ONS) has produced overall urban density estimates for the country's largest conurbations from the 2001 census. The methodology is similar to that used by census agencies in the other three countries, but relies on detailed mapping of land use rather than assembling census tracts, and therefore produces slightly higher density figures. The densities of the 20 largest urban areas in England are set out in Table 4.2, together with mode share figures for the journey to work, also from the census.

Table 4.2 *Density and method of travel to work in English cities, 2001*

City	Population	Density (per hectare)	Car (%)	Public transport (%)	Walking (%)	Cycling (%)	Other (%)
Greater London	7,172,091	51.0	39.2	45.9	9.2	2.5	2.7
Brighton/Worthing/Littlehampton	461,181	49.0	61.2	16.7	15.5	4.1	2.2
Portsmouth	442,252	46.8	68.1	9.7	12.0	6.8	3.5
Coventry/Bedworth	336,452	44.5	70.3	13.6	11.3	3.0	1.8
Merseyside Met County (Liverpool)	1,362,026	43.8	66.9	18.1	10.0	2.1	2.8
Leicester	441,213	43.4	66.6	14.6	13.6	4.0	1.6
Nottingham	666,358	42.0	65.2	16.8	12.2	3.9	2.0
Southampton	304,400	41.8	69.1	12.2	12.3	4.2	2.4
Tyne and Wear Met County (Newcastle)	1,075,938	41.7	62.7	22.6	10.2	1.7	2.4
West Yorkshire Met County (Leeds)	2,079,211	40.5	68.7	16.3	11.4	1.2	1.9
Greater Manchester Met county	2,482,328	40.2	70.1	14.6	10.6	2.0	2.2
Reading/Wokingham	369,804	40.0	69.2	14.0	11.0	3.6	1.7
South Yorkshire Met County (Sheffield)	1,266,338	39.5	69.5	16.6	10.8	1.5	1.6
Bristol	551,066	39.4	66.5	12.9	13.8	4.4	2.4
West Midlands Met County (Birmingham)	2,555,592	38.1	68.3	18.2	9.8	1.9	2.2
Kingston upon Hull	301,416	37.5	62.3	12.8	10.1	11.0	3.5
The Potteries (Stoke-on-Trent)	362,403	37.5	75.3	9.5	11.4	1.6	2.2
Birkenhead	319,675	35.9	71.3	13.7	9.2	2.6	3.3
Bournemouth	383,713	35.5	74.1	7.9	10.4	4.6	2.7
Teesside (Middlesborough)	365,323	32.0	72.7	11.2	10.8	2.6	2.6

Source: UK Census, 2001

Note: Population and mode share figures for London and the metropolitan counties are for the entire administrative area; density figures are for urban area only. For other places, all data are for urban area.

The English results confirm the absence of a relationship between public transport use and density. Although London has the highest density and by far the highest public transport share, there is no relationship between the two factors for the remaining urban areas. Brighton and surrounds is almost as dense as London, but has barely a third the mode share for public transport; Tyneside, which has the highest mode share outside London, is considerably less dense than Brighton (the difference in density is likely due to the fact that Brighton is largely residential and has little industrial and other urbanized, non-residential land).

English densities range from 51 per hectare in Greater London to 32 per hectare in Teeside (Middlesborough and surrounds), with the six large metropolitan counties ranging from 38 to 44. In his compilation of worldwide density figures, Wendell Cox has used the same figures for English metropolitan areas and has estimated European equivalents, mainly from satellite photographs. Although the results are not exactly comparable, Cox's European densities are generally lower than the British figures, with Zurich at 36.5 per hectare, Stockholm at 27, Rome at 32, Munich at 36 and Paris at 34.[31]

Many British commentators have attributed Europe's superior urban public transport to higher densities: it appears that, at least at the regional level, this view is mistaken. British cities have higher densities than many of the European urban areas that are case studies of successful public transport. And while British densities are much higher than those of Canadian cities, public transport mode shares are actually a little lower on the whole. For example, Greater Manchester houses a slightly smaller population than Greater Montreal at double the density (40 per hectare compared with 20), but only 15 per cent of workers use public transport, compared with 21 per cent in Montreal.

I have not been able to locate specific urbanized area densities for the 'outer suburbs' of London beyond the Green Belt, but these areas are also likely to be considerably denser than Canadian, Australian and US cities. But public transport use is at American, if not quite Los Angelean, levels in the 'South East' region surrounding Greater London – which actually houses more workers. The overall public transport share is only 11 per cent (mainly commuters to London), lower than in any Canadian city except Edmonton and Victoria, and most Australian cities. Walking and cycling are at 15 per cent and the car at 71 per cent. Public transport use is lower still in many places: 9 per cent in the local authority of Milton Keynes, 8 in Basingstoke and 7 in Aylesbury.[32] Los Angeles, it should be recalled, manages just under 5 per cent.

Walking rates are much higher in British than Canadian cities, although cycling is similarly insignificant – except in Kingston upon Hull, which may be influenced by the presence of a large university. This difference may well be due to density, but differing car ownership levels are also likely to be important. Residents of British cities have lower incomes than their Canadian counterparts, and correspondingly lower car ownership rates. This can be seen in the metropolitan counties, where between 32 (West Yorkshire) and 42 (Tyne and Wear) per cent of households own no cars; the London figure of 37 per cent may be influenced less by incomes than by parking difficulties and the higher quality of public transport.[33] The equivalent figures for Canadian urban regions range from 11 per cent in Calgary through to 28 per cent for Montreal, with Toronto at 22 and Vancouver and Ottawa both at 16.[34]

FORM OR STRUCTURE?

The mode shares for public transport and walking in US and Canadian cities correspond more closely to the share of economic activity in the Central Business District (CBD) than they do to density. Urban *structure* appears more important than urban *form*, an argument made three decades ago in J. Michael Thomson's *Great Cities and Their Traffic*. Thomson suggests that densities as low as 12 people per hectare would be sufficient to support an unsubsidized rail service supported by feeder buses,[35] provided the railway serves a strong centre with a significant share of the region's jobs and activity.

Although census data do not allow direct examination of this question (because census authorities have not adopted a common definition of the CBD), New York has by far the strongest centre of any US city, and this plays a major part in the high rate of public transport use there. Canadian cities have stronger centres than their US counterparts, thanks to historical differences including a greater propensity for the wealthy to reside in the inner city and the absence of a federally funded urban freeway programme.

But Australian cities have stronger CBDs and less extensive freeway networks than their Canadian counterparts, and their inner cities are even more comprehensively gentrified.[36] And Vancouver, which is not the provincial capital and has an awkwardly sited CBD, has a weaker centre than any other Canadian city, and even than many US cities. Urban structure is important, but it is not an insuperable barrier to change.

AND NOW FOR THE GOOD NEWS

So what can we conclude from our X-ray reports? All other things being equal, density does have an impact. But all other things are definitely not equal, and the effect of density is outweighed by other factors unless the differences in density are huge. This suggests both good and bad news.

The bad news is that the compact city is unlikely to solve the problem of automobile dependence, as the increases in density required to significantly change transport patterns on a metropolitan scale are impossible to achieve. 'Smart growth' policies might, after many decades, make Portland as dense as Los Angeles is now, Boston as dense as Las Vegas, or Brisbane as dense as Adelaide, but it is hard to see this producing big shifts away from the car. As the British Royal Commission on Environmental Pollution concluded in its exhaustive 1994 transport inquiry, 'there is no single pattern of land uses that will reduce the need for travel and so reduce the effects of transport on the environment.'[37]

This is not to argue that unplanned urban sprawl should continue to devour farms and forests. Most participants in the compact city debate are opposed to sprawl in the original sense of 'ribbon' development along roads or 'leapfrogging' of housing estates, producing an environment that is 'neither town nor country'. Vigorous critics of the compact city, such as Stretton and Troy, are equally critical of unregulated fringe development. Similarly, urbanists on both sides of the debate support clustering suburban activities into sub-centres instead of allowing them to spread randomly across the landscape. And since there is a demand for higher-density housing, it makes sense to locate it in these centres, or in other places well-served by public transport. Measures of this kind have a range of environmental advantages, including making it easier to provide public transport.

The good news is that we don't need impossible increases in density to provide viable alternatives to the car. The relative attractiveness of competing urban transport modes seems to influence mode choice much more than differences in density, and the notion that 400 or even 30 residents per hectare is a minimum density below which public transport cannot be provided is completely unsupported by evidence. It even looks as if greater usage of public transport might go hand-in-hand with higher levels of walking, which would be excellent news for the environment. Transport policy can be changed more quickly and cheaply, and with less disruption, than city density, so it might even be possible to make the necessary changes in time to save the planet.

Public transport can compete with the car in a dispersed urban environment, but this will require more ingenuity than is needed in a place like Tokyo or Hong Kong, where travellers have no real alternative. Services must be flexible to match the diversity of travel needs, but many observers question whether this can be achieved with old-fashioned public authorities in charge. They say the free market is the answer.

NOTES

1   CATS (1960, vol. 2, pp73, 53–54).
2   Rudlin and Falk (1999, p158).
3   Barton et al (1995, p80).
4   White (1976, p. 112, 2002, p97). The report also cites a 1981 manual called 'Urban Planning and Design for Road Based Public Transport', but this contains no reference to minimum densities at all.
5   CABE (2005, p7).
6   Bruegmann (2005, p55).

7 Moran (2006, p15).

8 Kahn-Ribeiro and Kobayashi (2007, p348).

9 CATS (1960, vol. 2, p52).

10 CATS (1959, vol. 1, p61, fig. 33).

11 Banister (2005, p98; see also ch. 6).

12 See Cox's websites www.demographia.com and www.publicpurpose.com (both accessed 30 August 2009).

13 Bruegmann (2005, p140).

14 US Census Bureau (2004, p5). One percentage point of the 3.1 per cent jump from 1990 was due to a change in the survey methodology. It should be noted that these are one-way trip figures, whereas the Canadian figures cited in the previous chapter are for the round trip between work and home.

15 Gordon and Richardson (2004).

16 Lowe (1994, p30).

17 Stretton (1993, p136).

18 Stretton (1975, pp5–6).

19 Gleeson (2008).

20 See Hall (1998, ch. 25).

21 Mindali et al (2004).

22 These definitions are based on Fooks (1946, ch. 4) and McLoughlin (1991). I have adopted McLoughlin's nomenclature.

23 CATS (1959, vol. 1, p. 17, table 1). Densities calculated by dividing the study area population into the various land areas.

24 Neutze (1981, p67).

25 Kenworthy and Laube (1999, pp27–32).

26 Kenworthy and Laube (1999, p375).

27 Bruegmann discusses US urbanized areas and densities at pp60–65 of *Sprawl* (2005).

28 Schaeffer and Sclar (1976); Bruegmann (2005, pp67–68).

29 Possible reasons for Victoria's high cycling rate are discussed in Pucher (2005).

30 EEA (2006, pp11, 18, 13).

31 Cox (2008).

32 ONS (2003, table KS 15).

33 ONS (2003, table KS 17).

34 Statistics Canada (2003, pp85–86, table 7).

35 J. M. Thomson (1977, p274).

36 My 2000 book *A Very Public Solution* provides an extensive comparison of centralization in Melbourne and Toronto (see 2000, ch. 7).

37 RCEP (1994, p151).

5

Planning, Markets and Public Transport

Chairman WAXMAN	*Dr Greenspan, I am going to interrupt you. The question I had for you is you had an ideology. You had a belief that ... 'Free competitive markets are by far the unrivalled way to organize economies.' [Do] you feel that your ideology pushed you to make decisions that you wish you had not made?*
Mr GREENSPAN	*Well, remember... To exist, you need an ideology. The question is whether it is accurate or not. What I am saying to you is, yes, I found a flaw. I don't know how significant or permanent it is, but I have been very distressed by that fact. But if I may, may I just finish an answer to the question –*
Chairman WAXMAN	*You found a flaw?*
Mr GREENSPAN	*I found a flaw in the model that I perceived is the critical functioning structure that defines how the world works, so to speak.*
Chairman WAXMAN	*In other words, you found that your view of the world, your ideology, was not right, it was not working.*
Mr GREENSPAN	*Precisely. That's precisely the reason I was shocked, because I had been going for 40 years or more with considerable evidence that it was working exceptionally well.*

US House of Representatives, Committee on Oversight and Government Reform. Hearings on the financial crisis and the role of federal regulators, 23 October 2008.[1]

THE TIDE TURNS

Alan Greenspan's mea culpa put him in good company. As 2009 dawned, policy makers across the western world were re-discovering the old truth that markets do sometimes fail, and that societies and economies need state intervention.

The idea that governments should be replaced by markets also had its heyday in transport planning. In the 1980s and 1990s, the dominant school of economists and transport planners advocated what one influential book called Free Enterprise Urban Transportation.[2] Congestion pricing on the roads would dovetail with a free market for public transport to provide the flexibility needed to cater for contemporary travel needs.

The push for the market was driven by economists in free-market think-tanks, universities and public bureaucracies. An international conference series was started in 1989 devoted to 'Competition and Ownership in Land Passenger Transport' (it is called the Thredbo series, after the Australian ski resort where the first conference was held).[3] The World Bank exported free enterprise urban transport to developing countries. Governments began to follow suit, beginning in 1986 with the deregulation of urban bus services in British cities outside London. The free market tide spread to New Zealand, where urban bus operations were deregulated in 1989, and then crossed the Tasman Sea to Melbourne, which franchised its railways and tramways to private firms in 1999 (buses had always been privately run). In the mid-1990s, British Rail was broken up and privatized, with passenger and freight operations franchised to a multitude of different operators.

The high-water mark of enthusiasm for applying the market to public transport came in 1995, when the Commission of the European Communities produced its urban transport green paper, *The Citizens' Network*.[4] Although residents of English-speaking countries regard the European Union as a citadel of left-wing and green politics, this strictly applies only to its parliament based in Strasbourg. The Brussels-based European Commission is dominated by academically trained economists who, like their bureaucratic counterparts in the UK, the US and Australasia, shared Alan Greenspan's ideology. This is one reason why it has been so difficult to persuade European voters to agree to EU treaties, such as the Maastricht accord on economic integration or the more recent European Constitution.

The European Commission deregulated the markets for long-distance passenger and freight services in the early 1990s, fully aware that this would increase road traffic and contradict the organization's own environment policies.[5] Switzerland, which is not an EU member, threw a spanner in the works in 1994, when 52 per cent of voters agreed to amend the country's constitution to protect the Alpine region from road transit traffic. Article 84 of the Swiss Constitution now expressly states that 'Transalpine freight ... shall be carried by rail' and [t]he capacity of transit roads in the alpine regions may not be increased.'[6] The European Commission's transport department was apoplectic, but when the Swiss refused to budge, agreement was eventually reached to implement the new policy.

The European Commission's 1995 green paper proposed extending the market to urban public transport. It shied away from full deregulation, because even by that stage it was widely accepted that this policy had failed in Britain, instead advocating 'systematic tendering of concessions' and 'public–private partnerships'.[7] Concession is another word for franchise, so the Commission was proposing the same system that, as we saw in Chapter 2, virtually destroyed urban public transport in the US even before the widespread availability of the car. In a 1998 follow-up report, the Commission lamented the fact that under current EU regulations 'there is no comprehensive requirement for authorities to bring market forces to bear' on urban public transport. It announced that new legislation would be brought forward to compel competition.[8]

No further public reports on urban transport emerged until 2007, when the Commission released a new green paper, entitled *Towards a new culture for urban mobility*[9]. This document adopts a much more conciliatory tone than its 1995 predecessor, which it barely mentions. 'The European Union must play a role in helping to bring about ... change, but without imposing top-down solutions which may not necessarily be appropriate for the diverse local situations.'[10] The report does not explain why priorities have changed, but the reason is that the 1998 proposals were opposed by public transport agencies concerned that they would create the kind of dis-integration seen in UK cities. A decade-long tussle between Brussels and Strasbourg ensued. The Commission brought forth two proposed regulations, both of which were rejected; a third version was released in mid-2005 and finally passed in modified form in December 2007, becoming effective from December 2009. The new 'regulation on public passenger transport services' represents a victory for the parliament, as it allows operators to choose whether or not to bring market forces to bear on service provision.[11]

The new EU approach emphasizes 'subsidiarity', knowledge-sharing and data gathering, rather than competition. Unfortunately, the background paper accompanying the 2007 green paper suggests that the new approach has a long way to go before it offers serious solutions. It outlines 52 EU-funded 'success stories' that emphasize alternative fuels and 'awareness campaigns'; none of them even claims to have brought about mode shift away from the car. There is, however, an 'innovative parking management scheme' from the Irish city of Cork, which enables motorists to use their mobile phones to pay parking fees – thereby making it even more convenient for them to keep driving.[12] After reading this catalogue, even die-hard supporters of state involvement might develop a sneaking sympathy for the idea of reducing the role of bureaucrats in urban transport!

And here we come to the nub of the dilemma. There are problems with state provision of public transport, just as there are problems with leaving it to the market. As the ideological fog of the free-market era lifts, it might be a good time to review the pros and cons of both, and consider what markets and governments can do best.

The European Commission has provided some assistance with this task. In early 2008, it released a commissioned report on different methods of awarding contracts for public transport services. Although the authors are well-known enthusiasts for the market, the report maintains a neutral stance on the range of possible operating models, and provides an excellent discussion of the differences between the models. The following discussion relies on this work, as well as recent analyses from the US by Jose Gomez-Ibanez, Eliot Sclar and Vukan Vuchic.[13]

COMPARING THE OPTIONS: PUBLIC AND PRIVATE

The first thing worth recalling is that there is no such thing as fully public or fully private urban transit anywhere in the developed world. The Railways Department of Victoria, Australia, used to manufacture trains at its own workshops and print timetables at the departmental printing press, but these functions were eventually outsourced to private suppliers. At the other end of the spectrum, even the 'deregulated' buses in British cities outside London receive government subsidies. All systems have a mix of state and private involvement: the question is which tasks are best performed publicly or privately.

To answer the question, it helps to consider the range of activities that must be carried out to provide public transport across an urban region. It has become customary to consider three levels of activity: strategic, tactical and operational.[14]

- The *strategic level* is where system objectives are set. These may relate to equity (e.g. provision of a defined level of region-wide accessibility), environment (e.g. targets for mode shift away from the car) or efficiency (e.g. subsidy or cost-recovery levels).
- The *tactical level* is where objectives are translated into system-wide service strategies, such as designing networks, selecting appropriate modes and technologies, and co-ordinating timetables.
- The *operational level* sees tactical planning translated into day-to-day operations, such as hiring and scheduling crews, maintaining equipment, collecting fares and providing information to passengers.

There is a range of possible ways of distributing these functions between public and private bodies, forming what Gomez-Ibanez calls a 'continuum of strategies'. At one end, all three levels are performed 'in-house' in a public agency; at the other, all are delegated to the market. In a sense, any movement towards the market end can be described as privatization, but strictly speaking the term should be reserved for those options which place private firms in charge of tactical, as well as operational, matters. Starting with the most 'public', the possibilities are as follows.

1. *Government or municipal department.* The public transport operator is simply a department of the relevant national, state or municipal government, like the Foreign Office or the Water Supply division. Having a minister or mayor at the head of the department will ensure the highest degree of political oversight of all three levels of operation: strategic, tactical and operational. Examples include the former Railways Departments of the Australian states and nations like Germany and Switzerland, and the municipal transit departments of present-day cities as diverse as Detroit, US, Ottawa, Canada and Kyoto, Japan. This model is much less popular than it used to be, because close political control can work against efficient operations, while the bureaucratic culture of a government department may not be the best environment to foster innovative tactical planning.

2. *Public corporation.* This model is intended to retain the advantages of state control, while giving more scope for efficiency and innovation at the tactical and operational levels. Services are provided by a public agency, established either under statute or as a 'private' company in which the state or municipality owns the shares. The public agency handles tactical and operational matters, but strategic planning is effectively shared with the political arm of government, which provides funding and sets overall policy goals. This relationship may be formalized through a contract between the agency and the government. Examples include the Toronto Transit Commission, the Paris RATP (the A stands for 'autonomous'), the Swiss Federal Railways and municipal operators in much of Europe.

3. *Public transport federation or verkehrsverbund.* This model is often called by its German name, because it originated in that country. The first verkehrsverbund was established in Hamburg in 1965 to deal with dispersed urban growth that had spilled over city boundaries. The city's public transport agency ran trams, buses and the metro; the national railways ran suburban trains; private firms ran suburban buses. Coordination was poor: timetables rarely connected and separate fare systems added insult to injury for transferring passengers. The Hamburger Verkehrsverbund, or HVV, was established to handle tactical planning, leaving the pre-existing agencies and companies responsible for operations. The model was so successful that it was copied by Munich in 1972 and has since spread throughout Germany. It reached Switzerland in 1990 with the establishment of the Zürcher Verkehrsverbund.[15]

4. *Public agency with sub-contracted, tendered services.* This approach has similarities to the 'federation' model, but evolved out of a concern to reduce operating costs while preserving service integration. Tactical planning remains the responsibility of the public agency, but operations are competitively tendered based on cost and quality. This model was introduced for buses in London in the 1980s, and across Sweden in 1989. Competition advocates in Vancouver hoped that the establishment of the Translink agency in 1999 would lead to a similar outcome, but this has not transpired. In some cases, 'in-house' operators

participate and bid against external firms; in others, no in-house capacity is retained. London Transport's own depots competed successfully against outside firms, but were eventually privatized. By contrast, in Gothenburg, Sweden, the city's transport company has competed successfully for bus tenders for two decades (tendering is not used for trams because the city company has no real competition).

5. *The concession system, or franchising.* Many economists argue that tendering is not enough, and that competition is needed to spur innovation at the tactical level. Under the concession or franchising model, governments set strategic goals and invite private firms to tender for the provision of tactical and operational realization of those goals. The franchise agreement will usually specify maximum fares and minimum service requirements. The franchisee bears 'revenue risk' (i.e. the risk that revenues will be lower than expected), as well as the 'cost risk' borne under sub-contracting/tendering. Franchises usually cover single modes across a specified territory rather than integrated networks, but could in theory be extended to become multi-modal. Franchising was, as we have seen, popular in US cities a century ago; today it is found on the former British Rail network, where it was introduced in the mid-1990s, and since 1999 on trams and trains in Melbourne, Australia.

6. *Private operation with discretionary regulation.* Some public utilities cannot be franchised, because they are too complex or operate across too many jurisdictions, but still require measures to restrain the abuse of monopoly powers. The preferred solution in the US was to establish a public regulatory agency with jurisdiction over price and service levels. So while the Los Angeles Railway was franchised by the city council, the Pacific Electric System, which ran across many jurisdictions, was regulated by the California Railroad Commission. Over time, regulation of US ground transport was replaced by nationalization of unprofitable passenger services – regional systems were taken over by local agencies, while Amtrak was established for long-distance rail services – and deregulation of profitable freight services. These days, this option is found mainly in non-transport privatized utilities, such as electricity supply.

7. *Private operation with deregulation.* Under this approach, public transport is treated as a normal consumer product, like cars or bread, and left as much as possible to private contracts between customers and suppliers. Competing private firms determine strategic, tactical and operational decisions and suffer financially if they get them wrong. However, in most cities, public transport is different from bread, because supplying it is unprofitable. So deregulation is supplemented by two forms of government intervention. First, operators are required to carry some passengers at concession fares or even for free, and are reimbursed for the revenue forgone. Secondly, some services may be unprofitable even with concession reimbursement; in these cases public authorities can supplement the market with contracted services – usually at

night, on weekends, or on low-demand cross-city and rural routes. Although deregulated public transport is common in third world cities, and was tried for two decades in New Zealand, its only application in developed nations now is in British cities outside London

All sorts of theoretical arguments can be presented for and against most of the options described here, but public transport is provided in the real world. What does the experience in real cities tell us about their relative merits? We begin with the 'market' approach.

FREE ENTERPRISE PUBLIC TRANSPORT?

The enthusiasm for markets was partly a response to problems with state-provided urban public transport. In the US, the Federal funding made available by the Urban Mass Transportation Act of 1964 and its successors did not stem the steady decline in the share of Americans travelling by public transport. Mode share for the journey to work has declined with each successive census, although the 1990–2000 period did see modest reversals, generally in the range of half a percentage point, in a minority of urban areas, including New York, San Francisco, Boston and Seattle. Portland had the largest increase, a full percentage point.

Critics of Federal funding claim that the main result has been a blowout in operating costs, as organized labour secured higher wages and inefficient operating practices, thanks partly to a provision in the US legislation requiring public transport agencies to sign labour agreements with unions before being eligible for federal funding. Even some supporters of federal involvement concede that there are problems: Vukan Vuchic acknowledges that in some cities, at least, the criticism may have validity.[16] Significantly, however, most observers accept that public ownership and funding (generally from provincial rather than national sources) in Canada have not led to inflated operating costs.[17]

The difficulties of publicly operated transit systems were not confined to the US. British cities neglected their public transport after World War II. They pursued similar pro-automobile policies to US cities despite having relatively high urban densities, low car ownership and publicly owned transit systems. The result was that by the 1970s, hardly any higher-performance urban public transport (i.e. employing separate rights-of-way, such as busways or rail) existed outside London. Patronage declined precipitously, and most systems began incurring operating deficits. Governments in Europe adopted more balanced policies, and generally upgraded public transport as well as roads. Although ground was lost to the car, the decline was less severe than in the US or Britain. But quality public transport in Europe did not come cheaply: large subsidies and low cost-recovery were common.

Competition was proposed as a solution to both these problems. Competitive forces would drive efficiency gains and keep costs down, but would also spur innovation, producing more flexible services that would better suit contemporary travel patterns. For many competition advocates, the model was the jitneys which sprang up in US cities at the end of World War I. These free-enterprise services operated without public subsidy until regulatory authorities suppressed them to protect the private tram franchisees. This move is criticized as a mistake that prevented the development of flexible public transport that could match the convenience of the car. Critics point to Manila, where the jitney evolved into the jeepneys that now dominate public transport, and similar free-enterprise micro-bus services in other developing cities, as illustrations of what might have been achieved.

Could jeepney-like services provide the answer to the transport problems of dispersed, wealthy cities? As Vuchic points out, conditions in Manila are precisely the opposite to those found in Los Angeles, or Manchester, or Melbourne. Population densities are very high, car ownership rates are low, and so are wages. This ensures heavy demand for public transport regardless of service quality, while enabling the economical operation of labour-intensive vehicles like jeepneys.[18] Few of the commentators praising Manila's public transport can have taken the time to speak to the city's residents. Had they done so they would have discovered that middle-class Manilenos never use jeepneys, because the service is unattractive and inconvenient. Jeepneys crowd the busiest roads, but services are sparse or non-existent for cross-city trips and travel to low-density, middle-class suburbs – in other words, the environments that most resemble western cities.

The 'British disease'

Nevertheless, the market model seemed very attractive to policy makers in colder climes, and so bus services were deregulated in both Britain and New Zealand. However, even the Thatcher government baulked at applying the market to London: the British capital was spared, initially temporarily, but eventually permanently. London was required to competitively tender its bus services, but under the control of a public agency which determined timetables, routes and fares. Without intending to, the British government set up an experiment to compare market-based public transport with the planned variety, and the excellent data published by the UK Department for Transport enables the results to be assessed. Table 5.1 compares trends in London and the six 'metropolitan counties' that cover urban regions like Greater Manchester and Greater Birmingham.

The near-consensus, which includes pro-market observers like the European Commission and Wendell Cox, has been that the London model dramatically outperformed deregulation. In the decade following deregulation, operating costs per bus were reduced, and the number of bus-kilometres operated increased, in

Table 5.1 *Bus patronage in English cities (million)*

	London	English metropolitan counties
1985/1986	1152	2068
1995/1996	1205	1292
2005/2006	1881	1111
2007/2008	2090	1121
Change (%), 1986–1996	+4.6	–37.5
Change (%), 1986–2008	+81.4	–45.8

Sources: DfT (2003, table 10); DfT (2008, table 6.13).
Note: 1985/6 was the last pre-deregulation year.

both London and the other cities. This was due partly to wage cuts and partly to increased use of regular buses and minibuses instead of the traditional double-deckers. But costs per passenger did not fall in the deregulated cities, because patronage declined drastically: the promise that deregulation would produce more customer-focused services was not fulfilled. In London, by contrast, patronage held steady so the cost per passenger was significantly reduced.

In the last decade, the differences have become more pronounced. Wage rises have seen operating costs increase at similar rates in London and the other cities. Operators outside London responded by withdrawing much of the service added after deregulation (by 2008 bus-kilometres were 16 per cent lower than in 1996) and raising fares faster than inflation. Patronage continued to fall, and most English metropolitan regions now have lower public transport mode shares than Canadian cities and even some in the US, despite having much higher densities and lower incomes. Meanwhile, bus patronage in London has spectacularly rebounded, and is now almost twice as high as in 1985/1986, the year before deregulation. Patronage increases in London are partly a response to service levels, which have grown rapidly. But patronage has grown faster than service, so occupancy rates have risen.

Before deregulation, London produced about one-third of urban bus patronage in England; now it accounts for two-thirds, despite housing only 7 million people, compared with 12 million in the six metropolitan counties. But while only carrying a third of the passengers, the metropolitan areas consume nearly two-thirds of 'concessionary fare reimbursement'[19] – a result that appears to be due to the higher fares charged and the increasing domination of ridership by those travelling on concession tickets.

British bus deregulation has not produced free-enterprise public transport at all; nor has it produced innovative services that respond to contemporary needs. Instead, it has produced a new version of the 1970s 'British disease' that Thatcherism was supposed to have cured: a mendicant, declining industry that relies increasingly on carrying 'captive' passengers at concession rates or even for free, and charging the government at full-fare rates.

Similarly disastrous results in New Zealand prompted the repeal of deregulation, which was replaced by the 'London model' from 1 January 2009. Even the leader of New Zealand's ultra-dry ACT party supported the change, pointing out that following deregulation 'Auckland moved from being the second-highest user of bus transport in the Australia and New Zealand region to the second-lowest on a population–patronage ratio.'[20] Britain is now the only part of the developed world where the policy persists.

Every independent inquiry into urban bus deregulation in Britain has concluded that it has been a failure – from the Royal Commission on Environmental Pollution's (RCEP) transport report in 1994 to the House of Commons Transport Committee's report on deregulation in 1995, to the 2006 Eddington Transport Study.[21] But Whitehall remains unmoved, and the policy remains in force despite the defeat of the Conservative government in 1997. The only change permitted has been the introduction, in the Transport Act of 2000, of 'quality bus partnerships', an impressive-sounding concept which has produced little real change.

In 2006, the UK Department for Transport released a report with the equally impressive title *Putting Passengers First*. The report was said to be the result of a 'long hard look' at problems with buses, which confirmed the contrast between success in London and failure elsewhere. 'We need to learn the lessons of the London experience', the authors piously intoned, then proceeded to ignore them. The capital's success was attributed to the congestion charge,[22] despite London having outperformed the deregulated systems for 16 years before charging came in. The report recommended giving other cities the power to introduce road pricing, together with 'tweaking' of the failed quality partnerships scheme. Alan Greenspan was by no means the only public official to be blinded by a pro-market ideology.

It is all rather depressing: no wonder British planners would rather talk about road pricing or compact cities. But as we have seen in previous chapters, and as the RCEP observed back in 1994, these measures are no substitute for a functioning public transport system.

THE LONDON – OR SWEDISH – MODEL

To many people, the difference between the way bus services are organized in London and other British cities may not seem all that great: after all, both systems involve using private firms to provide operational-level tasks. But the dramatic difference in outcomes shows the importance of tactical planning.

In London, central planning by a public agency ensured that the new services made possible by reduced operating costs were deployed strategically, in ways that attracted new riders. Buses were added on routes and at times that had previously seen infrequent services, for example evenings and cross-suburban routes. In deregulated environments, additional services usually consisted of two operators competing head-to-head on already well-served routes: because timetables were not coordinated, waiting times remained just as long as before. London also used newer, higher-quality buses and retained multi-modal 'travelcards', which largely disappeared in the deregulated cities.[23]

Following the election of Ken Livingstone as Mayor of London in 2000, public subsidies were made available for expanded bus services (the congestion charge was introduced to help defray the expense) that accelerated patronage growth. But even with this increased support, the total subsidy per passenger in 2006/2007 was 37 pence, not that different to the average of 34 pence across other British cities.[24]

There are, of course, external factors that have helped bus patronage in London, such as high job growth in the city centre that has boosted patronage on the Underground and surface rail systems, and London's higher population density. The importance of these may have been exaggerated. The central city travel market is, as we saw in Chapter 3, dominated by rail; most bus passengers travel in suburban areas. And the density of these areas is not significantly higher than that of other English cities; as we saw in Chapter 4, the UK Office for National Statistics (ONS) estimates Greater London's overall urban density at 51 persons per hectare. So London's suburbs, which produce most bus passengers, would have similar densities to the range of 32–49 per hectare found in other English cities. And car ownership is higher than in the metropolitan counties, with only 29 per cent of households without cars in 'outer London', compared with 32–42 per cent in the other cities.[25] The collapse in public transport use that occurs as soon as one leaves Greater London for the rest of the south-east (see Chapter 4) occurs even in places where one can cross the boundary without observing any change in urban form.

Bus services in London are by no means perfect; they still have a long way to go before meeting the standards of the best European cities, particularly in the area of integration with rail. But when compared with the experience in other English cities, London can certainly be considered a triumph of tactical planning by a public agency.

Most analysts have also presented London as a triumph for the privatization of operational service delivery, but this may not be correct. There were substantial reductions in operating costs per bus-kilometre after 1986, partly due to the replacement of many double-deckers with smaller vehicles. But most of the savings occurred before 1994, the year London Buses (which had been split into a number of smaller companies) was privatized. Cost savings stopped only two years after privatization: the inflation-adjusted cost per bus-kilometre in 2002/2003 (the most recent year for which figures are available) was 7.5 per cent higher than in 1993/1994.[26]

So were the savings due to competitive tendering, then, if not privatization? It appears not, because by the end of 1993 less than half of London's bus routes had even been subject to tender.[27] Bus operating costs in London were already falling before tendering was announced, as a result of efficiency improvements initiated under public ownership. These improvements continued under tendering, then stopped after privatization. Tendering may have helped the process by providing an additional spur to improve efficiency, but it also imposed substantial costs of its own, as did the privatization process of 1994.

Would cost reductions have continued after the mid-1990s had London Buses remained in public ownership? Would a better result have been produced had the organization been left to pursue the efficiency improvements initiated in the late 1970s and early 1980s? We don't know, because nobody has done the necessary analysis – possibly because London has done so much better than elsewhere in the UK.

This result is consistent with the message of Eliot Sclar's *You Don't Always Get What You Pay For* (2000), which provides case studies of sub-contracting exercises that failed to produce the anticipated cost savings, and often lowered service quality. The most notorious example is defence contracting in the US, exemplified in the (possibly mythical) story of the $600 toilet seat. As Sclar points out, every organization, public or private, is faced with the 'make–buy' decision: whether to produce something in-house or acquire it from an outside supplier. It is easy for organizations to get this decision wrong, but the probability of an incorrect decision increases substantially with political interference, such as a requirement to use private suppliers no matter what.

France illustrates the pitfalls of an uncritical adoption of private sector provision. While public transport in Paris is operated by the public RATP and SNCF (the national rail undertaking), services in other cities have traditionally been run by private firms under contract to regional governments. The industry has become an oligopoly dominated by three large companies; collusion has been more common than competition; there have been numerous corruption scandals, involving politicians accepting bribes from private contractors. This has led to one of the lowest cost-recovery rates anywhere in the world, with only 17 per cent of expenses covered by fares in the late 1990s; even Paris managed 35 per cent.[28]

I discovered another illustration of the need for caution in 2002, when I was asked to review a proposal for competitive tendering of the Toronto Transit Commission's (TTC) bus services. The proposal had come from the Ontario Motor Coach Association, and was supported by a report from Wendell Cox comparing the TTC's costs with those of small municipal systems provided by contractors. Sclar discusses a similar report prepared a decade earlier by private bus firms in Canada, and points out that costs per bus hour tend to be lower in smaller systems than larger ones, regardless of public or private provision, for reasons including lower 'peaking' and minimal night and Sunday service offerings.[29] Ten years later, I found that the TTC did have higher costs per bus-hour than smaller systems. But it also had very much higher bus utilization, with annual passengers per bus between two and five times as high as the smaller systems.

The average Toronto bus carried 23 per cent more passengers per year than the average London bus, even though the TTC operates no double-deckers or articulated vehicles, and serves a much less transit-friendly urban environment.

The high utilization is the result of a sophisticated programme of closely matching service to patronage on busy routes, by adjusting frequencies, operating 'short' runs over busy sections and regularly moving vehicles from less- to more-crowded routes. Each month, the Commission announces service changes like: '85 Sheppard East service will be increased to reduce crowding... During the afternoon peak period, the combined service between Don Mills Station and Meadowvale will be improved from every 5 minutes to every 4 minutes 38 seconds.' Matching service this closely to demand is rare internationally. It increases costs per bus hour, since it requires skilled scheduling staff and well-trained drivers, but reduces overall costs (and greenhouse emissions). Regular service adjustments like this would be impossibly complicated if sub-contractors were involved, which is one reason why they are not even attempted in London.[30]

One final example of why private isn't always best came during the 2000 Olympic Games in Sydney. I include it here for the record, since the story was hushed up at the time to avoid international embarrassment. Most spectators travelled to the Olympic stadium by rail, but a large fleet of buses was also used to transport spectators, athletes and officials. The majority of these were provided by Bus 2000, a national consortium of private operators overseen by the Bus and Coach Association of New South Wales. Shortly before the games commenced, it became apparent that a debacle was imminent: the logistical difficulties of rostering and scheduling such a large operation, and even parking buses in overcrowded depots, were beyond the private industry. At the last minute, the Games Organising Committee contacted Sydney's public bus operator, the State Transit Authority (STA), for assistance. STA sent a team of managers, supervisors, inspectors and dispatchers to take charge of operations. Disaster was averted, the games went ahead to international acclaim, and free-market advocates in the NSW Treasury and elsewhere resumed their campaign to privatize the allegedly inefficient STA.[31]

As Sclar says, one should always compare three alternatives: existing in-house provision, outsourcing and more efficient in-house provision. The comparison should be carried out dispassionately, without ideologically imposed distortions. Doubtless there will be many cases in which tendering and private provision are the right answers for the operational level, and it may be that London is one of them. In other cases, the threat of competitive tendering can be enough to start the process of improving in-house operating efficiency. What London and the Swedish experience with contracting really show, though, is the importance of keeping tactical-level planning in the hands of a public, regional agency.

NETWORKS AND NATURAL MONOPOLY

A central argument of this book is that multi-modal network planning is the key to public transport success in dispersed urban regions, and that this is only possible with a public agency in charge of tactical-level functions. This in turn suggests that genuinely privatized systems – models 5, 6 and 7 in the continuum of strategies discussed above – where private firms are responsible for tactical planning as well as operations, will fail. Urban public transport is a natural monopoly, the economist's term for an activity that works best with a single body in charge.

Traditional neo-classical economics holds that unregulated natural monopolies can lead to inefficiency or exploitation, and that governments are entitled to intervene to prevent these 'market failures'. The neo-liberal views espoused by regulators like Alan Greenspan downplay the importance of monopoly and emphasize the danger that government intervention might do more harm than good. Even before the recent world financial crisis showed that market failure is alive and well, analysts in the transport and infrastructure fields conceded that monopoly problems are real: Gomez-Ibanez's *Regulating Infrastructure* (2003) is an example of this from a strong advocate of markets. Nobody thinks it would be efficient to have competing water supply companies lay separate networks of mains under city streets.

Most discussions of monopoly in public transport have focused on economies of scale (whether bigger operations are more efficient than smaller ones) and the high cost and durability of infrastructure. In theory, these issues need not require a public agency, because infrastructure can be separated from services, allowing competition in the latter area. This is what occurred when British Rail was privatized in the 1990s, but the experience showed that 'vertical separation' greatly increases complexity, potentially negating any benefits of competition. Even Gomez-Ibanez now argues that railways, and in particular passenger services, are less suited to this approach than other kinds of infrastructure, with separation producing high costs and low benefits.[32]

Monopoly is not just relevant to operating costs; there are also economies of service integration, and these are most important in dispersed environments. Many commentators have assumed that the way for public transport to compete with the car is to employ car-like vehicles operating without fixed routes or timetables and above all, without the need to transfer; hence the enthusiasm for jeepneys, dial-a-bus, car-pooling and other forms of 'paratransit'. This kind of thinking mistakes the nature of public transport and the reason why it produces less environmental damage than the car.

The essence of public transport, reflected in its name, is carrying people with different trip origins and destinations in the same vehicle. The travellers can then be transported with lower social and environmental costs than if they travelled separately. This is public transport's strength, but also its weakness, because people don't all have the same trip origins or destinations. If people live at very high densities, that solves one half of the problem, because they can walk to the station or bus stop; but they would all need to travel to the same place. The Spanish engineer Arturo Soria y Mata proposed a linear city as the answer: everyone would live and work in dense communities clustered around stations on a single rail line. But no cities like this exist anywhere in the world: the near-universal trend is towards dispersal of homes and workplaces, of trip origins and destinations.

Traditional transport planners have responded to diverse, 'anywhere to anywhere' travel patterns by either giving up on public transport, or proposing car-like paratransit solutions. But the problem with paratransit is that the more it becomes like the car, the more it surrenders its environmental and economic advantages. A 'tailor-made' public transport system offering a direct route between every origin and destination would have low frequencies, low occupancies, high costs and high greenhouse emissions per passenger. Taxis already provide this kind of service in most cities, and while an important part of urban life, they are not cheap and don't reduce greenhouse emissions or fossil fuel consumption. So what's the alternative?

The alternative is networks. Instead of 'tailor-made' public transport, a 'ready-made' service is provided that relies on transfers.[33] This is the only way to enable anywhere-to-anywhere travel while keeping occupancy rates high. Visitors to Paris soon learn that this is how the famous Metro works: nearly every trip requires a transfer, but transfers are free and high frequencies ensure minimal waiting. Even in the dense urban setting of the City of Paris, it is not feasible to economically provide high-quality, transfer-free services; in dispersed environments the difficulties are much greater. Public transport is even more likely to be a natural monopoly in a dispersed area, because without network planning little or no service can be economically supported.

This question has received surprisingly little attention in the transport literature, but there are exceptions. Gregory Thompson has recounted the way California's Pacific Greyhound Lines used network planning to compete with jitney operators and the state's railroads during the 1930s. Inter-city bus services do not generate economies of scale (in fact costs often rise with fleet size), but Thomson demonstrated that there are 'economies of scope' arising from network planning. It was this network effect, not government regulation, that drove free enterprise inter-city transport in California out of business. And network planning, rather than a conspiracy, saw coordinated Greyhound buses outperform fragmented, non-connecting railroads. Planning, Thomson concludes, beat the market.[34]

In *Access for All*, Schaeffer and Sclar make a similar point when explaining why the car, a European invention, took off so early in rural America. This was a response to differences in railway service policy. 'In Europe, most railroads operated as regional and national ... systems ... schedules were devised to permit relatively convenient transfers on journeys that involved more than one train ride, since it was to the economic benefit of the railroads to increase system-wide ridership.' In the US, by contrast, competing operators served fragmented markets. 'Interline and off-hour travellers were served if it was profitable to do so, otherwise they might as well wait until the railroad was good and ready to run a train.' They give the example of an Ohio town where the 14-mile journey to the local regional centre involving a transfer took 6 hours 25 minutes, and could not be accomplished as a day-return trip. Interviews with older residents confirmed that even before the car, nobody made the trip by train.[35]

This problem was not confined to private rail systems. The Victorian Railways Department focused its inter-city services on Melbourne, and ignored travellers with other destinations. Mark Twain visited Victoria in 1895 and travelled from Ballarat, the state's second-largest city, to Bendigo, the third-largest, a distance of around 125km. He described the experience in *Following the Equator*:

> *Got up at 6, left at 7.30; soon reached Castlemaine, one of the rich gold-fields of the early days; waited several hours for a train; left at 3.40 and reached Bendigo in an hour… It has actually taken nine hours to come from Ballarat to Bendigo. We could have saved seven by walking.*[36]

In the 21st century, network economies drive the mergers and alliances that are transforming the airline industry into a worldwide duopoly. Few airlines today can survive without being part of a network.

The same network effect is being increasingly exploited by the most successful European regional transit systems. Integrated, multi-modal, transfer-based systems of the kind seen in Zurich (see Chapter 8) are enabling high-quality 'urban' service to be extended to suburban and even ex-urban hinterlands, and the lessons have even reached the Americas.

The strongest resistance to network planning in public transport comes from what are by now the usual suspects: academically trained economists and the English-speaking governments and agencies that follow their advice. Deregulation in the UK was launched with the 1984 White Paper *Buses*, whose title alone makes it clear that multi-modal planning was not contemplated; the tradition is maintained with the 2006 *Putting Passengers First* report, sub-titled 'proposals for a modernised national framework for bus services'. Over at the World Bank, the current urban transport strategy discusses buses and rapid transit in separate chapters, while 'public transport integration' is glossed over in half a page.[37]

Transfer-based systems won't work, the critics counter, because travellers dislike transferring. The objection to integration becomes a self-fulfilling prophecy, as market-based systems make transfers inconvenient or even impossible, with extra fares, poor facilities and non-connecting timetables. When patrons respond rationally by not transferring, this is taken as proof that no effort should be made to change things. This can even be 'proven' using transport models that incorporate large penalties for trips involving transfers, guaranteeing the models will predict low mode shares for networks that require them. The problem is that the assumptions behind these models directly contradict real-world evidence; as Vuchic notes:

The superiority of the transit network type with fewer, frequent lines relying on transfers over the network with numerous, infrequent lines is demonstrated by the fact that cities with the highest transit riding habit, such as Boston, Paris, Toronto and Zurich, generally have transit systems with the highest transfer ratios.[38]

Advocates of market-based public transport are usually the strongest critics of transfer-based systems, because an integrated network requires a single agency to plan it. With different organizations running different modes, integration is virtually impossible, as we saw in Chapter 2 with the case of 1950s Auckland, where bus interests helped block plans for a rail service with feeder buses. Half a century later, the same problem afflicts British cities.

The West Yorkshire conurbation, based on Leeds and Bradford, has 2.2 million residents, 70 per cent more than the Canton of Zurich. The overall urban density – 41 per hectare[39] – is also higher than Zurich's, and incomes are much lower. But annual public transport patronage is around 200 million trips, compared with 542 million (and rising) in Zurich.[40] Bus usage in West Yorkshire has been in decline for decades and local rail services are sparsely used, despite upgrading by the regional authority. The authority wants to improve services and move towards a network, but the local private oligopoly will not allow it, as the current regional bus strategy confirms:

Operators have largely been supportive of the Bus Strategy but some areas remain difficult, for instance:

- *bus services as feeder services for rail (one major operator has stated that they would not 'condone or support' such a proposal)*
- *ticketing and smartcards*
- *branding.*[41]

It was similar problems in Auckland that finally led to the repeal of bus deregulation in New Zealand. The Auckland Regional Transport Authority (ARTA) led the charge after receiving a report from its marketing consultants outlining the impossibility of 'selling' uncoordinated public transport. The consultants cut through the ideological rhetoric about choice to explain what competition really means for passengers:

Jack is waiting for a bus home at the bus stop. He hasn't come to this bus stop before and only catches the bus at odd times, but his car is at the panel beater and he thought he would give it a go. A bus arrives, but it is yellow and red, and the one he knows is purple. So he waits, but he notices that this bus has the same destination as where he is going but is unsure what route it actually takes. Three more buses arrive, they are different colours, one has Company 1 name but it has green advertising on it, and he knows his bus is purple. He also notices as the bus pulls away that the number corresponds to his normal route. So he asks a fellow traveller what bus he should catch and they suggest ... numbers 027, 028, 025, 31 or 37... Very soon after that a nearly empty number 31 arrives, he boards and presents his ticket however the bus driver says they don't accept that ticket – he is an ABB bus and that is a company 1 ticket. Jack despondently gets off and waits another 30 minutes for his purple bus ... the next day he collects his car from the panel beater and tells his friends about the nightmare he had trying to get home last night.[42]

The second half of this book explains the alternative that New Zealand's cities now have the legal authority to implement.

THE IDEAL CONTRACT

Before we turn to examine public transport systems that have exploited the network effect, one last objection must be mentioned. With the exception of the die-hards in the UK bureaucracy, next to nobody advocates deregulated urban public transport any more. The British experience has convinced most analysts that coordination is important, and even the World Bank has gone cold on deregulation. But putting a public agency in charge of tactical planning prevents the kind of service innovation that supposedly comes from competitive markets. How about the compromise of concessions or franchising, where the public agency calls for competitive bids for network planning? As we saw at the start of the chapter, this was the preference of the European Commission until it was rebuffed by legislators, and bodies like the World Bank seem to have come around to the same position.[43]

So why not try franchising rather than rushing back to central planning? The first answer would be that franchising has already been tried in many countries, especially the US, and has failed, as we saw in Chapter 2. Unless societies have become less complex, politicians more honest and regulators more intelligent in the last century, why should it work any better the second time around? Jose Gomez-Ibanez is a strong supporter of franchising, and argues that it is working better in the US now than a century ago. But 'it is possible that franchises are performing better because they are being applied in situations more favourable to the contractual approach ... where the chances of drafting a complete contract are greatest.'[44] In other words, franchising is working in North America this time because it is not being applied to public transport!

The main reasons Gomez-Ibanez doubts the applicability of franchising to public transport are, first, the lack of a genuinely competitive market; and second, the problem of incomplete contracts. Because the tactical-level aspects of public transport are complex, and franchises usually last for five or more years, it is very difficult to cover every eventuality. Situations will arise that are not covered by the contract, leading to complex renegotiations and the potential for disputes. A particular problem has been the practice of 'low-balling', where franchisees submit optimistic bids to secure contracts, and then demand increased subsidies once they are entrenched. As Peter Kain notes: 'Under the systems employed to date, it is the willingness to gamble rather than to operate efficiently that is rewarded.'[45] A sub-contractor that behaved like this would probably be sacked, especially if the public agency maintained an in-house operating capacity, as in Gothenburg. But a franchisee is more difficult to replace, because under the concession system the public authority has no easy way of replacing it.

There is also the problem of assessing franchise bids. With sub-contracting, the cheapest tender usually wins, subject to any concerns about service quality. Sclar reminds us that it is easy to make mistakes when assessing such tenders, but it is much more likely that things will go wrong when franchise bids are assessed. The public authority is making an assessment of competing 'packages' of tactical and operational elements, in which the cost to the public purse is only one factor. It is like judging a beauty contest, as Kain points out: there is no clear right answer.[46] How can public officials – who apparently cannot be relied on to do their own tactical planning – correctly judge a 'beauty contest' which requires them to second-guess tactical planning proposals submitted by private tenderers? And if, as seems likely, they make the wrong decision by hiring a 'low-balling' franchisee, will they admit the mistake, or will they take the easy option and team up with the franchisee to defend the 'system'?

These questions raced through my mind at the closing session of the 10th Thredbo Conference on Competition and Ownership in Land Passenger Transport in 2007. The series had returned to Australia for the anniversary, this time to the tropical resort of Hamilton Island. The closing forum was 'the ideal contract roundtable', and a panel of contributors from Australia, the UK, the Netherlands and Norway took a mainly bullish view of the possibilities. Regulators must stimulate entrepreneurship and 'let [private] operators make (their own) money and expose them to the test of the market!' Operators should assume revenue and patronage risks to force them to chase customers: revenue should be proportional to patronage, but additional 'performance incentives', or bonuses for growing the market, may be needed. 'The marketing tools should as much as possible be on the side of the operator, including fares', which means that 'one must allow operators freedom of tactical planning to enhance innovation and entrepreneurship'.[47]

It all sounded very convincing, but also rather familiar. The panellists had just described the regime under which public transport in my home city of Melbourne was privatized in 1999.

NOTES

1   Hearing transcript, pp36–37, http://oversight.house.gov/story.asp?ID=2256 (accessed 30 August 2009).
2   Roth and Wynne (1982).
3   www.thredbo.itls.usyd.edu.au (accessed 30 August 2009)
4   CEC (1995).
5   Whitelegg (1993, ch. 8).
6   www.alpeninitiative.ch/e.
7   CEC (1995, p27).
8   CEC (1998, pp12–13).
9   CEC (2007b).
10   CEC (2007, p5).
11   EC Regulation No. 1370/2007, preamble (5); see discussion in Stanley (2003) and Goldberg (2006).
12   CEC (2007b, p19).
13   Inno-V et al (2008); Gomez-Ibanez (2003); Sclar (2000); Vuchic (2005).
14   Vuchic (2005, pp456–459); Inno-V et al. (2008, pp32–35).
15   Vuchic (2005, pp438–440); Pucher (1996).
16   Vuchic (2005, pp305–308).
17   Frankena (1982).
18   Vuchic (2005, pp445–448).
19   DfT (2008, table 6.14).
20   Rodney Hide, 9 September 2008, *New Zealand Hansard*, vol. 650, p18,656.
21   Eddington (2006, section 4.3 & recommendation 5(b)). Eddington incorrectly calls the London model 'franchising'.
22   DfT (2006, p21).
23   White (2002, pp184–187); White (2008).
24   DfT (2008, tables 6.13 and 6.14; concessionary reimbursement plus 'support' divided by passenger journeys).
25   ONS (2003, table KS 17).
26   DfT (2003, table 26).
27   J. Toner (2001, p20).
28   Bouf and Hensher (2007, p523); see also Vuchic (2005, pp460–461).
29   Sclar (2000, pp49–55).
30   Mees (2002).
31   See STA Annual Report 2000–2001, pp4, 6.
32   Gomez-Ibanez (2003, p328).
33   These terms are taken from Nielsen (2005, p35).
34   Thompson (1993).
35   Schaeffer and Sclar (1975, pp40–44).
36   Twain (1899, p245 (ch. XXV)).
37   World Bank (2002, chs 7 and 8, p121). The report also discusses integration in ch. 11, which deals with institutions.
38   Vuchic (1999, p209).
39   Population is for whole region; density for urbanized area, from Table 5.1.

40 181 million by bus – DfT (2003, table 16) – plus PTE's estimate of 20 million rail trips; Zurich total from ZVV Annual Report (2007, p14).
41 West Yorkshire PTE (2006, p22).
42 Quoted in Harris (2007, p152).
43 World Bank (2002, ch. 7).
44 Gomez-Ibanez (2003, pp186–187).
45 Kain (2007, p100).
46 Kain (2007, pp49–50).
47 Reported in Hensher et al (2008).

6

Toronto and Melbourne Revisited

If what the honourable member is asking for is some sort of direct subsidy in place of the TTC reviewing its business practices and doing what they have done in other jurisdictions, for example, in Australia, where lots of places have contracted out certain routes for public transit – in one case, I forget whether it's Adelaide or Melbourne, they actually have 52 different entities contributing to the overall mass transit system in that city, and it functions a heck of a lot better than the TTC does here in Toronto.

Ernie Eves, Premier, Ontario Legislative Assembly,
22 October 2002.[1]

TWO TORONTO MODELS

The Premier was right on one point: Melbourne (not Adelaide) does have dozens of fingers in its public transport pie. However, on the main issue he was either seriously misinformed or employing an odd definition of functioning. The Toronto Transit Commission (TTC) outperforms its Melbourne counterparts on every criterion of effectiveness, from cost-recovery to market share.

As we saw in Chapter 4, use of public transport for travel to work is much higher in the Toronto census area than in Melbourne's, the 2006 shares being 22.2 and 13.9 per cent (Table 4.1). But the TTC only serves the City of Toronto, which houses half the region's 5 million residents, and there public transport carries 34.4 per cent of workers.[2] Comparing overall travel is more difficult, because census data only cover work trips. Toronto has a regular Transportation Tomorrow Survey conducted in the same year as the census,[3] but Melbourne's surveys have been less systematic, partly because it decided in the early 1990s to use more intensive survey techniques to catch short walking trips. Unfortunately, these methods are expensive, and Melbourne has struggled to achieve regular surveys with statistically valid sample sizes. The Melbourne surveys show many more walking trips than Toronto, but this reflects different survey methodologies, not actual differences in

Table 6.1 *Public transport patronage, (unlinked trips per annum), 1950–2000, Melbourne and Toronto*

	Melbourne			Toronto		
	Patronage (million)	Pop. (m)	Per capita patronage	Patronage (m)	Pop. (m)	Per capita patronage
1950	584	1.3	449	350	1.2	292
1960	441	2.0	222	330	1.8	183
1970	355	2.5	142	480	2.6	185
1980	258	2.7	95	660	3.1	213
1990	292	3.0	97	869	3.9	223
2000	343	3.3	103	810	4.7	173

Sources: Mees (2000, p178); operating authorities; census (population from the following year's census).

walking rates: census data show more walking in Toronto. The 2001 Transportation Tomorrow Survey found that 24 per cent of motorized trips (i.e. excluding walking and cycling) in the City of Toronto were by public transport; the equivalent figure for Melbourne was probably around 9 per cent.[4] Comparing changes over time is even more difficult, so I have used easier-to-obtain figures on the number of trips per head (Table 6.1).

Although the TTC outperforms Melbourne's public transport operators, there is more to the story than this. Public transport in Toronto's outer suburbs, beyond the boundary of the City of Toronto, is much less effective, and utilization rates are not much different from those in the equivalent areas of Melbourne. Most of the region's population growth has occurred in these areas, so as the years go by the outer areas drag the region-wide average down. The decline has been exacerbated by problems in the TTC's own heartland. Between the early 1960s and the late 1980s, public transport in the regional Municipality of Metropolitan Toronto (which became the City in 1998) held its own against the car, with average trip rates rising so rapidly that they lifted the average for the whole region (see Table 6.1). This was a time of rapid decline in other places, particularly Melbourne, where tripmaking fell by more than half. The contrast led observers to speak of a 'Toronto model' for successful public transport. But the last two decades have seen a turnaround in performance, with big falls in trip rates and mode share in the TTC's heartland.

So there are two Toronto models: the TTC's success in turning the tide of car dominance up to the end of the 1980s, and the less impressive performance found in outer areas, and recently even in the TTC's territory. The most popular explanation for the difference between the TTC and outer suburban systems is the much higher urban density in the City of Toronto, but this cannot explain the problems there in the last two decades, as the city's density has increased over that period. So what is the explanation? To answer this question, it is necessary to look at the two different policy models employed in Toronto, the successful one and the approach that seems to be failing.

A TRIUMPH FOR PUBLIC OWNERSHIP: HOW THE TTC COMPETED WITH THE CAR

I examined the reasons for the TTC's 'golden age' at length in my 2000 book *A Very Public Solution*. The main conclusion was that Toronto's success was not, as had been widely claimed, a result of land-use planning that clustered high-density housing around subway stations. There was much less of this clustering than had been generally believed: observers from outside Canada had confused the aspirations in regional planning documents with on-the-ground reality. More recent analysis of census data by researchers from the University of Waterloo confirms these findings. There was 'weak correspondence between high residential density and subway stations', and 'on its own density has a weak effect on modal shares'.[5]

The real difference between Toronto and Melbourne was not in the share of residents living within walking distance of rail stations: the share in Melbourne was actually higher, at 20 per cent to Toronto's 15, because its rail network is much larger and has many more stations. The critical factor was the behaviour of the 80–85 per cent of residents who *didn't* live near stations. In Melbourne, these residents rarely used public transport, especially outside peak hours: across the day, 69 per cent of rail passengers walked to the station and 17 per cent travelled by car. In the part of Toronto served by the TTC, residents who lived beyond walking distance from stations used public transport nearly as often as those who lived nearby: only 20 per cent of rail users walked to the station and a tiny 3 per cent took cars. The big difference was in the use of feeder buses (and trams): 76 per cent of TTC rail passengers travelled to the station in this way, against only 10 per cent in Melbourne.

The TTC's bus network operated as an extension of the subway system, linking it to the whole of the city (or Metro Toronto as it then was). This enabled the provision of a 'Paris Metro' style frequent rail service, running every five minutes or better until 1:45 am seven days a week. Frequencies like this would require extremely high densities if patrons walked to the station, but the TTC's rail–bus strategy circumvented the density problem in precisely the way Thomson suggested in *Great Cities and Their Traffic* (see Chapter 4). Because of the economical densities of patronage generated by the feeder bus network, the Toronto subway returned an operating surplus, which helped defray the loss incurred by the buses. Conventional economists might object to this apparent cross-subsidy, but in reality the performance of the two modes cannot be separated: the rail service would not carry enough passengers to make a profit without the loss-making buses that fed it. The net result was that Toronto's much smaller rail system outperformed Melbourne's large network, by using buses to extend its reach.

High passenger loads generated by the rail-feeder role – around half of all bus trips were made to and from subway stations – also supported high service levels on the TTC's bus routes. The main routes operated at high frequencies (10 minutes or less) until after 1:00 am, every day of the year – better than on bus routes in the City of Paris, only half of which operate at all after 8:30 pm, and those generally every 20 minutes. The network followed the grid pattern of Toronto's road system, which like Melbourne's was the product of 19th-century British surveyors armed with T-squares, providing direct routes to subway stations, which are located in accordance with the same grid pattern. As well as linking with the radial rail system, the bus routes link with each other to form a network catering for cross-suburban travel. The single most surprising observation I made while riding the TTC's network was the high rate of bus-to-bus transferring, which occurs all day and evening at most points where different routes intersect. Combining radial and cross-city travel on a single bus network produced high occupancy rates, resulting in relatively low subsidies, and greenhouse emissions, per passenger.

This integrated network did not come about by accident: the TTC's system was designed to be multi-modal from the time the first section of subway opened in 1954. Transfers are free because the fare system is fully multi-modal, and at most subway stations passengers proceed directly between buses and trains without the inconvenience and delay of ticket checking. These 'free-body transfers' are possible because buses, and even trams, enter the station precinct on specially designed roadways, placing the whole bus–rail interchange inside the station fare gates. Even bus-to-bus transfers are encouraged by physical design: stops are located immediately adjacent to intersections where routes cross, with approach- and departure-side stops on wide roads, to minimize walking for passengers transferring between bus routes. This means that stopping buses block a road lane at each intersection, but the TTC justifies this by pointing out that on many roads, buses carry more passengers than cars.

The contrasting situation in Melbourne is illustrated in the story of Monash University in Chapter 1. Without a functioning feeder bus network, Melbourne's rail system relies mainly on walk-on custom, which is insufficient to support high all-day frequencies or even staffed stations. There are also some park-and-ride commuters, who travel mainly in the peak period, exacerbating the problem of peaking, which leaves staff and vehicles idle for most of the day. The rail system requires a large operating subsidy and does not generate a surplus that could support good bus services. Buses are infrequent and poorly coordinated with trains, and many routes do not operate at all in the evenings or on Sundays. Rather than following the arterial road grid, as in Toronto, Melbourne's buses meander in a vain attempt to avoid transfers by directly linking as many origins and destinations as possible. The result is a slow, inefficient network that is difficult for passengers to understand and makes cross-city travel a nightmare. Rail–bus transfers are uncommon in Melbourne and bus-to-bus transferring is unheard of. Naturally, bus stops are located well away from intersections, to avoid delaying important people in cars. Cost-recovery is poor and bus occupancies so low that, like the American services discussed in Chapter 3, greenhouse emissions are no better than would be the case if passengers used cars instead.

HOW THE DIFFERENT MODELS EVOLVED

The differences between public transport planning and operating philosophies in the two cities did not come about as a result of 'deterministic' factors like urban form, income or car ownership. Nor can they be attributed to national or political culture, since in these respects it would be hard to find two cities more alike: the constitutions of Ontario and Victoria were drafted by the same officials at the British Colonial Office, and their political histories show remarkable parallels. The differences are the result of policy decisions taken in response to transport challenges, and just as in Chapter 2, the critical periods were those following World War I and then World War II.

The Toronto Transportation Commission, the initial version of the TTC, was established in 1921, the year after President Woodrow Wilson received the report of the US Federal Electric Railway Commission. In 1919, the year Wilson set up the Commission and Auckland municipalized its privately operated tramway service, Melbourne's equivalent body, the Melbourne and Metropolitan Tramways Board (MMTB), commenced operations. The TTC and MMTB were both founded in response to problems with private tram systems run under 30-year franchises. The problem with the private operators was not financial unsoundness, as in the US, but inadequate service due to the franchisees' reluctance to extend routes to keep up with urban growth. The two cities chose not to renew the franchises when they expired, but instead established public agencies.

In Toronto, where the city's boundaries covered most of the urbanized area, the solution was a municipal body. In Melbourne, with its patchwork of 'pocket-handkerchief' municipalities, the solution was less clear, so the state government established a Royal Commission into public transport well before the tram franchise expired. The Royal Commission reported in 1911, recommending the establishment of the MMTB, but with one critical difference from the model chosen in Toronto. The TTC was given a monopoly over all forms of public transport in the city, except taxis and steam railways, while the Melbourne Board only had power over trams. The different decision in Melbourne was partly a response to the existence of a substantial suburban rail service operated by the Victorian Railways Department, but also due to the fact that in 1911 nobody foresaw the rise of the bus. Toronto had no suburban rail service, and by the time the TTC was established in 1921, buses could not be ignored.

These small initial differences became crucial to the evolution of policy and operating philosophies. The TTC became an exemplar of coordinated, multi-modal central planning, while Melbourne was a laboratory for competition. Melbourne's public transport operators competed with one another; the TTC competed with the car.

The government-owned railways and tramways of Melbourne were rivals, and both competed with a burgeoning private bus industry. Melbourne, uniquely among developed cities, chose not to abolish jitneys, or 'cabs' as they were called locally; indeed, they were given special treatment when legislation was enacted to regulate buses. The Motor Omnibus Act of 1924 applied to vehicles with 'seating capacity for not less than eight passengers', so seven-seat cabs (which often included unofficial extra fold-up seating) proliferated, operated by owner-drivers – usually returned servicemen who had learned to drive during the war. These operators were the pioneers of the private bus industry in Melbourne: even today, many firms are run by their grandchildren or great-grandchildren.

Jitneys in Melbourne did not provide the kind of flexible, customer-friendly service envisaged by commentators hailing from cities that never had them. The surviving pioneers themselves conceded this, when interviewed by a local historian in the early 1990s. 'Cab-style operation was a very haphazard affair; service was provided as traffic warranted and if the owner decided he'd rather spend the afternoon at the races or elsewhere he'd simply do that and passengers would have to find other means of transport or walk.' Another informant agreed: 'It was pretty rough and ready, to say the least, and the system was somewhat unreliable as far as the paying public was concerned.'[6] Gradually, the system evolved toward a more familiar pattern, as operators swapped cabs for buses, and formed companies and associations to regularize routes and timetables. But the industry's shambolic beginnings left a legacy of convoluted, inefficient routes and limited service that has lasted into the 21st century.

Competition had been a feature of rail-based transport in Melbourne since the 1880s, when the suburban steam trains of the Victorian Railways fought private cable trams for patrons. One result was rapid network growth, with public transport extending to the very edge of urban development and even beyond, leading rather than following suburbanization in much the same manner as Henry Huntingdon's Pacific Electric Railway in Los Angeles two decades later. Extensive public transport, combined with the Eight Hour Day and high wages won by local trade unions when Henry Ford was still a schoolboy, allowed Melbourne to spread earlier and further than any US city. Mark Twain reported in 1897 that 'Melbourne spreads around over an immense area of ground', while a British visitor of 1883 observed: 'Terraces and attached houses are universally disliked, and almost every class of suburban house is detached and stands in its own garden.'[7]

The 1920s saw a second round of this competition, as the railways and the now-public tramways electrified their lines, sparking a new round of suburban dispersal. Melburnians were spoiled for choice when it came to radial trips to the city centre, but travel to other destinations was inconvenient, as rail and tram lines usually parallelled one another rather than meeting up, timetables never connected and an additional fare was required for each transfer. Buses were almost useless, as the city's new metropolitan planning agency pointed out in 1953, in a comment that echoed Mark Twain's observation made the previous century (see Chapter 5): 'On account of infrequent service and poor co-ordination the saving in walking time by use of a feeder bus is largely offset by waiting time ... there are relatively few who can save much time by using these services.'[8] Low car ownership and wartime petrol rationing (which lasted until 1950) meant most people had little alternative, but the planning agency's 1951 travel survey recorded high rates of cycling to non-central locations: 17 per cent of non-CBD workers rode bikes; 18 per cent travelled in cars.[9]

Meanwhile in Toronto, comprehensive planning had enabled a different kind of service to be provided using much less infrastructure than in Melbourne. The TTC provided a comprehensive service across the whole area within city boundaries, employing uniform minimum service standards. It used buses to supplement trams on low-demand corridors, including cross-suburban runs and thinly settled districts, converting heavily used bus corridors to tram operation. It laid routes out along the grid of the arterial road network and encouraged transfers through route and stop design, and by offering a fully multi-modal fare system. As a municipal agency, the TTC was reluctant to extend service beyond municipal boundaries, but provided some service on contract for suburban municipalities, which were also served by private bus firms. Efficient management enabled the Commission to weather the Depression and, during the wartime patronage boom, accumulate a large surplus intended to finance construction of a subway under the main artery of Yonge Street.

Frances Frisken of York University calls this result 'a triumph for public ownership', contrasting it with the contemporary collapse of private, franchised services in US cities like Los Angeles and Chicago (discussed in Chapter 2). Critics respond that the TTC faced a more favourable operating environment than its US counterparts, since Canada had lower incomes and car ownership levels.[10] Melbourne's experience supports Frisken's conclusion, since car ownership and incomes were lower than in Toronto, but public transport operators barely survived the depression and emerged from World War II with run-down systems and without the financial reserves to modernize them. Equally importantly, Melbourne's public transport operators also entered the post-war period without the knowledge or organizational capacity to provide services that could compete with the car.

The two cities again diverged in their response to the rapid post-war rise in incomes and car ownership. In Toronto, pre-war growth had been held in check by the TTC's reluctance to extend services into the suburbs; now, the region exploded as bungalows, factories and strip malls spread outwards along main roads. The high-density city was soon surrounded by sprawling suburbs characterized by fragmented development scattered through farm and vacant land. Melbourne changed much less: it had already been a spread-out city, and post-war suburbs grew by accretion to the existing urban form. Much of it simply filled the vast reserve of empty blocks that had been prematurely subdivided in the booms of the 1880s and 1920s.

In both cities, however, increasing car ownership meant that people were no longer required to constrain their lives to fit the available public transport. In Toronto, this meant that suburban living became possible; in Melbourne, it meant cross-suburban trips and the extension of suburbs beyond walking distance of tram and train stops. Urban planners in both cities saw that public transport would have to change to meet the new challenge, but only Toronto rose to the occasion.

The situation in Toronto in the early 1950s was similar to that in Chicago at the same time (see Chapter 2): a higher-density city served by a public transport network was surrounded by sprawling suburbs with minimal services operated by private firms and municipalities. There were two critical differences: first, bigger and wealthier Chicago had much more passenger rail infrastructure; second, the Toronto Transportation Commission was well-run and financially sound, while the Chicago Transit Authority (CTA) was hamstrung by the legacy of failed private operation. In Toronto, suburban municipalities wanted to join the TTC; joining the CTA was much less attractive.

Toronto's transport planners, unlike their Chicago counterparts, did not use low suburban densities as excuse for doing nothing about public transport. Instead, the provincial government created a federal arrangement, with a new Municipality of Metropolitan Toronto serving higher-level functions across the entire urbanized area, covering the old City of Toronto and half a dozen surrounding municipalities. The TTC became an agency of Metro in 1954, the same year the Yonge subway opened. The suburban bus firms were bought out and the TTC's pattern of comprehensive service expanded to cover the entire urban area.

Initially, the organization's management adopted a cautious approach to extensions, believing that suburban densities were too low to justify comparable standards to those in the city. By the early 1960s, suburban population growth changed the balance of power on the Metro council, and 'urban' service levels were extended across the whole region. Continued expansion of the subway system led to additional feeder buses, establishing the Metro-wide grid network. Despite continued growth in incomes and car ownership, the decline in per capita patronage was halted and reversed (see Table 6.1).

In Melbourne, post-war public transport patronage collapsed almost as rapidly as in Auckland. The city's planning agency had pointed out the inadequacies of public transport in its 1953 report, concluding: 'it is apparent that, if the public transport system is to play its proper part in the essential movement of people and goods, there will have to be effective coordination of all forms of surface transport – trains, trams and buses.'[11] But how was this to be achieved? The public rail and tram agencies, and the multitude of private operators, continued to compete with one another and ignored the car. By the late 1950s, all three modes were trapped in a spiral of falling patronage and revenue, reduced services and fare rises. A decade later, public and private operators were on the verge of bankruptcy, and the State was forced to step in with subsidies to cover the deficits.

A TALE OF TWO FREEWAY REVOLTS

The different planning and operating philosophies influenced the way Toronto and Melbourne responded to their own versions of the freeway revolts that swept the western world in the early 1970s. In Toronto, the lightning rod was the proposed Spadina Expressway, which would have cut a swathe through inner city neighbourhoods to the north of the University of Toronto – one of which was home to the American urbanist Jane Jacobs, who had moved there from New York in 1968. In Melbourne, where freeway construction had been minimal due to lack of funds, the controversy was ignited by a 1969 plan for a network of freeways covering the whole inner city, that would have required the removal of some 40,000 residents.[12]

The political environment was remarkably similar in both cities. Long-standing conservative governments at state/provincial level with new, reformist leaders – Bill Davis (Premier of Ontario from 1971 to 1985) and Dick Hamer (Premier of Victoria from 1972 to 1981) – faced difficult elections. Davis cancelled the Spadina Expressway in 1971 and won an increased majority in the election held later that year. In an oft-quoted explanation, Davis said: 'If we are building a transportation system to serve the automobile, the Spadina Expressway would be a good place to start. But if we are building a transportation system to serve people, the Spadina Expressway is a good place to stop.'[13] The message was not lost on Davis's Victorian counterpart, who in 1972 said: 'Action must be taken so that the motor car adds to the amenity of life … without assuming such proportion that the city is a place for the motor car to move rather than for people to live.'[14] Shortly before the 1973 state election, Hamer cancelled most of the inner city freeways from Melbourne's 1969 plan; he was also returned with an increased majority.

Each Premier offered improved public transport as the alternative to the cancelled freeways, backing the statement with increased funding. In Toronto, this funding was used to accelerate the public transport recovery that had been underway since the early 1960s. In Melbourne, nobody knew how to revive public transport, and the decline in patronage continued apace.

Melbourne's public transport operators used their additional funding to buy new vehicles, but operated them in the same uncoordinated way as the old ones. Throughout the 1970s, off-peak, evening and weekend services were cut back in established areas, while new suburbs were provided with minimal service. Patronage continued to decline and deficits mounted: by the end of the decade, fares were covering less than half of operating costs. The conservative government appointed an inquiry into public transport, which recommended closure of large sections of the train and tram systems, with the funds saved diverted to freeway-building. The report's release coincided with the opening of the first stage of Melbourne's underground rail loop, constructed at vast expense in anticipation of patronage increases that never came. The main result of the report's proposed cuts and closures was the defeat of the conservatives at the 1982 state election and the election of a Labor government on a pro-public transport platform.

The Labor government of the 1980s proved barely more successful at reviving public transport than its conservative predecessor. A multi-modal fare system had been introduced in the dying days of conservative rule, and this produced the first patronage increase since the days of war-time petrol rationing. The new fare system probably saved the private bus operators from extinction, because it required their incorporation into the public system as sub-contractors. The logical next step would have been the introduction of Toronto-style integrated services to match the integrated fares, and the new government actually amalgamated the railways, tramways and bus regulatory authorities into a single Metropolitan Transit Authority.

One of the government's early acts was to commission a group of local 'experts' to produce an agenda for the new MTA. The group evaluated a high-standard direct-route bus network following the arterial road grid – in other words, a service strategy like that of the TTC. The evaluation, which did not mention Toronto, used traditional economic analysis and concluded that the bus upgrade would attract few new passengers, leading to a large increase in subsidies. The team insisted that demand was constrained by 'land use characteristics and car availability'.[15] The MTA followed the experts' advice and never attempted to integrate its services – as generations of Monash University students, among others, can testify (see Chapter 1). Instead, it argued that population density was the major barrier to improved public transport in Melbourne, a convenient view which absolved the Authority of any responsibility.

The TTC used its new provincial funding to move further towards equalizing city and suburban service standards. The subway system was originally intended as a replacement for the busiest tram routes, with subways confined to the dense environment of the old City of Toronto. Between 1973 and 1980, the subway system doubled in size, as lines were extended into suburban areas where densities had previously been regarded as too low to justify rail transport. The high suburban bus service levels inaugurated in the 1960s, along with excellent bus–rail integration, overcame the density problem. Provincial subsidies were also used to eliminate a two-zone fare system inaugurated in 1954, which had required suburban residents to pay higher fares than city dwellers to compensate for lower densities and longer trips. And it is in these 'middle suburbs' of Toronto, not the dense inner city, where patronage turned around from the 1960s onwards; this is also the area where the TTC outperformed Melbourne by the largest margin.

THE TORONTO MODEL COMES UNSTUCK

The TTC achieved its post-war success during decades of rapid suburban growth and falling population densities. These trends were eventually halted and partially reversed, which should have made public transport's job easier. But this change coincided with a reversal of the TTC's gains in patronage and mode share. Public transport patronage in Metro Toronto reached an all-time high in 1988, having grown by a third in 10 years despite a static population. A decade later, Metro's population was growing modestly thanks to widespread urban redevelopment, but the number of trips made on the TTC had fallen by 20 per cent, and mode share by a similar amount. Since the late 1990s, patronage has steadily recovered, but still remains below the 1988 peak, despite a 10 per cent increase in population within the service area.

Changes in urban form do not explain the turnaround, so what does? The trends in TTC patronage before and after 1988 match changes in service levels.[16] A long strike in 1989 initially depressed patronage, then the 1990 recession exacerbated the trend. This created a budget problem for the Commission, which responded by substantially cutting services in 1991. Patronage declined further, and the financial consequences were exacerbated by reductions in provincial subsidies, culminating in their complete elimination in 1996, following the election of a conservative government committed to reducing outlays and taxes. A vicious cycle of decline had been established. Most of the cuts fell on bus services, which are easier to adjust to changes in patronage, and in off-peak periods, where it was felt that service reductions would not increase crowding.

Because the TTC's transfer-based system operates on the basis of frequent headways rather than the coordinated timetables employed in places like suburban Zurich (see Chapter 8), it is very sensitive to service frequencies. It appears that the cuts of the early 1990s disrupted the functioning of the network by increasing waiting times on many routes beyond tolerable levels.

Public confidence in the TTC suffered a further blow in 1995, when two subway trains collided, killing three passengers. The collision resulted from the failure of a 'trip arm', intended to stop trains running red signals, and led to a focus on repairing and updating existing infrastructure. Subway extensions were placed on the back-burner, with only one short extension opened during the two decades after 1980. Subway growth had ceased some time before, largely in response to what Richard Soberman of the University of Toronto calls 'provincial government fixation on novel technology'. Soberman argues that the TTC 'lost about ten years of transportation planning responding to technology based, rather than demand based initiatives.'[17] The only outcome of this period was the use of 'automated light rapid transit' (ALRT) to serve a subway extension to the regional centre of Scarborough, an area that was thought to have densities too low to justify subway expansion. Within a decade of opening the Scarborough ALRT was overwhelmed by higher-than-anticipated patronage.

In the last decade, service levels on the TTC have been progressively reinstated, assisted by the advent of modest federal funding and, following the defeat of Premier Eves at the 2003 election, provincial assistance. Patronage has gradually recovered in line with the improved services, and has almost reached the 1988 record figure, although with a higher population in the area served, per capita tripmaking remains below the peak.

The TTC still accounts for 80 per cent of regional public transport trips, despite serving only half the population. The critical issue now is in the outer regions beyond the boundary of Metro Toronto – which in 1997 became the new City of Toronto, as the province abolished the lower-tier municipalities. Most regional population growth is occurring in these outer areas, where public transport is similar to that in equivalent parts of US urban regions: small-scale municipal bus operations are supplemented by peak-period-only 'commuter rail' services focused on the CBD. Travel by public transport to non-central locations, and even to the CBD outside peak period, is extremely inconvenient. For example, the two largest outer-suburban municipalities are neighbouring Mississauga and Brampton, with a combined population of 1.1 million. Each houses one of Canada's largest shopping malls. The two municipalities have separate bus systems, so residents of Brampton have no direct link to the Mississauga shopping mall, or to the nearest TTC subway terminal. Mississauga residents have no bus link to the Brampton mall either: travellers must change at the municipal boundary to the neighbouring system's infrequent, uncoordinated service, and pay an additional fare.

The largest change in urban density in the Toronto region comes when one moves from the inner city, the old City of Toronto, to the 'middle' suburbs that comprise the remainder of the new city: overall urban density (see Chapter 4 for explanation) drops from 70 per hectare to 34. Public transport use declines more modestly when this boundary is crossed: mode share for work trips drops from 41 to 31 per cent. The fall in density from Toronto's 'middle' suburbs to outer areas is smaller, from 34 to 20 per hectare, and much of the difference is due to the greater amount of non-residential urbanized land – indeed, it is difficult to tell when one crosses the municipal border, as the form of development is so similar. But public transport usage rates drop dramatically, with the share of work trips falling to 11 per cent. The modes where changes do relate to density (or at least proximity to the CBD) are walking and cycling, with a big fall from 17 per cent to only 4 between inner and middle areas, then hardly any change to outer areas, where the figure is 3 per cent.[18]

Gilbert and Perl's *Transport Revolutions* gives figures for total (work and non-work) travel from the 2001 Transportation Tomorrow Survey. The same pattern is revealed, with mode share falling from 27 to 18 per cent from inner to middle areas, then to only 8 per cent in outer areas. They also give urban density figures, showing a big fall from 61 to 31 per hectare from inner to middle, and only a small drop, to 25 per hectare, from middle to outer. Strangely, the authors seem to think that density explains the differences in mode share, when the results clearly show that the two factors are not closely related.[19]

The decline in the TTC's performance since 1988 and the continued poor performance of outer suburban public transport present serious challenges for the region's policy makers. However, the challenge is not necessarily more difficult than those that were successfully tackled in the 1920s, 1950s and 1970s. And the fact that the regional and temporal differences in performance are not related to population density suggests that the contemporary challenges can be met, since public transport funding, service levels and organizational arrangements are easier to change than the urban density of a region with five million residents.

It is not clear that local policy makers understand this, however, as the emphasis in most discussions remains on density. The Province of Ontario established the Greater Toronto Transportation Agency in 2006, with a remit to plan for public transport and roads across the Toronto region, and the adjoining regions of Hamilton and Oshawa. The Agency, which adopted the name Metrolinx in 2007, has consulted widely and published a series of discussion papers emphasizing the need for more sustainable transport outcomes. The discussion paper on public transport, released in 2008, identifies the need for substantially improved services and better integration. But 'context is essential', Metrolinx argues. 'Transit modes and services that are appropriate to a given corridor can be determined almost exclusively by land-use density and trip density in that corridor.' This is illustrated with a table showing the supposed 'relationship between Land Use Density and Transit Potential'. Below 20 persons per hectare, no transit is possible; 20–40 per hectare permits 'marginal transit'; 40–90 can support a 'good bus service'. An excellent bus service requires 120–130 per hectare, trams need 140–250 and a staggering 200–350 per hectare is the density required for 'subway and feeder bus network'.[20]

The transport planners at Metrolinx seem unaware of the lessons of their own region's history. The TTC's success came from providing comparable service levels across areas of differing urban density, each major expansion involving a foray into territory where densities had previously been regarded as too low to justify a high-quality service. As we shall see shortly, this lesson is currently being applied by transit planners in Vancouver, undeterred by densities considerably lower than even Toronto's outer suburbs. The Metrolinx planners are by no means alone in this ignorance of the lessons of local history, of course. As we saw at the start of the chapter, former Ontario premier Ernie Eves even suggested that the TTC should imitate public transport in Melbourne – at the very time Melbourne was grappling with the unravelling of the privatization scheme he was praising.

MEANWHILE IN MELBOURNE

Given its long history of inter-modal competition, it is probably not surprising that Melbourne should have privatized its rail and tram services following the election of a 'new right' state government in 1992. After all, even after a decade with a single Metropolitan Transit Authority (later amalgamated with the rural rail operator to form the Public Transport Corporation, or PTC) in charge, the city's trams, trains and buses were as far as ever from forming a genuine network. However, the conservative government, which privatized many profit-making public utilities, chose initially to keep public transport in public hands and pursue cost reductions through a mixture of genuine efficiency improvements and cuts to service. Anticipated union opposition was avoided with a deal that abandoned most of the cuts proposed for metropolitan Melbourne (although retaining closure of many rural rail lines). The Victorian Auditor-General reported only five years later that the 'public transport reform program' had reduced the PTC's operating subsidy by half while improving the reliability of suburban train and tram services.[21] Patronage, which had fallen in the early 1990s in response to service cuts, began to recover as services were restored and the economy improved. A particular feature of the economic recovery has been a sustained increase in employment in Melbourne's CBD, with an additional 100,000 jobs added between the 1996 and 2006 censuses, raising the total by nearly half.

In late 1996, the transport minister responsible for the reform programme retired, and free-marketeers in the State Treasury made their move. The following year, the government announced that Melbourne's trains and trams would be privatized, using the 'franchising' model employed in the UK for British Rail, in which private firms handle tactical as well as operational matters. In his 1998 report on the public transport reform programme, the Auditor-General called for caution, expressing scepticism about the prospects for future cost savings.

When details of the new franchises were announced in 1999, it seemed that the Auditor-General and other critics (including the present writer) had been proven wrong. Melbourne had achieved the ideal contract, and the responsible officials from the Public Transport Reform Unit wasted no time in boasting about their achievement to a worldwide audience that apparently included Premier Eves of Ontario. The agreements promised the best of all possible worlds: an innovative subsidy regime would gradually wean the private operators from fixed subsidies, which would be replaced by incentives for improving customer satisfaction and attracting new patrons. Fares would be capped, subsidies would fall, services would expand, and patronage would rise substantially. It all sounded too good to be true – and so it proved to be.

The new franchisees commenced operations in August 1999, a fortnight before a state election at which the conservative government was expected to be returned with an increased majority. Instead, the election saw an upset, as rural voters angered by cuts to government services (including trains) swung to independents and the opposition Labor Party.

The new Labor government, which had opposed its predecessors' privatizations, appointed an Audit Review of Government Contracts to investigate them. The Audit Review gave public transport franchising a bill of health so clean it positively glowed. The effusive praise sounded as if it had been written by the Public Transport Reform Unit itself – which it had been, specifically by the Unit's former Director, Jim Betts, who had served as 'special advisor' to the Audit Review.[22] The Review sounded a single note of caution: 'In relation to the financial outcomes for trains and trams it needs to be kept in mind that financial savings, new investment and patronage growth on which train and tram franchise contracts are based are yet to be delivered.'[23] But what if these outcomes were not delivered? What was Plan B? It soon became apparent that there was no Plan B.

The Audit Review's glowing assessment of franchising was delivered in June 2000. A year later, or only two years into franchise agreements supposed to last up to 15 years, the three firms operating Melbourne's trains and trams began grumbling that costs were proving higher, and revenues lower, than they had anticipated. The franchise agreements had been based on the assumption that patronage would skyrocket from the moment the new operators took over, with growth of 25 per cent expected in the first two years alone. In fact, the whole franchising scheme had been based on assumptions so unrealistic that Peter Kain, of the Canberra-based Bureau of Infrastructure, Transport and Regional Economics later queried whether 'those negotiating on the government side genuinely believed that risk would be transferred successfully.'[24] The franchisees threatened to pull out of Melbourne unless their subsidies were increased and their obligations reduced.

The government faced a classic instance of 'low-balling' (see Chapter 5). It responded, understandably perhaps but extremely unwisely, by turning to the only people it knew with expertise in public transport, Jim Betts and a fellow-director from the old Public Transport Reform Unit. When this decision finally leaked out to the press most observers were gobsmacked, but one party was happy. The head of one of the franchisees said: 'There are great advantages in having people involved who have intimate knowledge of how we got to where we've got to.'[25]

After two years of negotiations, new arrangements were announced in 2004. One franchisee, the UK firm National Express, withdrew from Melbourne, leaving two French-based consortiums, one operating trams, the other trains. Very large increases in subsidies, to around three times the levels in the original contracts, were agreed – with the result that, as Kain concludes 'the new agreements are costing the taxpayer more than public sector operation.'[26]

No sooner were these arrangements announced than the franchisees and Betts (now in charge of the Public Transport Division of the Transport Department) identified a new problem: patronage was growing and the rail system faced a 'capacity crisis'. In other words, shortly after gaining over a billion dollars in additional subsidies on the basis that patronage had been too low, the franchisees claimed patronage was suddenly too high. Although some of the rise was an illusion generated by changes to the formula used to estimate trips from ticket sales (since privatization, no comprehensive patronage counts have been conducted), the more reliable data from the census does show a modest increase for trains and trams, commencing in 1996, following a severe decline in the previous five years. The share of work trips by train rose from 8.5 to 10.1 per cent in a decade, while the tram share increased from 1.9 to 2.4 per cent. Similar trends have been seen across other Australian cities, and appear to be the result of a substantial re-centralization of metropolitan employment. This explains why the share of Melbourne workers using buses, which cater mainly for non-central travel, continued to decline.[27]

The increased numbers should have been good news: after all, only two decades earlier, a government inquiry had proposed closing large sections of the network in response to the decline in patronage since the post-World War II peak. Now, absolute passenger numbers were almost as high as those recorded at this time (although mode share was, of course, much lower since Melbourne's population had tripled). Given that Melbourne had built an expensive underground rail loop to allow a doubling of train services from 100 per hour to 200, the city should have been well prepared. Instead, the private rail operator and its regulators convinced the state government to pay for a multi-billion-dollar second city underground railway, designed to allow hourly train numbers to be lifted from just under 100 to 140 – fully 30 per cent below the capacity of the existing infrastructure. Efficiency levels had declined so much that the option of using infrastructure as efficiently as planners of the 1970s intended was dismissed as too difficult.[28]

Whatever was driving the increase in rail patronage, it was certainly not improved service. Cleanliness and reliability deteriorated following the 2004 bailout, culminating in the system's near-collapse during the hot summer of 2009. Temperatures climbed above 40°C for three days in a row, and nearly half of all scheduled trains were cancelled on the third of these days, Friday 30 January, when the mercury hit 45° (this was a week before the terrible February bushfires, which occurred on a weekend). Melbourne's trains, which date mainly from the 1980s, simply weren't designed to operate in hot weather, the franchisee explained, and the air conditioning systems had broken down. Mr Betts, by now promoted to Secretary of the Transport Department, backed the operator's story. Nobody tried to explain why the cancellations had begun a fortnight beforehand, when temperatures were still mild, or why the same trains, built at the same Melbourne factory, ran without incident through the contemporaneous heatwave in Adelaide, which saw six days in a row above 40°, and a maximum of 46°.

When asked why, in light of all these problems, she persisted with the franchise system, the State's Transport Minister replied: 'We get that innovation, we get that international experience, not only in running the system but in responding much more quickly to problems'.[29]

VANCOUVER TAKES THE LEAD

The lessons from the success of the 'Toronto model' seem to have been forgotten in the model's home, and are certainly not being learned in Melbourne. In the first decade of the 21st century, the city that seems most determined to apply them is Vancouver.

Vancouver's density is a third lower than Toronto's and about the same as Melbourne's, when the effects of methodological differences are taken into account (see Table 4.1, Chapter 4). The share of work trips by car is 3.3 percentage points higher in Vancouver than in Toronto, but the difference has narrowed since the 1996 census, when the gap was 6.7 points. The change has been due to a significant increase in public transport use, and a modest rise in walking.[30] Although Vancouver has a long way to go, these trends, especially when combined with the reduction in trip lengths discussed in Chapter 3, suggest it is at least heading in the right direction.

Vancouver's 'freeway revolt' began in 1968 and climaxed in 1972, when anti-freeway activists won control of the city council. It had a more dramatic impact than those of Melbourne and Toronto. In contrast with Toronto, it came before many regional freeways had been built; in contrast with Melbourne, it virtually stopped freeway construction in the region. As a result, Vancouver has a very limited expressway network, comprising the Trans-Canada Highway and a few outer-suburban links; none of these roads serves the CBD.

The newly formed regional planning agency, the Greater Vancouver Regional District (GVRD), began work on a regional transport and land-use plan in the aftermath of the freeway controversy. There was general agreement that a public transport alternative to freeways was required, but what form was this to take? Vancouver's public transport was like Chicago's and Toronto's had been two decades earlier: a comprehensive, publicly run service across the City of Vancouver, but with infrequent, uncoordinated private and municipal offerings in the suburbs. A 1970 consultant's report on regional transit proposed an intensification of the divide, recommending two subway lines serving the city, supplemented by buses in the middle suburbs, and nothing at all in outer areas where the car was to remain king.[31]

This proposal offered nothing to suburban residents to replace the now-cancelled freeways, so the GVRD's transport committee took a second look, assisted by in-house staff. By this time, as we saw earlier, the Spadina Expressway controversy in Toronto was leading to a new policy of extending rapid transit into the suburbs. The GVRD report recommended a similar change for Vancouver, with a regional light rail system serving the entire urban area, not just densely populated inner regions, supported by high-quality, integrated, region-wide bus services. This would require a single public agency to take control of City of Vancouver buses and trolley-buses, and private and municipal routes in the suburbs. The new policy was confirmed in 1975 by the first Livable Region plan, and was followed up with the establishment of a regional public transport bureau, which eventually evolved into today's South Coast British Columbia Transportation Authority, better known as TransLink. The authority integrated and expanded regional bus services, and began planning a light rail system. Public transport usage rebounded, with substantial gains in mode share in suburban areas. The first light rail line opened in 1986, and the system has grown steadily ever since.[32]

Unlike Toronto, Vancouver has a single public transport agency responsible for upgrading services across the entire urbanized area. An integrated network of buses and light rail lines spreads from the city centre to the ex-urban fringe, with a single fare system. A Toronto-style high-frequency grid operates in the City of Vancouver, but in outer areas where demand is thinner, something closer to the coordinated 'pulse-timetable' approach of suburban Zurich (see Chapter 8) is employed.

While Translink's history has not been without its controversies and setbacks,[33] the Vancouver region offers greater Toronto an excellent example of how to revive the model of success Toronto itself pioneered.

NOTES

1   Ontario Hansard, 22 October 2002, 37th Parliament, p2308.
2   Statistics Canada (2008a).
3   The survey is conducted by the Data Management Group at the University of Toronto: www.dmg.utoronto.ca/transportationtomorrowsurvey/index.html (accessed 30 August 2009).
4   2001 TTS Survey Summary: City of Toronto (2006 results were not available at the time of writing); Victoria (2002) *Melbourne 2030*. Comparison is further complicated by the fact that Toronto operates separate school buses, which are not counted in public transport figures, while Melbourne carries schoolchildren on regular services.
5   Filion et al (2006, p1388).
6   Maddock (1992, pp22–23, 29); see also Mees (2000, ch. 9).
7   Twain (1899, p162 (ch. XVI)); Twopeny (1973, p37).
8   MMBW (1953, vol. 1, p184).
9   Mees (2000, p265).
10 Frisken (1984); Davis (1978).
11 MMBW (1953, vol. 1, p192).
12 MMBW (1971, p72).
13 Bill Davis press release, 3 June 1971 (in possession of the author).
14 Dick Hamer, press release, 21 December 1972 (in possession of the author); see also Davison (2004, ch. 8).
15 Ministry of Transport (1982, pp32–35).
16 See Soberman (1997, p21, table 3.1).
17 Soberman (2002, p392).
18 Mode shares calculated from Statistics Canada Community Profiles for Toronto CMA, Toronto City and 'Toronto (City/Dissolved)'. Densities are for same areas, except that the Toronto urban centre is used instead of the CMA. Figures are for 2001, the last census for which separate data was published for the old City; in the other two regions, there was little change in density or mode share between 2001 and 2006.
19 Gilbert and Perl (2008, pp72–73). Inner ('outer core') and middle ('inner suburbs') areas are defined slightly differently from the areas I have used to discuss work trips.
20 Metrolinx (2008, pp17–18).
21 Auditor General (1998).
22 Audit Review of Government Contracts (2000, vol. 2, pp139–162, Appendices, pp51, 52).

23 Audit Review (2000, vol. 2, p150).

24 Kain (2007, p100); see also Mees (2005).

25 'Ministry stands by privatisers' *The Age*, 20 August 2002, p5.

26 Kain (2007, p91, fig. 5).

27 Mees et al (2007, tables 1.1–1.8). These figures are for 'main mode' and exclude feeder services.

28 State of Victoria (2008); Mees (2008).

29 'Kosky stands by privatised trains', *The Age*, 24 January 2009, p1.

30 Statistics Canada (2008b, tables 11a, 11b, 11c).

31 Lash (1976, ch. 4).

32 S. Al-Dubikhi (2007, ch. 6); Stone (2008, chs 6 and 7).

33 See Translink (2008).

7

The Busway Solution

FROM FUTURAMA TO FOZ DO IGUACU

Urban transport in the 21st century is provided using technologies that developed in the 19th century – cars, bicycles, buses, electric trains and trams – and walking, which has been around for much longer. Some transport planners find this frustrating. Why should travellers in the age of the i-phone use vehicles that haven't substantially changed since the days of the Edison phonograph?

The answer is that the proposed replacement technologies have proven impractical, or at least less effective than those we already have. The most popular exhibit at the 1939 New York World's Fair was Futurama, a General Motors-sponsored depiction of the city of 1960: 'trains' of electronically controlled cars ran efficiently on freeways, with vehicles de-coupling to operate individually on local roads. Despite promises, name-changes and lavish government funding, the concept, most recently re-christened Intelligent Vehicle-Highway Systems, has gone nowhere in 70 years. *Futurama* is now better known as a cartoon series satirizing technology-based utopias.

Most other new urban transport devices have gone the same way. The 'aerocar' never managed to fly from *The Jetsons* into a real city; monorails have remained an expensive toy; and 'personal rapid transit' looks unlikely to transport any persons in real urban applications. Automated 'people-movers' such as Vancouver's Skytrain and the Scarborough line in Toronto are best thought of as variants on rail rapid transit, which is also capable of being automated, as seen on the most recent line of the Paris Metro.[1]

The reason the obsession with gadgets has produced so few results is that the difficulties of urban transport cannot be eliminated by technology. The car offers the convenience of door-to-door travel, but uses space and energy inefficiently. Public transport improves efficiency by transporting people together, but requires travellers to walk, wait and transfer. Attempts to join the two modes risk combining their disadvantages, as with personal rapid transit, which seeks to eliminate the inconvenience of transfers with automated individual capsules on computer-controlled city-wide monorail systems. The small vehicles and complicated routings produce low passenger-carrying capacity, but the expensive guideway systems require high densities of demand. The result, as Vuchic concludes, is that PRT is 'impractical under all conditions'.[2]

The previous chapters have already suggested that success in urban public transport is not really about technology: Vancouver, the Toronto Transit Commission and London use much the same transport technologies as Los Angeles, Auckland, Melbourne and Manchester. The difference is that the successful cities have deployed those technologies as networks designed to minimize the inconvenience associated with the necessary walking, waiting and transferring – the same approach that underpins Zurich's success, as we shall see in the next chapter.

Buses do not appear high-tech or glamorous, but they are the newest of the urban transport modes, having reached maturity in the 1920s. And they can, in theory at least, provide something close to door-to-door service, reducing walking distances and eliminating transfers. Their principal disadvantage is low speeds and capacity relative to rail-based modes, but these problems stem mainly from having to share streets with other vehicles. The busway concept originated in the late 1950s as an attempt to eliminate this problem by providing separate roadways for buses. Bus 'freeways' would offer the speed and capacity of rail on busy corridors, but buses could continue their journeys on regular streets, thus avoiding the need to transfer. 'Bus Rapid Transit' (BRT) would offer the advantages of rail at lower cost, and without the need to coordinate trunk and feeder services.

Some enthusiasts have acclaimed BRT as a genuinely new travel mode that would make rail-based public transport redundant. Like most public transport technologies, BRT has developed passionate supporters and detractors, with a particularly virulent dispute between partisans of BRT and enthusiasts for light rail. Sydney University's David Hensher argues that BRT is usually ignored for political reasons, and that support for light rail is driven by 'blind commitment' rather than a sober assessment of the alternatives.[3]

So is BRT the way of the future? Can it square the circle, by combining the advantages of rail with transfer-free direct service – and, in the process, reduce the need for centralized planning? Or is it simply another element of traditional public transport that requires network planning like the rest? Fortunately, it may be possible to answer these questions, because in contrast with other futuristic urban transport technologies, busways have actually been built, and have now been in operation for decades. The first genuine busway opened in 1973 in the English New Town of Runcorn, near Liverpool, but the most influential system is that of the Canadian capital, Ottawa.

OTTAWA: THE FIRST MODEL BUSWAY CITY

Transport planners must have done something right in Ottawa. As Table 4.1 shows, the region has the lowest private car use for travel to work of any city in Canada,

Australia or the US, apart from New York. And if taxis (included among 'other' in the table) are counted as cars, which they are, then the figure for Ottawa falls below that for New York. Ottawa combines high public transport mode share with above-average rates of walking and cycling, and importantly, the share of work trips made by these 'sustainable modes' has been growing since the 1996 census.

Ottawa has not always been a public transport success story. Four decades ago, the region was dominated by the car, and expected to remain so. A large freeway network was planned, supplemented by 'residual' public transport that was only expected to carry a small share of travel. Since then, Ottawa has cancelled most of the planned freeways, built an extensive busway network and become one of the least car-oriented cities in the English-speaking world – until recently, without any rail-based transit. Its busways inspired other cities, including Curitiba, Brazil, and Brisbane, Australia, both of which are discussed below. Ottawa has been hailed as a model of successful BRT by authors who disagree on most other urban transport policy questions, such as Berkeley's Robert Cervero and Sydney's David Hensher.[4]

All is not as it seems, however. Ottawa experienced rapid public transport growth that began in 1972 and continued for about 12 years. Per capita ridership – the best available measure, since the Canadian census has only included a question on the mode of travel to work since 1996 – nearly doubled over this period, one of the most dramatic turnarounds recorded anywhere in the world (see Figure 7.1). But the busway system was not responsible for this growth, because it was not in operation. Although construction began in 1978, the first section of busway did not open until 1983, with the remaining stages opening progressively through to 1996. Patronage actually declined after the first section of busway opened, reaching a low-point in 1996, since which time there has been a steady recovery. Bus usage

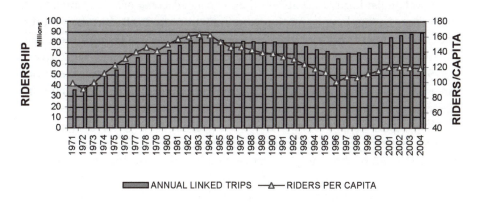

Source: Al-Dubikhi (2007)

Figure 7.1 *Public transport ridership in Ottawa, 1971–2004*

and mode share in Ottawa are both lower today than immediately before the first busway route opened, although much higher than they were in 1972.

So what did cause the increase in patronage that has been erroneously attributed to the busway system? The answer will by now be familiar.

Ottawa had its own version of the Toronto and Vancouver freeway revolts discussed in the previous chapter. The target was the Ottawa-Hull Area Transportation Study of 1965, which recommended an extensive freeway system covering the region of Ottawa, and the adjoining region of Hull (now called Gatineau) across the Ottawa River in Quebec (the data cited in this chapter are for the Ottawa region on the Ontario side). Much of the network on the Ontario side would be carved through existing neighbourhoods. In obeisance to the new orthodoxy of 'balanced transport', the study proposed busways for central business district (CBD) commuters, to be provided in the medians of radial freeways.

The study had been commissioned by the National Capital Commission (NCC), a federal agency that shared responsibility for regional planning with the provinces of Ontario and Quebec and local municipalities, since there is no equivalent of the District of Columbia or the Australian Capital Territory. The NCC had planned Ottawa around the automobile since the 1950s, a policy which began to create conflict with inner city municipalities; meanwhile, the NCC's policy of maintaining a green belt around the inner city was unpopular in the suburbs. The Ontario legislature responded with a federal solution modelled on Metro Toronto, establishing the Regional Municipality of Ottawa-Carleton. The region commenced operations in 1969, and its first task was to prepare an 'official plan' to replace those of the NCC.

Public disquiet over freeways soon turned this process into a debate about transport priorities. The region officially abandoned balanced transport, replacing it with a policy of 'transit first', under which major new roads were to be a last resort. This required attention to the problems of the region's public transport, which took a by-now familiar form. The City of Ottawa operated a reasonably comprehensive bus service, having bought out a private franchisee in 1948. But the suburbs, where most growth was occurring, received minimal service from private firms. The solution adopted was the same as in Toronto in the 1950s and Vancouver in the 1970s: a regional public transport agency was established to replace the private and municipal systems, and upgrade and integrate services. Just as in Toronto, the provincial government stepped in with subsidies to help defray the costs.

The Ottawa-Carleton Regional Transit Commission, better known as OC Transpo, started operations in 1972, and it is no coincidence that this year marked the end of the long post-war decline in patronage and the start of the dramatic turnaround (Figure 7.1). Region-wide fares were introduced, together with new suburban routes and higher suburban service levels. These measures were complemented by bus-only lanes on busy streets and agreement by the federal government, the region's major employer, to eliminate free parking for its employees and stagger working hours to spread the peak on buses. Patronage and mode share increased throughout the region, but the biggest change was in low-density outer areas. The rise in oil prices after 1973, growing environmental consciousness and an effective moratorium on new freeways probably also helped, as did the failure of the NCC's attempts to reduce road congestion by dispersing government offices away from the CBD.[5]

The busway system was intended to build on the success of these policies, particularly the bus lanes and other on-street priority measures. Busways, or transitways as they are called in Ottawa, would follow the routes of the now-cancelled radial freeways, with buses running through the CBD in priority lanes on a pair of one-way streets. The basic service pattern that currently operates was actually put in place before any transitways opened, initially using temporary bus lanes and shifting to the reserved roadways as they were completed (the pattern is described in detail in Cervero's *The Transit Metropolis*, 1998).

So why did patronage decline after the first section of transitway opened? The main reason appears to be an earlier commencement of the problems seen in Toronto in the late 1980s (see previous chapter): an initial fall in patronage due to a recession, leading to service cuts and further patronage decline, exacerbated by the progressive elimination of provincial subsidies during the 1990s. Restoration of service levels from the mid-1990s has seen patronage rebound.

Ottawa's busways do not appear to have stemmed the decline, suggesting again that service levels and integration were the most important factors. But did they make things worse? Are there features of the system's operation that exacerbated the effect of the service cuts?

One clue can be found from the fact that the decline in patronage was most severe in off-peak periods. At these times, Ottawa's BRT operates in the same way as a rail system served by feeder buses: dedicated 'transitway' routes operate along each arm of the system, and passengers must transfer to and from feeder services at transitway stations. In peak periods, this basic network is supplemented by express routes that run directly between residential areas and the CBD via the busway, obviating the need to transfer, but the more diffuse pattern of off-peak patronage does not permit such services outside the peaks.

Transfers from feeder to transitway routes are convenient, owing to the high frequency of the trunk services, but 'outward' transfers are less attractive because timetables are not coordinated and off-peak local feeders only run every 15 or 30 minutes. And it may be that the design of the transitway stations themselves discourages transfers. They spread over large sites in order to accommodate large numbers of buses at peak periods, forcing transferring passengers into lengthy walks without protection from the weather, and frequent climbs up and down stairs. Alan Hoffman, an enthusiastic BRT advocate from the US, concedes this point: 'It may also be worth asking whether the stations ... are perceived as desirable by users and potential users of the system (passengers are still exposed to potentially harsh weather when accessing vehicles, and the hard materials, such as exposed concrete, do little to create a warm and welcoming environment).'[6]

The ability of Ottawa's transitways to offer transfer-free services in peak periods may have led its planners to pay less attention to making off-peak transfers as convenient as possible, as well as leading timetablers in the 1980s to underestimate the importance of service frequency at these times. However, these limitations should not be allowed to obscure the fact that Ottawa outperforms peer cities in North America and Australasia.

Public opinion in Ottawa has been less mindful of this fact, with many observers blaming the decision to choose busways instead of rail for the decline in performance since the peak of the early 1980s. Comparison with Toronto suggests that this diagnosis may not be entirely fair, but the new City of Ottawa, which replaced the Regional Municipality of Ottawa-Carleton in a similar merger to that seen in Toronto,[7] decided in 2008 to replace the main transitway routes with light rail. An important factor behind the decision was increasing bus congestion on the CBD section of the system, but concern was also expressed about the lack of off-peak and non-CBD usage of the current system.[8]

So Ottawa is a public transport (and walking) success story, but not one that lends support to those who argue that BRT is the ideal urban transport mode. Rather, it seems to be another example of successful, region-wide network planning.

CURITIBA: THE NEW MODEL BUSWAY CITY

One theme that is beginning to emerge from cities with successful public transport is the role of public debate and controversy in modifying the designs of planners; Zurich, as we shall see, provides another case. This does not sit easily with the most popular model of city planning, which focuses on the work of 'great men'. There is no equivalent for Ottawa or Vancouver of the Burley Griffin Plan for Canberra, the Abercrombie Plan for London, or even Ken Livingstone's role in congestion charging.

Curitiba offers a more comforting story, with its city plan and public transport system presented very much as the work of one man, Jaime Lerner. Lerner was an architect-planner at the local university before becoming head of the city's development agency and eventually mayor. He served three terms and then became governor of Parana State, of which Curitiba is the capital. Few town planning academics could remain unmoved by the wisdom of a populace that would vote for one of us, and this almost too-good-to-be-true history helps explain the near-universal praise the 'Curitiba model' has received. As is so often the case, however, the received version of the story is not the full one. Lerner began his first term as Mayor of Curitiba in 1971, but not as the result of an election: he was appointed to the post by the military dictatorship which governed Brazil from 1964 to 1985.

Brazil is like that, always confounding expectations of who is on the progressive side. The country became a republic in 1889 because the liberal Emperor Pedro II, who had abolished the slave trade in 1850, freed the remaining slaves. International opinion applauded, but angry local elites staged a coup and appointed a general as the first of many military leaders. They also pursued a policy of 'racial whitening' designed to reduce the influence of the newly freed slaves, encouraging immigration from Europe and even Japan. Many of the migrants went to Brazil's more temperate southern region, which includes Parana; this area now has the highest standard of living in the country.[9]

Parana was originally part of neighbouring Sao Paulo State, and its citizens developed a habit of comparing themselves favourably to the rest of the country – particularly the former mother province which, along with its coffee-producing neighbours, dominated the political life of the republic. This history of civic boosterism dovetailed nicely with the flair for self-promotion of Lerner and his fellow-architects at the city's planning agency.

We shall shortly examine whether Curitiba's public transport is as good as is claimed, but there is no doubting the city's prowess in the field of self-promotion. Unfortunately, most outside observers have been content to echo this self-praise; the major exception is a comparison of Curitiba and Portland by Clara Irazabal of the University of Southern California. Irazabal suggests that urban planning in Curitiba has been predominantly top-down and technocratic, a trend that continued even after the restoration of democracy (Lerner won his third term as mayor, and two terms as governor, in democratic elections).[10]

The city has been developed under a master plan adopted in 1966, with a determination matching that shown by the planners of Canberra and Singapore. Like their counterparts in those two cities, Curitiba's planners were influenced by the contemporary enthusiasm for linear cities. Outward growth follows transport corridors, the main arteries lined with high-density office and residential buildings, and lower densities in surrounding areas. Each corridor was to be served by rapid transit, and after some debate it was decided that this would take the form of busways – partly because the World Bank refused to fund rail systems. The first busway corridor opened in 1974, evolving into the Integrated Transport Network (*Rede Integrada de Transporte*, or RIT) in 1979, and subsequently expanding to five main bus corridors, plus branch lines.

Curitiba's busways were provided at much lower cost than Ottawa's by the simple expedient of using the centre lanes of the wide boulevards that follow each of the radial axes. Buses are separated from traffic with barriers, but must stop at intersections, unlike in Ottawa's grade-separated system. The busways imitate European metros with stops every 400–800m, served by express routes operated with articulated buses and even extra-large bi-articulated vehicles manufactured especially for the city. Passengers board and transfer at 'stations' designed to speed movement, with platforms at the same height as the bus floor and ticket sales performed at the station entrance, rather than on the bus. Many stations are 'boarding tubes' with distinctive designs that show the influence of the city's architects.

Curitiba is a model of busways, but also of network planning, as the RIT's name would suggest. The express bus routes along the busways, and faster 'direct' services with fewer stops, are complemented by feeder and inter-suburban routes, with free transfers available at interchange stations. Data from 1993 supplied to Hensher by the system's operator showed that 37 per cent of express bus passengers, and 66 per cent of those using direct services, transferred from other routes; conversely, 46 per cent of feeder and inter-suburban route passengers transferred to other services.[11]

This high level of integration is possible because the city agency *Urbanizacao de Curitiba*, or URBS, controls bus services, setting routes and timetables, collecting fares and paying the private firms who actually provide the service by kilometres travelled, rather than passengers carried. This arrangement was introduced in the mid-1980s, to replace a long-standing system of area-based franchises. Lerner had left the franchise system in place while building the RIT to avoid antagonizing the existing oligopoly of nine firms – and possibly also because, like his architecturally trained colleagues, he regarded 'institutional' issues as being of lesser importance. The franchise system led to secrecy and claims of overcharging; it also prevented the establishment of a fully multi-modal fare system and inhibited network planning, as each company refused to allow rivals to service its 'territory'. The result was what Irazabal calls 'a major scandal': operators were found to have inflated their costs and understated revenues.[12]

Lerner's successor Robert Requiao, the first democratically elected mayor, cancelled the companies' franchises and replaced then with a more transparent system of sub-contracting, overseen by URBS. This was necessary, he said, to allow 'the re-establishment of legality and public morality'.[13] Requiao had intended to use competitive tendering and partial nationalization to bring the oligopoly to heel, but Lerner won a third term as mayor at the 1989 election, and reversed these measures. The oligopoly remained, although as sub-contractors instead of franchisees, and World Bank funding allowed the modernization of vehicles and an expansion of the fleet, including the introduction of bi-articulated vehicles.[14]

Despite the chorus of praise for Curitiba, reliable information on trends in mode share and patronage is hard to find (the Brazilian census does not include a question on the mode used for travel to work). It is true that patronage on the busway increased substantially as the network was expanded, but since the RIT replaced conventional services, much of this simply reflected existing public transport users moving to the new services. A number of authors have reported that public transport carries 75 per cent of work trips, although the source for this estimate is unclear; the URBS website reports the same figure, but as the mode share for 1965, the year the city's master-plan was prepared.[15]

Good information about recent trip-making rates is available from URBS. Cervero reports ridership of 350 unlinked trips per capita (see explanation in previous chapter), or 205 linked trips, in the mid-1990s, a higher figure than those recorded in Sao Paulo and other Brazilian cities. The difference is at least partly due to higher incomes: *favela*-dwellers in Sao Paulo don't have jobs and can't afford bus fares. Recent reports claim that Curitiba's buses are losing market share to the car, and the municipal public transport agency URBS reported a 20 per cent patronage decline from 1997 to 2004, with a more recent partial recovery to around 320 million linked trips in 2007.[16] This would represent 188 linked trips per head if divided by the 1.7 million residents of the City of Curitiba, but just as we saw with Toronto, the city is now part of a larger region of 3.3 million, in which most regional growth is occurring beyond city boundaries.[17] URBS services were extended, on a limited basis, into the suburbs in the late 1990s, and around 19 per cent of trips are now made on non-urban routes.[18] So the trip rate for the City of Curitiba is really 153 linked trips per head, a significant decline from the 1990s rate of 205. By way of comparison, the equivalent figure in the (new) City of Toronto for 2007 was 184 linked trips per resident per annum, although comparisons should be made with caution as the two cities are so different.

Curitiba's Integrated Transport Network has experienced difficulties in the last decade, but some of these are problems of success. Even with bi-articulated buses, congestion is becoming an increasing problem, particularly in the CBD, where busway corridors converge. Some local observers, including the head of URBS, argue that Curitiba, like Ottawa, has reached the point where a rail system is required to replace the busiest busway routes. There seems to be resistance to this idea from people convinced that busways are the ideal public transport mode in all circumstances.[19] BRT can also attract the 'blind conviction' Hensher identifies as a feature of much rail advocacy, especially when the World Bank and some sections of Curitiba opinion seem to regard the absence of a metro as a reason for pride vis-à-vis cities like Sao Paulo. A less ideologically constrained analysis might suggest that a busway attracting so many patrons that it requires upgrading to rail could also be an occasion of pride.

Although Curitiba's Integrated Transport System does not live up to the most extravagant accounts of its success, it remains well-patronized and efficient – especially compared with public transport in most Latin American cities. It has inspired progeny from Bogota to New Delhi, and even Los Angeles. The planners of Bogota's *Transmilenio* and similar systems in other places understand that the success of the Curitiba system is not just the result of building busway infrastructure. Even more important has been the provision of integrated network planning by a single public agency, as opposed to the Manila-style free-for-all that applied previously. Robert Cervero makes this clear in his detailed analysis of the RIT, which stresses the high level of integration. David Hensher, generally a strong advocate for markets, concludes that Curitiba's superior performance relative to Porto Alegre and other Brazilian cities with busways shows that '[a]n efficient busway requires a firm and coherent system of regulation'.[20]

A LESS SUCCESSFUL TRANSPLANT

Another lesson in the importance of network planning can be had by travelling from Curitiba to Foz do Iguacu, at the other end of Parana State.[21] Foz is a city of 300,000 adjacent to the Iguacu Falls world heritage site (the falls are at the intersection of Brazil, Argentina and Paraguay, and are spelled Iguazu in Spanish). Tourism is the major industry, and for most of the year visitors outnumber locals. In 1998, a municipal public transport agency was established, called FozTrans. The agency was modelled on URBS, and planned an integrated transport system modelled on the state capital's. Curitiba-style 'boarding tubes' were erected along dedicated bus lanes provided in the medians of main roads, with an enclosed terminal in the city centre allowing for free transfers.

The FozTrans system is a major improvement on the deregulated free-for-all that prevailed previously, but it has hit a series of snags. These arise from the fact that the system's designers copied Curitiba's architecture, but not its organizational arrangements. Four private companies have area-based franchises and retain their own revenues. The operators' support for integrated fares is half-hearted at best, since it means carrying non-paying passengers who have transferred from other companies' services. The result has been intractable wrangling between the authority and the operators, which in turn has prevented the development of truly integrated services. The Curitiba model uses high-capacity vehicles on busy routes, generating surpluses that cross-subsidize feeder and cross-suburban routes, just as the Toronto subway cross-subsidizes TTC buses. But because the operators in Foz do Iguacu keep their fare revenue, they prefer to concentrate on profitable trunk routes rather than running loss-making services. So feeder routes are poorly serviced, cross-city services do not exist, and busy radial corridors are over-serviced with a bewildering array of offerings. Routes are hard to understand, services infrequent and irregular, and operators cancel departures at whim.

The overall system is less convenient to locals than Curitiba's integrated model, and completely incomprehensible to tourists, who avoid it entirely. By contrast, the Curitiba RIT is a tourist attraction in its own right.

BRISBANE: BLAME THE KOALAS

Brisbane should be *the* model busway city, as it has spent considerably more on bus rapid transit than Ottawa and Curitiba combined. However, this investment has produced fewer passengers than the cheaper systems in other cities. Perhaps the koalas are to blame.

The big difference between Brisbane and the two other cities is that it already had an extensive electrified rail passenger system before moves were made to build busways. The trains are run by the state-owned Queensland Railways, while buses within the boundaries of the City of Brisbane are operated by the city council.

Brisbane is the only city in Australia with a municipal council big enough to be entrusted with tasks like public transport, but even there the suburbs now account for nearly half the 1.8 million residents of the census area, and two-thirds the population of the broader South-East Queensland region, which includes the tourist resorts of the Gold and Sunshine Coasts. Suburban buses are run by private firms.

Just as in Melbourne in past decades (see Chapter 6), the council-owned buses – which replaced trams in the 1960s – have competed with the state-owned trains, with almost no coordination between the two. Only 7 per cent of rail passengers reached the station by bus in the mid-1990s, a lower figure even than in Melbourne.[22] Bus routes parallelled rail lines and provided extremely poor cross-suburban connections; fare systems were completely separate. The city centre was dominated by parked buses, until a large underground terminal was built beneath the pedestrianized central shopping artery of Queen Street.

The Queen Street bus terminal actually occupied the site proposed for the central station of an underground rail line recommended by American consultants in a 1970 plan for Brisbane's rail system. This recommended electrification of the suburban system, then run by diesel trains, and a new central city line – a similar proposal to that made for Auckland in 1950 (see Chapter 2). Just as in Auckland and Los Angeles before it, the consultants advised that the rail system would only work effectively if bus services were recast as feeders and cross-suburban links, with an integrated fare system and a single agency in overall control.[23] The rail system was electrified in the late 1970s and early 1980s, funded by a short-lived federal programme, but the city council resisted changes to bus services and organizational arrangements. The busways have literally set the rail–bus rivalry in concrete.

As in Curitiba, the prime mover behind busways was a long-serving mayor, Jim Soorley, Lord Mayor of Brisbane from 1991 to 2003. Soorley was elected with the support of the Greens party, and claimed to support 'sustainable transport'. In practice, this meant something like the balanced transport approach of the 1960s, because Soorley combined investment in public transport with major new inner-city bypass roads. The first major public transport initiative was the introduction of fast river ferries serving the University of Queensland and green-voting inner-city neighbourhoods. This was followed by a study of the city's bus services by John Bonsall, formerly General Manager of Ottawa's OC Transpo, now President of the transport consultancy firm McCormick Rankin.

The McCormick Rankin report recommended that Brisbane construct four major busway corridors: one each to the north, south, east and west. Each of these corridors parallelled an existing electrified rail passenger line: indeed, the western route was to be constructed by removing 'at least one track' on a four-track section of the western rail line, as 'this would allow a busway to be constructed in the railway corridor'![24] The explicit intention was to shift demand from rail to bus. The report noted that on existing corridors where the two modes competed, rail captured just over half of travellers; it proposed a shift from rail to bus of between

5 and 20 percentage points, depending on the corridor, resulting in an overall majority for bus travel. The railways would serve long-distance commuting, with 'short distance trips being transferred to the busway system.'[25] The argument for the proposal relied almost entirely on the success of Ottawa's busways.

The obvious, but unanswered, question is what public benefit would be achieved by spending many millions of dollars to transfer passengers from trains to buses?

The busways report was released in July 1995, the same month as a state election in which the Queensland Labor government lost office to the conservative National Party on an environmental issue. The issue was a proposed freeway connecting Brisbane to the Gold Coast, which threatened the habitat of some of Australia's famous koalas. Nobody remembers the road's official name, because it was soon dubbed the 'koala freeway'. Labor insisted that there was no alternative to building it, because its transport planners had said so (actually, their modelling study didn't even consider the possibility of improved public transport: it assumed at the outset that the share of travel by different modes would remain constant). The Nationals announced that they would instead widen the existing Pacific Highway, gained the support of the Greens, won a series of seats in the corridor and took the reins of government early in 1996. 'We are all environmentalists now,' the new Transport Minister proclaimed.

The state government was persuaded by Lord Mayor Soorley that the widening of the highway should take the form of the southern busway proposed in the McCormick Rankin report. By this time, the cost of the 'South East Transit Project' had risen to $520 million (£230 million), and that of the full network to $1 billion, compared with McCormick Rankin's estimate of $600 million. While spending this sum on a busway doubtless made more sense than using it to widen a freeway serving an already congested city centre, was it really the best use of available funds?

The Queensland Parliament's Public Works Committee finally asked the difficult questions in a 1997 report on the project. The committee, comprised of six back-benchers assisted by a secretariat of three, expressed its concerns plainly.

> *The committee was astonished to see that the BCC employed McCormick Rankin to do a study on the potential for busways in Brisbane. As the committee understands that McCormick Rankin designed the Ottawa busway system it came as no surprise that [they] recommended a busway system as the answer to Brisbane's transport problems.*[26]

The committee pointed out that 'Ottawa does not have an existing rail system and when Ottawa decided to build a busway it was a choice between rail or bus.'[27] It noted that the proposed busway routes all duplicated existing rail lines and rejected the government's response that only passengers within walking distance of stations could be considered served by rail. Rail catchments could be expanded by use of feeder buses, and the main problem in the region was not lack of infrastructure, but lack of service coordination:

> *The committee saw no evidence that Queensland Transport, Brisbane City Council, Queensland Rail and private bus and ferry operators ever spoke to one another other than to plan more major infrastructure projects. The classic example is the lack of an integrated ticketing system. Why Brisbane does not have one, the committee does not know. Southern capitals seem to have managed it.*[28]

Nobody in the committee or its secretariat had any background in transport planning, but this actually seemed to help. Their analysis was more consistent with the approach of cities like Zurich, Toronto, Vancouver and even Ottawa than that of the local experts. When Queensland Rail objected that its huge heavy rail system, which carried fewer passengers than the single light rail line in Vancouver, could not accommodate any more demand, it received a curt response:

> *The committee does not agree. It would like to see more work go into looking at improving the rail service. It would like to see a comparison between the increase in public transport patronage caused by either $1,000,000 spent on the busways and $1,000,000 spent on improving City Train services.*[29]

The committee called for more attention to operational efficiency and coordination, calling for integrated ticketing and a region-wide public transport map within 12 months. It also recommended that no more busways be built until the effectiveness of the original corridor had been comprehensively evaluated – and that 'an organization independent of Queensland Transport conduct the evaluation'.[30]

The committee's report was not so much ignored as buried. The government passed a parliamentary motion demanding the committee re-examine the issue: it did so, reaching the same conclusions as before, and noting that the cost of the busway scheme had now risen to $1.3 billion.[31] The South-East Busway opened in 2001, but has never been independently evaluated. Instead, more busways have been built and still more are under construction. The total cost is approaching Aus$3 billion, and Brisbane now has some superb pieces of infrastructure that have won all kinds of architectural and engineering awards.

But what about patronage? The South-East Busway opened in April 2001. The Brisbane City Council's bus service carried 42 million passengers in the financial year ending on 30 June 2001, a million fewer than in the previous 12 months. Patronage remained static until 2005, when a large increase commenced which has continued since.[32] This increase had nothing to do with busways, however; it followed the introduction of a multi-modal fare system, a delayed result of the Public Works Committee's report and subsequent work by other parliamentary committees. Bus patronage increased 35 per cent in only three years in the City of Brisbane, and by up to 118 per cent in suburban regions, a result an order of magnitude greater than anything achieved by the busway programme.[33]

The fare system has been followed by the establishment of TransLink, a multi-modal public transport agency charged with integrating the region's rail, bus and ferry services. The new body's name has been copied from Vancouver, hopefully indicating that the real lessons of Canadian cities including Ottawa may finally be learned. But Brisbane's Translink has also been charged with extending the busway system, creating more competition for rail and making the provision of adequate feeder bus services that much harder.

A BUS NAMED PARADISE: ADELAIDE AND ITS O-BAHN

Brisbane might have built the world's most expensive busway system, but Adelaide holds a special place in the hearts of busway enthusiasts: the South Australian capital has the world's only complete O-Bahn, or guided busway, system.

Adelaide has always been an innovator. The city's original plan of 1837, featuring a township and a satellite settlement separated by parkland and the Torrens River, inspired Ebenezer Howard's idea of the Garden City. In the 1950s, Adelaide built Australia's first British-style new town at Elizabeth, along the rail corridor to the north. Adelaide was also the site of Australia's first freeway revolt.

The South Australian government lost office in 1970 mainly because of public anger over a freeway plan prepared by American consultants using the techniques pioneered in Chicago. The new Labor administration led by Premier Don Dunstan shelved the freeway plans and gave priority to public transport. The city's sole remaining tram route, a light rail line to the seaside resort of Glenelg that had been slated for closure, was retained, and the small suburban rail system extended and upgraded with new diesel rail cars. The biggest change was the establishment of the State Transport Authority, which took over the railways, the public buses (operating on former tram routes in the inner city) and privately operated suburban bus lines. Services were upgraded and multi-modal fares introduced.[34]

Dunstan's new policies seemed to be working. Public transport patronage rose modestly in Adelaide over the 1970s, contrasting with dramatic declines across the rest of Australia. By the 1981 census, mode share for travel to work was 16 per cent, nothing to boast about by world standards, but the third-highest in Australia, after Sydney and Melbourne. And in contrast to those cities, the figure had increased since 1976, the year the census first asked about mode choice. But the quarter century following saw a reversal of the Dunstan era gains: Adelaide experienced the sharpest drop in public transport patronage and mode share of any Australian city, with the share of workers travelling by public transport falling below Brisbane by 1986 and Perth by 1996, bottoming out at 8.9 per cent before recovering modestly to 9.9 in 2006.[35]

Despite having few freeways, and none at all in the inner city, Adelaide is now a car-dominated city, even by Australian standards. What went wrong?

Dunstan retired in 1979 and his party was defeated at the state election two years later. Although the conservative government only lasted a single term – Labor has reigned for the majority of the last 30 years – it effected a permanent change to transport policies. The expansion of the 1970s had increased subsidy levels and the new government and its successors were determined to bring them under control. Their transport advisers argued that the main problem was the decision to retain Adelaide's antiquated, poorly patronized trains and trams, which should be replaced by cheaper, more flexible buses.[36]

It proved politically impossible to close Adelaide's rail lines: they had too much public support. But the investment tap was turned off, allowing infrastructure and rolling stock to decay, leading to even bigger deficits as patronage fell and operating costs rose. Express bus services were introduced in competition with rail, by the same organization that was paying the rail deficit; by contrast, feeder services were under-developed and cross-suburban links practically non-existent. Off-peak, evening and weekend timetables were steadily cut back during the 1980s and early 1990s.

One of the first acts of the conservative government elected in 1981 was to scrap plans to modernize the Glenelg tram line and extend it across the city to the new growth area of Tea Tree Gully. The tram proposal replaced an unpopular freeway, which was to run through parkland along the Torrens River valley and incorporate an express bus service. As a replacement for the tramline, the government settled on the O-Bahn, then an experimental system operating on a short section of track in the German city of Essen. Although various consultants' reports backed the decision, it was a political choice.

The first stage of the 12km busway, to Paradise Interchange (named after the adjacent suburb), opened in 1986; the final section to the Tea Tree Plaza shopping mall in 1989. The operation of the O-Bahn, described in detail in chapter 14 of Cervero's *The Transit Metropolis* (1998), is much like a freeway express, with peak-period buses collecting passengers from residential areas, then joining the O-Bahn for a fast run to the city centre. In off-peak periods, many routes revert to shuttle services, requiring a transfer at the O-Bahn interchange.

A dozen routes share the O-Bahn in peak period, leading to a high combined service frequency. Many passengers drive to park-and-ride stations at Paradise and Tea Tree Plaza, instead of using buses for the whole trip. Service levels on regular route sections off the O-Bahn offer little incentive to those with cars available, especially outside peak period: typical frequencies are half-hourly on weekdays and hourly evenings and weekends.

Has the O-Bahn been a success? Supporters argue that it has, because patronage has grown in the corridor it serves, while declining across Adelaide as a whole. But the O-Bahn was introduced to serve Adelaide's fastest-growing suburbs: the City of Tea Tree Gully grew from 67,000 residents to 96,000 in the 25 years to

2006. Patronage has grown because the population served has grown, which tells us nothing about the performance of the O-Bahn. Mode share figures are more instructive. In 2006, 11.1 per cent of Tea Tree Gully workers commuted by public transport, higher than the Adelaide-wide figure of 9.9 per cent. But the share of workers driving was also higher, at 84.2 versus 83.1 per cent, because walking and cycling rates are lower than average, reflecting the lack of local employment.[37]

The South Australian government has finally decided on the future of Adelaide's public transport. In 2007, it extended the Glenelg line into the heart of the city and introduced new rolling stock to replace the quaint, but decrepit, 1920s-vintage trams. In 2008, it announced plans to upgrade and electrify the suburban rail system, converting one line to light rail by linking it to the Glenelg service. There are no plans for new O-Bahns.[38]

The decision to upgrade Adelaide's rail and tram systems was partly motivated by embarrassment at Adelaide's poor performance relative to Perth, its neighbour across the Nullarbor Plain. The revival of public transport in Perth took place during the same 25-year period that saw steady decline in Adelaide, but has received virtually no international attention – possibly because it involved boring old technologies like electric trains and non-guided buses.[39]

Perth is of similar size to Adelaide, but presents an even more difficult environment for public transport planners, with a lower population density, a significant freeway network and higher average incomes. In 1981, public transport's share of work trips was 11.6 per cent, lower than in any other Australian city apart from Canberra. It declined further to 9.0 per cent by 1996, partially recovering to 10.4 per cent by 2006.[40] The figure is now higher than in Adelaide (Table 4.1), and the difference is likely to have widened since the census, with the opening of the major southern railway project in 2007. While hardly impressive compared with Canadian or European cities, the changes in Perth are a modest success story by Australian standards.

Like their Adelaide counterparts, Perth's transport planners decided to close the city's ageing diesel-powered suburban rail system; unlike in Adelaide, politicians took their advice. The first line to close was the line to the port of Fremantle, in 1979, prompting fierce protests from a local group called Friends of the Railways. A political backlash at the 1980 state election reduced the conservative Western Australian government's majority to a single seat, and the conservatives lost office at the following poll in 1983.

The change of government permanently changed transport policy, but in the opposite direction to Adelaide: support for a modernized, expanded rail network became bipartisan. The Fremantle line was reopened four months after the change of government, and then electrified along with the other two existing lines. The electrified service commenced in 1991, to be followed in 1993 by a completely new line to the northern suburbs, which had developed along a freeway. This line has since been extended twice, and in 2007 a much larger project created a new line to the south, including an underground railway through the city centre. Since no other location was available, the two lines run down the median of Perth's main north–south freeway, ensuring that transit-oriented development is infeasible at most stations.

Perth's new northern and southern lines are impressive engineering works, featuring high-speed, high-frequency operations and clean, comfortable, modern trains. But equally impressive, and quite unusual in the Australian context, is the close coordination with bus services: fares and timetables are integrated, and Toronto-style interchanges bring buses to the station door. At many stations, the majority of passengers arrive by bus, something unheard of anywhere else in the country. Although Perth's buses are operated by private sub-contractors selected through London-style competitive tendering, they appear to passengers to be just as much a part of the TransPerth system as the trains, which the public transport agency runs itself.

Interestingly, the key officials behind the revival of Perth's rail system and its integration with buses were the same people who tried to close the system in the late 1970s. They also resisted the plans for electrification and new lines, using familiar arguments like 'people don't like to transfer'. When a review by a team that included Vukan Vuchic rejected these arguments, and it became clear that the government was determined to persist with rail expansion, the officials accepted the verdict and worked to make the new model a success.

The success of the Perth rail revival presents another delicious irony, because the key figure behind Friends of the Railways and the rail expansion programme was none other than Professor Peter Newman of Murdoch University, a Fremantle councillor at the time of the 1979 closure. As we saw in Chapter 4, Newman and Jeffrey Kenworthy are renowned internationally for having revived the idea of the compact city. But by reviving Perth's rail system and extending it into suburbs that are sprawling even by local standards, Newman has demonstrated that high densities are not required for successful urban rail.

AND THE WINNER IS … NETWORKS

The results of the busway experiments are clear, and the story of rail in Perth reinforces them. Bus rapid transit does have a genuine role to play, and in appropriate contexts can provide effective trunk service at lower cost than rail. But BRT does not offer a way around the fundamental constraints on public transport, especially in low-density, high-income cities where demand is thin. Region-wide network planning is needed with busways, just as with older public transport modes, and this factor is more important than the type, or even the amount, of infrastructure provided.

This is a good time to leave the sunny southern hemisphere and head north to consider the paragon of public transport integration.

NOTES

1 See Vuchic (2007, pp456–475).
2 Vuchic (2007, p474).
3 Hensher (2007, ch. 17).
4 Cervero (1998, ch. 9); Smith and Hensher (1998).
5 Fullerton (2005).
6 Hoffman (2008, p20).
7 One result of the amalgamation was that OC Transpo changed from being a semi-independent commission to a department of the new city's administration.
8 Schepers (2008).
9 Skidmore (1993); see also Sorupia (2007, ch. 4).
10 Irazabal (2005).
11 Smith and Hensher (1998, p137, table 2 – express figure is the combined total of 'express' and 'bi-artic express').
12 Irazabal (2005, pp98, 105–106, 125–127).
13 Jane's Publishing (1988, p83).
14 Irazabal (2005, pp125–127).
15 'Historia do transporte de Curitiba', www.urbs.curitiba.pr.gov.br.
16 Lubow (2007, p3); 'Historia do transporte de Curitiba', www.urbs.curitiba.pr.gov.br.
17 www.curitiba.pr.gov.br (accessed 30 August 2009)
18 'Resumo Operacional 2007', www.urbs.curitiba.pr.gov.br. I have excluded 'metrop. nao integrado'; including them would lower the tripmaking rate for the city further.
19 Quoted in Lubow (2007); see also Irazabal (2005, p108).
20 Smith and Hensher (1998, p152).
21 This section is based on Sorupia (2007, ch. 4).
22 Queensland Government (1997, p78).
23 Wilbur Smith & Associates (1970).
24 McCormick Rankin (1995, vol. 1, p92).
25 McCormick Rankin (1995, p76, table 8b).
26 PWC (1997a, p15). I should come clean and admit that the Committee relied to a considerable extent on my work.
27 PWC (1997a, p15).
28 PWC (1997a, p26).
29 PWC (1997a, p11).
30 PWC (1997a, p8, recommendation 1).
31 PWC (1997b, p11). I acted as a consultant to the committee for this second report.
32 Brisbane City Council (2008, p72), and annual reports for previous years.
33 Queensland Transport (2007, p66, table 14).
34 Parkin and Pugh (1981, pp91–114).
35 Mees et al (2007, table 1.2, fig. 4).
36 Scrafton and Skene (1998, p271).
37 ABS (2003, table W18 – figures compiled on the same basis as for Table 4.1).
38 South Australia (2008) *New Connections* (brochure).
39 The following discussion is based on Al-Dubikhi (2007, ch. 7) and Stone (2008, especially chs 6 and 7).
40 Mees et al (2007, fig. 4).

8

The Zurich Model

In Italy for 30 years under the Borgias they had warfare, terror, murder, and bloodshed, but they produced Michelangelo, Leonardo da Vinci, and the Renaissance. In Switzerland they had brotherly love – they had 500 years of democracy and peace, and what did that produce? The cuckoo clock.

Harry Lime (Orson Welles), *The Third Man*, 1949

A VERY CIVIL WAR

Actually, it wasn't all brotherly love. The Swiss even fought a civil war in 1847.

The saga started in Zurich, where the liberal government appointed a controversial German freethinker called Strauss to the chair in theology at the local university. This scandalized pious Protestants – Zurich had been the birthplace of the Swiss Reformation – and a militant clergyman led thousands of armed, hymn-singing rural protesters in a march on the city. The *Zuriputsch* was successful: the government resigned and Professor Strauss accepted early retirement.

The Catholic canton of Lucerne responded with its own 'radical cure for Straussism', inviting the Jesuit order to run the local seminary. Freethinkers and Protestants dropped their differences and united in a crusade against 'Jesuitism'. Armed partisans from neighbouring cantons made two attempts to overthrow Lucerne's government, which repelled them with the assistance of Catholic neighbours. This triggered a slide to war between Protestant and Catholic cantons. Fortunately, the leader of the victorious forces, General Guillaume Dufour, was a master tactician as well as a moderate, and secured victory with only 100 casualties on both sides.[1]

The conflict resulted in two developments which proved critical to the success of public transport in Zurich. First, the victorious Freethinking Radical Party, which ruled Switzerland for decades, used the provision of efficient public services to promote national unity. Among these were the national postal office, which provided coach transport as well as carrying mails, and the Federal Railways (*Schweizerische Bundesbahnen* or SBB), established after a lengthy debate that culminated in a successful 1898 referendum. Secondly, the referendum was promoted as a more efficient way of settling political disputes than overthrowing the government.

A key demand of the *Zuriputsch* was a popular veto of government decisions, and the referendum has been most fully developed in the city and canton of Zurich. It is rarely used in theological disputes now, but it has played an important role in settling transport controversies.

A VERY CIVIL *ZURIPUTSCH?* THE DEBATE OVER TRAMS

In the 1950s, transport planners in Zurich followed similar ideas to their counterparts in other cities. A 'balanced' system of freeways and underground railways was the way of the future; trams were doomed to disappear. Zurich's tram system was popular with the community and well-patronized, with a tradition of frequent, reliable service dating back to the public takeover of 1894. But traffic congestion was making trams slower and less reliable, while traffic engineers argued that public transport was delaying motorists. The solution developed by the tramway operator VBZ (*Verkehrsbetriebe Zurich*) was to put the main routes underground and convert the rest to buses, thus speeding trams and creating more space on the surface for road traffic. This idea had been popular in some German cities, and the Zurich plans were finalized in 1962, with an estimated cost of 544 million francs. As cantonal law requires all projects costing more than 10 million francs to be approved by referendum, the scheme was put to popular vote – and soundly defeated, with a No vote of 61 per cent.[2]

The result came as a shock: all councillors and political parties had supported the plan. Some residents objected to the expense and disruption; others wanted a full metro rather than merely underground trams; others disliked the idea of having to travel underground instead of on the surface. The planners went back to the drawing board, and emerged with a proposal for a full metro system, plus an S-Bahn (short for *Schnellbahn*, or fast train) serving areas beyond the city borders. The S-Bahn also included a long tunnel, to overcome a bottleneck at the main railway station, which was a dead-end terminal that required trains to reverse. Again, the model was Germany, especially Munich, which had built metro and S-Bahn systems for the 1972 Olympics.

The new project required involvement by the cantonal government, and was therefore submitted to a canton-wide referendum in 1973. City planners may have expected suburban voters to be more supportive than their city counterparts had been a decade earlier, but the proposal was again defeated – the No vote this time was 57 per cent. The opposition was led by an informal coalition of students, academics and environmentalists, concerned about the high cost (1.2 billion francs) and the increased traffic that would follow once trams were removed from main streets.

The referendum's opponents developed an alternative 'People's Initiative for the Promotion of Public Transport' to upgrade the existing tram, trolley-bus and bus system, with exclusive lanes, priority at intersections and higher service frequencies. The proposal was inspired by the 'small is beautiful' message of E. F. Schumacher, as well as the success of priority measures in other Swiss cities, notably Basel and Berne. Developed with the assistance of some more adventurous transport planners, the initiative took priority much further, aiming to make intersections like railway level crossings: trams would not need to slow down or stop, except for passengers.

The proposal was presented to the city council a month after the defeat of the referendum. The city engineer responded negatively, and said that his department was already working on a less ambitious priority system that would not inconvenience motorists. Almost four years passed before the People's Initiative was put to a public vote, with a recommendation from the city council that citizens reject it. It passed, with 51 per cent of the vote.[3]

The passage of the referendum changed transport policy and practice. The city council adopted an explicit policy of giving priority to public transport in the allocation of funding and roadspace: the era of 'balanced transport' was over. It moved rapidly to implement the radical priority plan, which was largely complete by the mid-1980s.[4] 'Traffic-calming' on residential streets and pedestrianization of much of the 'old city' complemented the improvements to public transport. In 1991, the city council and VBZ sponsored a successful referendum to extend the priority programme.

The results have been dramatic. Public transport patronage in the City of Zurich, already among the highest in the world on a per capita basis, increased by about half during the 1980s, despite a small decline in the population.[5] VBZ currently carries around 287 million passengers annually, which would equate to 811 trips per capita – except that many of these trips are made by suburban residents (as discussed below).[6] In 2000, 66 per cent of people who lived and worked in the city travelled to work by public transport, with 16 per cent walking or cycling. Only 19 per cent travelled by car, down slightly from 20 per cent in 1990.[7]

Why is public transport use so much higher in Zurich than other central cities in Switzerland and elsewhere in Europe? Zurich city's density is not remarkable: it is actually slightly lower than the former City of Toronto and well below many European cities that have much lower public transport usage rates. Most analysts who have considered this question agree that while tram priority and pedestrianization have been important, the critical factor is the way the VBZ functions as an integrated network:

> *The most important aspect of Zurich's public transit system is that it is an excellent network. Passengers can get from anywhere to anywhere almost any time of the day throughout the year.*[8]

Zurich has avoided two extremes. Many cities that built metros have concentrated high service levels on the metro lines, leaving passengers wishing to reach locations that are not on the metro with an infrequent and unattractive service. By contrast, Zurich offers high frequencies and reliable services on all corridors, cross-city as well as radial, with multi-modal fares and excellent facilities easing transfers between routes. Zurich has also avoided the other extreme of a bewildering and inefficient array of low-quality routes, as seen in cities as diverse as Auckland and Foz do Iguacu. Bus routes serving city and suburban areas beyond the tram system terminate at tram interchanges or railway stations, and generally do not enter the city centre. Passengers must transfer to complete their journeys, but just as in Toronto and Curitiba, the economical densities of patronage this practice creates allow trams to cross-subsidize buses, ensuring high service levels all round – as well as keeping the city centre free of congestion from buses.

It is worth noting that all this has been achieved without congestion pricing, and has arguably produced better environmental outcomes than the policies employed in central London. While purists might object that the Zurich approach is less economically efficient than London's, it is difficult to see how this contention could be sustained in light of Zurich's continued prosperity. As two economists from the University of Aberdeen suggested back in 1992: 'Preoccupation with road pricing as the key solution to congestion is inappropriate because, even with road charges, private vehicles still obstruct the progress of spatially efficient buses and trams'. Under the alternative approach adopted in Zurich, 'welfare gains in terms of the efficiency of road use and the quality of urban life are striking'.[9]

EXTENDING HIGH-QUALITY PUBLIC TRANSPORT TO THE SUBURBS

In Zurich City, the high quality of public transport has made it easier to build public support for measures that restrain automobile use. The 1977 referendum on the People's Initiative for the Promotion of Public Transport was accompanied by a vote on whether to cancel cantonal plans for three radial freeways that would converge on the centre of Zurich city in the shape of a 'Y'. The initiative to scrap the freeways was passed in Zurich city, but defeated in the canton-wide vote. Although the result led to the *de facto* cancellation of the Y-freeways, it also showed that suburban residents were less attracted than city dwellers to restraints on the car. A key reason for this difference was the poor quality of suburban public transport.[10]

Public transport in Canton Zurich was a mess – by Swiss standards at least – with nobody in overall charge. The situation was similar to Chicago and Toronto in the early 1950s and Vancouver in the early 1970s (see Chapters 2 and 6). Zurich City, as we have seen, provided its residents with an excellent service, and also operated buses into adjoining municipalities. Some other larger municipalities, like the Canton's second-largest city, Winterthur, ran their own public transport systems. Rural municipalities were too small to provide any public transport; these areas were served by the PostAuto, the bus arm of the Swiss Post Office. The SBB operated infrequent suburban trains on an extensive network of lines dating largely from the 19th century, when private companies built them to serve towns and villages. In all, 42 separate organizations were involved, with at least a dozen fare and timetabling systems. Commuting to Zurich city was difficult, but inter-suburban travel was virtually impossible.

The population of Zurich City peaked at 440,000 in 1960, and declined for two decades before stabilizing at around 360,000. The population of the remainder of the canton rose from a little over 500,000 to just under a million over the same period, as the canton was gradually transformed into 'greater Zurich'. The Swiss statistical agency defines an 'agglomeration of Zurich' which is intended to cover the city's commuter-shed. This area includes the municipalities bordering the central city, but has rapidly become out of date as commuters criss-cross the entire canton.

In 1980, 306,000 workers were employed in Zurich City, of whom 42 per cent came from outside the city boundary; by 2000 the workforce had risen to 349,000 and the share coming from outside had risen to 55 per cent. Change in the opposite direction was even more rapid: 22 per cent of workers living within city borders in 2000 worked in the suburbs, up from only 9 per cent two decades earlier. The canton's second city shows the same pattern. Winterthur, 27km north-east of Zurich and housing 90,000 residents in 2000, is not part of 'agglomeration Zurich', because until recently there was little commuting between the two. In 1980, only 8 per cent of resident workers commuted to Zurich City, but since then the figure has risen to 15 per cent, while the number of Zurich residents commuting to Winterthur has tripled.[11]

With trends like these, even the excellent public transport within city boundaries was rapidly becoming irrelevant.

Zurich's transport planners and policy makers could easily have made the same density-based arguments against improved suburban transit that we have seen used in North American, Australian and British cities. The 'middle-suburban' districts of the agglomeration have much lower densities than the city, while the population of the remaining outer municipalities is more thinly scattered than much Australian or American exurbia. According to the Swiss Federal Statistical Office, some 20 per cent of the Canton is devoted to urban purposes, which would give a canton-wide overall urban density of approximately 38 per hectare. The urban density of Zurich City is 67 per hectare, but the average for the middle and outer suburbs is 32 per hectare,[12] much lower than the equivalent parts of London, similar to or lower than in other English cities, and only about 20 per cent higher than the figures for the equivalent parts of Toronto and Los Angeles (see Chapters 4 and 6). In fact, the overall urban density of the City of the Angels is closer to Zurich than it is to Boston or Portland, Oregon.

A mixture of professional pride and public participation ensured that Zurich's low suburban density was not allowed to stand in the way of canton-wide public transport improvements.

Commuter rail services began in 1968 with the inauguration of the 'Gold Coast Express' along the north shore of Lake Zurich. The express replaced an unpopular proposed freeway, and the cantonal government funded the track work that enabled the Federal Railways to operate the service. A year before, the first Government of Ontario (GO) Transit commuter rail service commenced in Toronto, but the two systems diverged significantly in their service philosophy and patronage. The first GO rail line operated hourly in the off-peak and more frequently in peak periods; subsequent GO lines have provided no off-peak services at all. The SBB tried out a quite different concept on the Gold Coast Express, introducing a regular timetable, with departures every half-hour, and trains leaving and arriving at exactly the same times past the hour all day long. The idea was to make the timetable easy to remember, partially compensating for the relatively low service frequency.

The underground S-Bahn link proposed in Zurich's unsuccessful 1973 referendum had been intended to enable a similar regular-interval service to be offered on other lines. The main reason for the project's defeat had been its linking with the unpopular metro proposal, so SBB planners developed a new proposal involving the S-Bahn only. This was approved at a 1981 referendum by 74 per cent of voters, and work began just over a year later. But faster and more frequent commuter trains were not going to be enough to create a real alternative to the car for suburban residents, especially those travelling to non-central locations.

By this time, a model for providing 'anywhere to anywhere' services in low-density environments was being pioneered by the SBB, partly as the result of another political setback.[13] The Swiss Federal Railways lost patrons during the 1960s, as car ownership increased and motorways began to open. The first deficit was recorded in 1966, and losses mounted rapidly. The organization responded by floating two alternative plans: either close unprofitable routes and concentrate on busy corridors, or invest massively in high-speed services. The fast rail proposal was modelled on Japan's bullet trains, which received worldwide exposure when they opened in time for the 1964 Tokyo Olympics.

Swiss voters and politicians rejected both options. Line closures were impossible to implement, as voters in the affected cantons could utilize the referendum to veto them. The high-speed lines were unpopular with affected communities, environmentalists and residents of smaller towns and cantons that would be bypassed by the fast services. The high-speed rail plan was eventually abandoned, as it looked unlikely to attract the double majority – of voters and cantons – necessary to pass at a national referendum.

In the meantime, a group of young SBB engineers had been working to refine the fixed-timetabling experiment introduced on the Zurich Gold Coast Express. They argued that the main factor attracting passengers to the car was not high top speeds, but the freedom to travel when, where and as often as desired. The national rail system needed to find a way of matching this flexibility, but could not rely on the high-frequency-service approach used on the Zurich tram system or the Paris Metro.

The alternative solution was the *integraler taktfahrplan*, or integrated pulse-timetable, launched in an internal SBB paper in 1972. All rail lines would be provided with regular-interval services at the same frequency, with schedules arranged so that different routes converged on key interchange stations at the same time. Passengers could then transfer in any direction, allowing 'anywhere to anywhere' travel all day long. This proposal replaced the unsuccessful high speed rail plan, and a nation-wide integrated pulse-timetable was inaugurated in 1982. All-day hourly services were introduced on the main SBB routes, and on connecting PostAuto services. The decline in patronage was halted and reversed, and in 1987 Swiss voters approved *Bahn 2000*, a proposal for capital investment to allow frequencies to be improved to half-hourly. This objective was met in 2004, and SBB is now working towards an 'S-Bahn Switzerland' with 15-minute frequencies on major corridors.

Hans Kunzi was Canton Zurich's Minister for Economic Affairs, with responsibility for transport, during the 1970s and 1980s. He was also the former Professor of Mathematics and Operations Research at the University of Zurich. Operations Research is the use of mathematical programming techniques to solve 'optimization' problems like railway timetabling. Kunzi and the SBB decided to use the S-Bahn as an opportunity to introduce the *integraler taktfahrplan* for regional travel, and include all modes of public transport, not just trains. This required a single organization to integrate trains, buses and trams across the canton, and a multi-modal fare system to ease transfers. They chose the model pioneered in Hamburg (see Chapter 5), and in 1988 prepared the legal basis for a *Zürcher Verkehrsverbund* (ZVV). The new organization would have a monopoly on public transport throughout the canton, and would be funded from fares and subsidies, with the latter split evenly between the canton and the municipalities. These changes required an amendment to the cantonal constitution, and therefore a referendum: the Yes vote was 77 per cent.[14]

THE *ZÜRCHER VERKEHRSVERBUND* IN OPERATION

The ZVV commenced operation in May 1990, along with the new railway tunnel and a canton-wide integrated fare system. The suburban rail lines of the SBB and two other operators were upgraded and integrated to form the Zurich S-Bahn, which incorporates around 20 separate rail corridors and 400 route kilometres, providing dense coverage of the canton. Some corridors have more than one route operating on them, so there are 26 S-Bahn routes in all, with a full-time express service provided on most major corridors.

Half-hourly services were initially provided on most routes, with hourly departures on remote lines serving rural parts of the canton. Trains were through-routed between the east and west through the new tunnel, catering for cross-city travellers, while timed connections at major interchange stations served cross-suburban travel. Post-buses in remote areas, and municipal services in the suburbs, were re-routed and re-timetabled to connect with the train system, with high-frequency trams and buses in the urban centres of Zurich and Winterthur providing timetable-free connections. Increasing patronage has led to service upgrades, with 15-minute intervals becoming the norm on busier corridors, and half-hourly frequencies progressively replacing hourly services on rural lines.

An illustration of the system in operation can be had by travelling to Hinwil, a town of around 5000 residents in the Zurich Oberland, the mountainous region in the far east of the canton. S-Bahn line 14 leaves Hinwil station at 8 and 38 minutes past the hour, from 5:38 am to 11:38 pm every day of the year; longer trains run at busy times. Five minutes down the line, each train arrives at the regional junction of Wetzikon, which has two 'island' platforms. A minute later, the S5 express service from Rapperswil pulls in on the opposite side of the platform. After passengers are exchanged, the express departs for Zurich, followed by the stopping-all-stations S14. A minute later, a third service departs: the S3, which uses the platform vacated by the express but follows a different route to Zurich, via the sub-regional centre of Pfaffikon. On the opposite island platform, the same procedure occurs in reverse, allowing transfers in all directions.

In the station forecourt, half a dozen bus routes perform a similar manoeuvre. Some of these service the town of Wetzikon, while others fan out across the countryside to neighbouring rail corridors. Connections are possible between all three train lines and all six bus routes, in all directions. Once the last bus has left, Wetzikon station is quiet until the cycle begins again. Until 2006, this meant a gap of half an hour, but in that year a second express service was added, doubling train frequencies to 15 minutes; three of the bus routes serving more urban areas were upgraded to match the increased frequency of the trains.[15]

The all-directions transferring available at Wetzikon is confined to major junctions, but timetables are still coordinated at other interchange points. If timed transfers cannot be ensured in all directions, they are guaranteed for the most popular connections, generally to or from Zurich or Winterthur. So, as we saw in Chapter 1, each bus from Bauma to Sternenberg is timed to leave four minutes after the arrival of the S26 train from Winterthur.

Zurich's approach to serving the suburbs contrasts with Toronto's. As we saw in Chapter 6, the Toronto Transit Commission (TTC) provides a grid of high-frequency services, allowing transfers at all points where routes intersect, but achieves this by using an extensive bus network to extend the catchment for its relatively small rail system. The ZVV's approach is the mirror image. Its rail system is much more extensive than the TTC's, with more than twice as many stations and six times the route-kilometres, but caters for only half the population served by the TTC subway. With many lines and stations, it is not practical to offer frequencies so high that timetables are unnecessary – and in any event, most S-Bahn lines are shared with freight and long-distance passenger services, imposing an additional limit on frequencies. Zurich offers most residents close access to the rail system – feeder buses mainly serve small villages and cross-suburban travel – with the 'pulse' system of regular departures and integrated timetables compensating for lower frequencies.

The service planning philosophy is specified in detail in the regulations made under the law establishing the ZVV. Every settlement with 300 residents, jobs or educational places must be provided with a basic service, within 400m (750m if served by rail). This service should link to major places of employment and education, and to the S-Bahn. Timetables should follow the *Taktsystem*, or pulse-system, and coordinate with the S-Bahn. Normal hours of operation are from 6:00 am to midnight, with minimum frequencies of 60, 30 or 15 minutes, depending on whether the area served is rural, suburban or urban.[16] In 2002, a 'night-network' was introduced, providing after-midnight services on Friday and Saturday nights to the far corners of Canton Zurich.

Integrated services are backed up with integrated fares and marketing: one of the ZVV's slogans is 'one ticket for everything'. Zurich Canton is divided into fare zones roughly corresponding to municipalities, and passengers pay by the number of zones traversed, regardless of the number of transfers made. Heavily discounted monthly tickets are offered, building on the 'Rainbow Card' environmental ticket introduced in Zurich City in the 1980s. Some 300,000 people, or a quarter of the canton's population, own ZVV season tickets; the share rises to half in Zurich City.[17] This approach is possible because all fares collected go to the ZVV, which reimburses operators for the service provided, avoiding conflicts over revenue distribution and enabling stronger services to cross-subsidize weaker ones.

Marketing is another critical function of the central body. This includes more than advertising campaigns: the ZVV provides easy-to-understand information about routes, fares and timetables. Tourists are targeted as well as locals, and there is more information available in English on the ZVV's website than can be found on those of many English-speaking cities. One important aspect of the marketing task is responding to the genuine concerns of passengers – for example, conductors were introduced on trains operating after 9:00 pm in response to concerns about security. The clear message is that people choosing public transport deserve nothing but the best.

The ZVV conducts its work with a very lean organizational structure: see Figure 8.1, taken from the English version of the authority's website. The entire staff complement amounts to only 35 – to supervise a public transport system that carried 542 million passengers in 2007. The 'traffic planning' division responsible

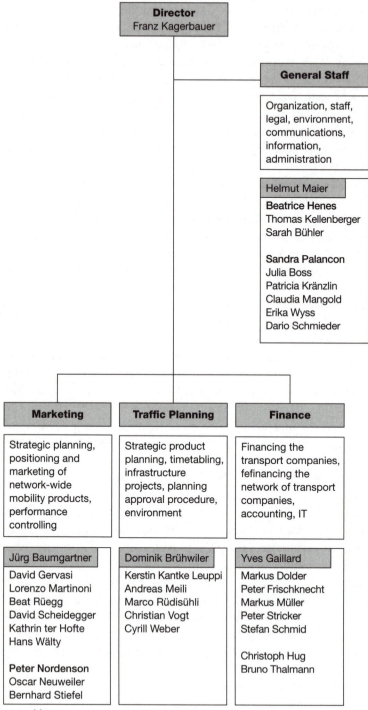

Source: www.zvv.ch/en

Figure 8.1 *Organization of the ZVV*

for timetabling and infrastructure projects has only six members. By way of comparison, regulating and subsidizing Melbourne's public transport franchisees, which carried 418.5 million passengers between them in 2006/2007, requires some 300 staff (this figure is an estimate, as nothing resembling Figure 8.1 is publicly available for Melbourne).

The reason the ZVV is such a lean organization is that it concentrates on the critical strategic and tactical planning tasks, leaving operations to eight major sub-contractors. These are SBB, PostAuto, the Zurich and Winterthur municipal transport agencies, three regional public transport associations formed by municipalities in Zurich's suburbs,[18] and the firm operating most of the ferries on Lake Zurich. All but the last of these organizations are public sector bodies, but they supervise smaller private providers and engage others as sub-contractors.

The private sector does play a role, albeit a small one, in the ZVV system: there are 26 small private bus companies and two private ferry operators. Another boat service is run by a cooperative. But the public sector exercises ultimate control, knitting private operations and public agency services into a single network. As the ZVV says, 'the loss of entrepreneurial autonomy is much more than matched by the radically improved customer friendliness'.[19]

ANOTHER TRIUMPH FOR PUBLIC OWNERSHIP?

The success of network planning is reflected in the high modal shares seen for all trip types. Canton Zurich has the same population as metropolitan Auckland, but the ZVV carried more than ten times the 52 million passengers carried in 2007 by Auckland's deregulated private operators.[20] Mode share for work trips was seven times as high in Zurich, and the ratio for non-work travel is likely to be even higher.

Daily patronage on the Zurich S-Bahn has risen from 159,000 in 1989, the year before the ZVV began, to 356,000 in 2007 – an increase of 124 per cent. The network is being upgraded in readiness for further increases, with capacity expansion centred around a second inner-city city tunnel.[21] Although this sounds impressive, the real question is whether there has been a shift in travel modes, or merely rapid suburban growth. The 1990 census was conducted in November–December, six months after the ZVV commenced operations. It revealed a large canton-wide shift to public transport since 1980, but this was the combined result of the ZVV and improvements within the City of Zurich earlier in the decade.

Public transport captures most of the market for travel to, or by residents of, central Zurich, but strong results are beginning to emerge in suburban areas. The canton's second city illustrates the trend. Between 1990 and 2000, industry in Winterthur declined, leading to a fall in the number of residents working locally. Walking and cycling fell from 25 to 19 per cent of work trips, but car use stayed at 40 per cent, because public transport made up the difference, rising from 35 to 42 per cent of trips. The most important non-local work destination was Zurich City, with a public transport share of 77 per cent in 2000 (71 in 1990). The second-most important destination was the industrial suburb of Kloten, home to Zurich Airport; public transport's share for these workers rose from 41 to 44 per cent. The biggest changes were for the most dispersed trip types. Only 151 workers travelled from Winterthur, north-east of Zurich, to Wetzikon in the south-east, but the share doing so by S-Bahn jumped from 23 per cent in 1990 to 49 per cent in 2000.[22]

These results are impressive, but are not the end of the story. Although Switzerland only conducts its census once a decade, there was a 'micro-census' in 2005, which included a national travel survey. Although the sample size is too small to allow analysis at the level of detail I have given for Winterthur, it does enable canton-wide trends to be tracked. These revealed a large increase in public transport's share of work and non-work travel since 2000, resulting in a small absolute decline in canton-wide car travel, and a larger fall in mode share for the car.[23] The rapid growth in ZVV patronage since 2005 suggests that the 2010 census may well record a significant drop in car trips across the canton.

The recent patronage growth has improved vehicle occupancies and contributed to an increase in cost-recovery. The large increase in suburban service levels that accompanied the establishment of the ZVV produced an initial fall in cost-recovery. Costs and subsidy levels rose through the early 1990s, leading to concern about the organization's financial sustainability. There were even service reductions in the mid-1990s, which temporarily halted the growth in patronage. By this time, the ZVV had developed the skills necessary to identify efficiency gains, and began to require cost reductions from its subsidiary operators. These savings, along with a resumption of patronage growth, saw cost-recovery rise from 58 per cent in 1999 to 64 per cent in 2007. The 271.5 million franc subsidy for 2007 was actually lower than the figures for the four preceding years, and works out at only 50 centimes per passenger.[24]

International cost comparisons are complicated by the dramatic exchange rate movements of recent years, which have made Swiss costs seem higher than they really are. Writing in 1995, Apel and Pharoah used an exchange rate of 3.36 Swiss francs to the UK pound; by early 2009, the pound only bought 1.60 francs. But even on a straight conversion at the rates of 2009, the ZVV subsidy per passenger works out at 30 British pence, below the figure for buses in both London and the 'deregulated' cities (see Chapter 5). Conversion to Australian currency gives 66 cents, a third the current Melbourne subsidy of $1.92 per passenger.[25] And importantly, subsidies in Zurich are falling, while those in Melbourne and British cities are rising.

So are there any negatives to the Zurich experience? The most striking discordant note is sounded by the continued decline in the share of work trips made by the only truly sustainable modes, walking and cycling. Analysis of census data shows that this is due to increases in trip lengths arising from declines in self-containment: more and more workers are travelling outside their local area to find jobs. The same pattern has been seen across Switzerland, not just in Zurich, and appears to be mainly caused by changes in the economy over which transport planners have little control. But have the high speeds and improved access created by the ZVV exacerbated the trend by encouraging long-distance commuting?

Critics suggest that the fast travel offered by S-Bahn rail services promotes 'sprawl' in Swiss urban regions just as freeways have in other countries. Commuter rail service may be one factor behind the very low suburban population densities in regions like New York and Boston (see Chapter 4). Swiss S-Bahn networks enable inner city dwellers to move to suburban and rural communities where, critics argue, they will do most of their non-work travel by car. These new residents also push up local property prices, especially in historic centres which are popular living locations, forcing established residents on lower incomes into less accessible locations. A review of the debate by Vincent Kaufmann, of the Federal Polytechnic of Lausanne, suggests that while these criticisms have some validity, they may be overstated. Cities with high levels of rail use do not appear to be suburbanizing faster than those that rely on cars (we saw in Chapter 3 that commute times continue to increase in US cities), and suburban residents in Zurich still have relatively low rates of car use, even for non-work trips.[26]

Kaufmann's conclusions are supported by census data. The Swiss census includes a question on travel by school and post-school students, and the 2000 figures show very low car use, and high rates of walking and cycling – even in suburban and rural areas. Across the canton, only 3 per cent of students of all ages travelled by car; nearly a third used public transport and two-thirds walked or cycled. There was a small shift from non-motorized modes to public transport between 1990 and 2000, but the share travelling by car actually fell, from 4 per cent in 1990. Even in remote Sternenberg, 59 per cent of students walked or cycled in 2000, with car use at 18 per cent.[27] By way of contrast, the most recent survey results for Melbourne, which date from 1994, show only 26 per cent of students walking or cycling and 19 per cent using public transport. The great majority, around 55 per cent, travel by car, and more recent data, although sketchy, suggests that this figure has risen since 1994, mainly at the expense of walking.[28] The most recent figures for the UK, while much better than in Australia, are still dramatically worse than Zurich, with 48 per cent of school students walking or cycling, 20 per cent using public transport and 30 per cent – ten times the share in Zurich – travelling by car.[29]

The major defect in Zurich's transport policies is the absence of disincentives for car use in suburban and rural areas. In Zurich City, the 'carrot' of excellent public transport is accompanied by the 'sticks' of traffic calming and public transport priority. But it has been more difficult to persuade voters in the rest of the canton to endorse measures of this kind. Indeed, the national and state road agencies are still working to complete the motorways planned in the 1950s, except for controversial projects like the inner-city 'Y' link and the Gold Coast route (see discussion above).

Using Vuchic's categorization from Chapter 3, Canton Zurich has a policy mixing strong incentives for public transport with significant, albeit weaker, incentives for car use. As the head of the city's planning office noted back in 1993, 'promoting ecological transport modes is not sufficient in itself. In addition ... it is essential to limit the attraction of private car travel.'[30] Zurich's suburban and rural areas could learn from Vancouver (see Chapter 6) and the Swiss Alpine Initiative to transfer freight to rail (Chapter 5) that incentives for more sustainable modes work better when accompanied by disincentives for private transport.

Although suburban Zurich has not left the automobile age behind, it is in an excellent position to do so once the necessary political support can be obtained. If oil supplies were interrupted, or urgent measures adopted against global warming, the transition would be relatively painless – and in the case of students, only 3 per cent would be affected.

Zurich's success deserves to be counted a triumph for public ownership, and for public strategic and tactical planning. Although the private sector does play a role in the ZVV's network, it is noteworthy that all the service innovations, from tram priority to integrated fares to the pulse-timetable system, came from public-sector bodies. But significantly, most of these innovations came about as a result of conflict between public sector experts and public opinion. The Swiss system of participatory democracy enabled the public to force city, cantonal and national public transport planners to come up with cheaper, more effective ways of competing with the car. Zurich is a triumph for public participation in transit planning as well.

SCHAFFHAUSEN: THE ZURICH MODEL IN MINIATURE?

When I read the chapter on Schaffhausen in Apel and Pharoah's *Transport Concepts in European Cities* (1995), I found it hard to believe. Could the 44,000 residents of this small town (including the adjoining municipality of Neuhausen) really make 11.3 million public transport trips per year? That's 257 per head.[31] I checked and found that in 2007 *Vehkehrsbetreibe Schaffhausen*, the local public transport authority, carried 13 million passengers on its buses and trolley-buses; the population served was 43,508, so the per capita trip rate has risen to 289.[32] That's higher than the most recent figure for Curitiba (261 unlinked trips, or 153 linked trips, per head), more than double Ottawa and four times the figure for Brisbane (counting rail journeys). Yet these three cities all have extensive busway networks, while Schaffhausen has none.

Apel and Pharoah were unable to confirm the effect of this high patronage on car travel due to a lack of data on mode shares, but this deficiency can now been rectified. The 2000 Swiss census reveals that across the two municipalities, 15 per cent of workers walked or cycled, 41 per cent took public transport and 44 per cent went by car.[33] The mode share for public transport is nearly twice as high as in Tyne and Wear, the English metropolitan county with the highest usage rate, and car use is almost as low as in London (Table 4.2).

Schaffhausen lies on the Rhine, 53km north of Zurich in the canton of the same name. Local public transport has been provided by buses and trolley-buses since trams were removed in the 1960s, but tram-like services are provided. Six full-time routes operate through the city centre to connect both sides of the town. The standard pattern is a 10-minute frequency from around 5:30 am to 8:00 pm on weekdays and Saturdays, as well as on Sunday afternoons; a 20-minute service is provided at other times. Articulated vehicles are used on the three busiest routes and midibuses on the quietest route. Buses finish around 12:30 am, but a limited 'night network' operates on Fridays and Saturdays, with services every 30 minutes until 2:00 am.

All buses stop outside the main railway station in the city centre, and wait there for two or three minutes so passengers can transfer. Every ten minutes, a dozen buses converge on the station, lining up on each side of the street outside the entrance, before moving off one after the other. Each convoy leaves at exactly 10, 20, 30, 40 and so on past the hour. With services this frequent, there is no need to specifically coordinate schedules with those of the trains, although the last night-buses are timed to meet the 1:00 am S-Bahn service from Zurich. Naturally, transfers are free, and the city's fares are integrated with those of the regional buses serving the 30,000 residents of rural parts of Schaffhausen canton. Heavily discounted periodicals are available, with a monthly ticket costing only twice as much as a weekly. Despite this, cost-recovery rates remain respectable, assisted by strong off-peak loads and full-fare-paying custom. Fare revenues cover just over half of costs, a further 10 per cent is covered by a levy on city parking, and the remainder is shared between the two municipalities and the cantonal government.[34]

The use of parking revenues to fund public transport is the result of a 1973 referendum on a citizen's initiative to improve services.[35] Like Zurich, Schaffhausen has achieved public transport success through a combination of efficient public enterprise and participatory democracy.

Schaffhausen has created its own version of the public transport 'network effect' that we have seen working in cities as diverse as Zurich, Toronto, Ottawa and Curitiba. If public transport can compete with the car across such an array of cultures, climates and urban forms, perhaps there is a generalizable model of successful transit. It is now time to consider what this model is – and why, and how, it works.

NOTES

1   Remak (1993).
2   This section is based on Cervero (1998, ch. 11); Apel and Pharoah (1995, pp127–154); Nash and Sylvia (2001), and Petersen (forthcoming).

3   The text is reproduced at Cervero (1998, p305).

4   The system is described in detail in Nash and Sylvia (2001).

5   Apel and Pharoah (1995, p137, fig. 28); FitzRoy and Smith (1992, p211, fig. 1).

6   www.vbz.ch/vbz_opencms/opencms/vbz/english/FactsFigures/number_of_
passengers.html (excluding district and regional services) (accessed 30 August 2009).
All figures cited in this chapter are for unlinked trips.

7   Swiss Federal Statistical Office, 2000 Census, 'pendler' table A2A, Gemeinde Zurich
(261). The figures in Chapter 3 are for all workers residing in the city, including those
employed in the suburbs. The 1990 public transport figure of 76% cited by Apel
Pharoah (1995, p145, table 22) is the share of motorized trips (i.e. excluding walking
and cycling).

8   Nash and Sylvia (2001, p41).

9   FitzRoy and Smith (1992, p213).

10 This section is based on the same sources as the previous section, plus Pucher
(1996).

11 Statistisches Amt des Kantons Zurich (2004).

12 www.bfs.admin.ch/bfs/portal/en/index/regionen/regionalportraets.html (accessed 30
August 2009) – portraits for the Canton and Commune of Zurich. This methodology
is not precisely comparable to those used in the UK and North America, so
comparisons are only approximate.

13 This section based on G. Hürlimann (2004, 2005) and Petersen (forthcoming).

14 www.wahlen.zh.ch/abstimmungen/zhresultate.php (accessed 30 August 2009); see
6.3.88, (a).

15 Photographs of trains and buses meeting at Wetzikon station appear at Vuchic (2005,
pp226, 227).

16 *Angebotsverordnung*, 740.3, 14 December 1988.

17 ZVV (2006, p7).

18 One of these, the Sihltal Zurich Uetliberg Bahn, is a partnership with the national
and cantonal governments to operate two S-Bahn lines and associated bus routes.

19 ZVV (2006, p8).

20 ARTA (2008, p15).

21 www.zvv.ch/en (accessed 30 August 2009); ZVV (2008a).

22 Swiss Federal Statistical Office, 2000 Census.

23 Moser (2008, p7, Grafik 4). The graphs measure distance travelled rather than the
number of trips, and as a result under-state the importance of walking and cycling.

24 ZVV (2008b, pp16, 22).

25 Victorian Government (2008, p130; 'payments for services' for 2006/2007; bus
reduced 20% to allow for fare revenue).

26 Kaufmann (2004).

27 Swiss Federal Statistical Office, 2000 Census.

28 ABS (1995, p2, table 2); cycling is not listed separately, but 'other' is assumed to be
mainly cycling, as suggested by comparison with table 3; see also: www.dhs.vic.gov.
au/__data/assets/pdf_file/0010/276607/WalkingCyclingSchoolBus.pdf (accessed 30
August 2009).

29 DfT (2007/2008, table 1 – results are for 2006).

30 Ott, quoted in Apel and Pharoah (1995, p150).

31 Apel and Pharoah (1995, pp223–227).
32 Vehkehrsbetreibe Schaffhausen (2008, p19).
33 Swiss Federal Statistical Office, 2000 Census.
34 Vehkehrsbetreibe Schaffhausen (2008, p12).
35 Apel and Pharoah give a brief history of transport policy in the city.

9

Towards a General Theory of Public Transport Network Planning

THE WAY TO CORK

A few years ago, an Australian newspaper published a cartoon satirizing economists. A stereotypically pointy-headed male was staring in rage at some example of successful government enterprise, shouting: 'It might work in practice, but it doesn't work in *theory!*'

Urban public transport seems a bit like that cartoon. The success stories reviewed in this book rely on measures condemned by the conventional wisdoms of neo-liberal transport economics: high transfer rates, central planning, government monopolies, cross-subsidization – and congestion instead of road pricing. Conversely, public transport systems that follow the conventional wisdoms have failed, from England to the Antipodes.

But the cartoon economist is right on one point at least. The conflict between theory and successful practice does need to be resolved. We need to understand not only what works, but why it works, if we are to apply the lessons learned from successful public transport systems to cities where transit is failing.

Graeme Davison recounts the old story of the motorist travelling in rural Ireland, who stops a grizzled local and asks the way to Cork. After a long pause, the oldtimer scratches his head and says: 'Well, if I wanted to go *there*, I wouldn't have started out from *here*.'[1] Most transport analysts agree on the desirability of moving beyond the automobile age, but are not convinced that the shift is achievable: even the Intergovernmental Panel on Climate Change is daunted by the challenge, as we saw in Chapter 3.

To re-state the central problem, public transport uses urban space and environmental resources more efficiently than the car if it can attract people with different trip origins and destinations to travel together. This task becomes more difficult as origins and destinations disperse, which is exactly what is happening almost everywhere in the world. Trip origins are spreading, as suburbanization lowers region-wide population densities; trip destinations are less concentrated, as the share of jobs and retailing in central business districts (CBDs) falls; traditional peaks are spreading, as working and shopping hours are deregulated.

The result is that public transport is usually infrequent and unattractive, poorly patronized and heavily subsidized. Attempts to improve services will often seem like throwing good money after bad: some additional patronage may be attracted, but not enough to fill the extra seats provided. So subsidies rise, cost-recovery falls, and greenhouse emissions per passenger increase until eventually – as we have seen with buses in the US and Melbourne – there is no advantage over travel by car.

The key to the dilemma is elasticity of demand, the economist's term for the way demand for a commodity changes when its price or quality changes. An elasticity of 0.5 means that a 10 per cent change in, say, the price will produce a 5 per cent change in demand. Most research into elasticities of demand for public transport has produced figures well below one, with typical figures around 0.2 for fares and 0.5 for services.[2] This means that patronage changes more slowly than the rate at which services or fares change. Since cutting fares and adding services is expensive, revenue from the new passengers is unlikely to cover costs. Therefore, the only way increased service can be sustained appears to be through alternative means of provision, such as minibuses or 'para-transit', leading us back into the realm of market-based solutions.

There must be something wrong with the studies of demand elasticities, at least for service levels, because they are flatly contradicted by real-world experience. Successful public transport systems offer higher service levels than unsuccessful ones operating in comparable environments, but usually have higher, not lower, occupancy rates. Bus services and occupancies are both better in London than the deregulated British cities; the same applies when Toronto is compared with Melbourne, and when Zurich and Schaffhausen are compared with just about anywhere.

So what's the explanation? To answer this, we must leave the road to Cork and visit another city, this time an imaginary one called Squaresville. I discussed Squaresville in 2000 in *A Very Public Solution*, and Gustav Nielsen, now of Norway's Institute of Transport Economics, developed it in his 2005 HiTrans manual.[3] I hope readers familiar with these books will forgive another visit, because it provides the key to understanding how low elasticities of demand can be overcome, and why expanding services need not lower occupancy rates.

THE WAY TO SQUARESVILLE: DISPERSED CITIES AND THE NETWORK EFFECT

The hypothetical city of Squaresville is a worst-case scenario of urban dispersal, illustrated in Figure 9.1A. It will be familiar to readers of *Great Cities and Their*

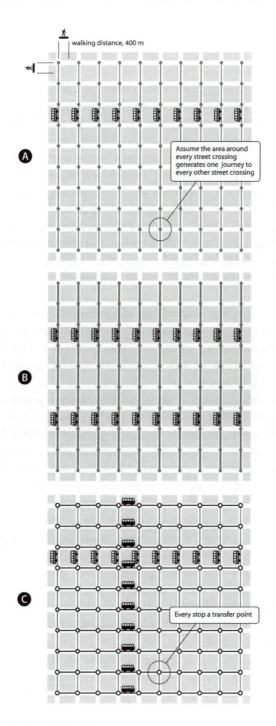

Sources: Mees (2000, p140); Nielsen (2005, p86).

Figure 9.1 *'Squaresville' and the network effect*

Traffic, as it is based on Thomson's dispersed 'full motorization' archetype of city development.[4] The city has a grid road network, with ten north—south and ten east—west roads, at intervals of half a mile or 800m. Travel patterns are completely random, with no dominant pattern of movement. Each of the city's 100 square blocks produces 100 trips a day: one internal trip (made on foot), and one external trip to each of the 99 other blocks of the city – giving 9900 external trips in total.

Squaresville has ten bus routes that grew up in a free-market environment, with each operated by a different firm. There is one route along each north—south road, reflecting a past era when this was the dominant pattern of movement (Figure 9.1A). This means that each resident of Squaresville has a bus within 400m walking distance, but can only reach the nine other city blocks lying along her or his bus route, giving access to 900 daily trips out of the total of 9900. Assume that public transport attracts a third of the trips it can theoretically serve; this gives a total of 300 trips (a third of 900), or a city-wide mode share of only 3 per cent (300/9900).

Now, imagine that the government of Squaresville wants to do something about the low rate of public transport use in the city. It pays the bus operators to double service frequencies on Squaresville's ten bus routes (Figure 9.1B). With a typical demand elasticity of 0.5, this would increase patronage by half, to 450 trips per day or 4.5 per cent of the market. Occupancy rates will fall, since patronage has grown more slowly than service levels, and fare revenue will not cover the extra costs. Subsidies will rise, cost-recovery will worsen and so will greenhouse emissions per bus passenger. Public transport is still of marginal importance, but it has become less efficient in economic and environmental terms.

Imagine instead that the additional buses are used in a different way. Ten east—west routes are introduced to complement the ten existing lines and create a grid network, as shown in Figure 9.1C. The number of trips served directly doubles, to 1800, but by transferring between routes, passengers can now access the entire city, so the network also serves the remaining 8100 trips. Squaresville's planners do everything possible to make transfers convenient, providing integrated fares, convenient facilities and coordinated timetables. But since so many transport analysts say that passengers dislike transferring, let's assume that the mode share for trips requiring a transfer is only half that for direct trips, that is one-sixth. So the total number of public transport trips is one-third of 1800 plus one-sixth of 8100, giving a total of 1950.

Under the second model of service provision, public transport's mode share has jumped dramatically, from 3 to 20 per cent. Service has increased 100 per cent, but patronage has grown 550 per cent, giving an elasticity of 5.5. Increased revenue would more than cover the costs of the additional service and occupancies would rise substantially, reducing subsidies and greenhouse emissions per passenger.

Although Squaresville is not a real city, it illustrates why real cities with integrated public transport networks can have their cake and eat it too, combining high service levels with high occupancies and high efficiency. It also illustrates why uncoordinated service additions, such as those seen early on in deregulated English bus systems, can lower efficiency. The elasticity of demand for service additions doesn't have to be less than one if the new services are added in a way that serves new trip demands by creating a network.

Significantly, this 'network effect' becomes stronger as travel patterns become more dispersed: in a hypothetical city where all trips are made to a single centre, there is no network benefit at all. This contradicts another arm of the conventional wisdom in transport economics, which assumes that public transport is only likely to be a natural monopoly (see Chapter 5) in dense, centralized cities where strong demand produces economies of scale. The network effect is an example of 'economies of scope' and, as Thomson's study of Pacific Greyhound in Chapter 5 showed, it applies in the opposite situation – namely where demand is weak and dispersed. In a more recent paper, Thomson argues that US cities that have followed a similar strategy, turning radial systems into multi-destinational networks, have achieved better patronage and efficiency outcomes than those that concentrated on providing transfer-free trips to a limited range of destinations.[5]

Australians get the opportunity to see the network effect in action each time they travel to Europe. At the time of writing, it is not possible to travel directly from Australia to any European airport other than London Heathrow. To reach Paris, Berlin or Rome, Australians must transfer, either at London or at an intermediate hub like Singapore or Dubai. I once spent five hours waiting for connections at Singapore at around 2:00 am and did not enjoy the experience! But the demand for travel between Australia and any other European port is so thin that direct services cannot be economically supported, unless they are to run only weekly or fortnightly. Nobody will wait a week for a direct service when there are competing daily services with transfers, so no direct trips are provided. There were once infrequent direct services between Australia and other European cities, but this was at a time when fares were so high that airlines could run half-empty planes and still make money. The transfer at London or Singapore is one of the costs of the dramatic fall in real airfares in the last three decades, but it has also allowed Australians easier access to a larger range of European cities. For example, the quickest route to Copenhagen is through Singapore, rather than London.

In the airline industry, network planning has enabled firms to connect a wider range of origins and destinations, while at the same time increasing occupancy rates and lowering fares. In urban public transport, the network effect also allows the apparently impossible to be achieved: genuine networks can serve a wider range of destinations, increase frequencies and operating hours, and improve occupancies – thereby lowering pollution and subsidy levels per passenger.

Network planning also changes the rules of the debate between rail and bus enthusiasts. It allows buses to provide the high service levels and easy-to-understand route structures that were once regarded as the exclusive property of heavy or light rail – as Ottawa, Curitiba and Schaffhausen, among others, have demonstrated.

But the network effect also allows high-quality rail to be provided when regional populations are lower or more thinly spread than in the big, dense cities which were once believed to be the only places suited to it – Toronto, Vancouver and suburban Zurich are cases in point.

The network effect even offers a solution to another dilemma faced by transit planners, namely guessing where passengers want to go. One of the traditional arguments for competition in public transport has been that public authorities will be insufficiently dynamic to track changes in travel patterns and respond with new service offerings. But with a full network provided, the passengers themselves will answer this question by using transfers to reach new destinations as they arise, just as motorists use a road network to make new trips. And provided trends in patronage are monitored properly, the agency in charge of tactical planning can track changes and respond appropriately. A good example is the Translink bus network in the City of Vancouver, which operates as an interconnecting high-frequency grid. 'B-Line' express bus service is being introduced progressively on key corridors, which are easily identified as those with the highest and fastest-growing patronage. The busiest B-Line services are in turn being replaced by extensions of the regional light rail network.

Given its obvious advantages, it is often asked why network planning requires public control to succeed. Why don't private transit firms adopt it voluntarily, in order to reap the benefit of increased demand and higher occupancies? The answer is that networks require cross-subsidy. Because real cities are not exactly like Squaresville, demand is not evenly dispersed: some routes and periods of the day are more profitable than others, but all must be run at high standards to create a functioning network. Under a genuinely privatized system, who will volunteer to run the loss-making routes that, by creating a network, increase profits on the strong lines, most of which are operated by rival firms? The answer is, nobody. No rational private firm will be the 'sucker' who bears a loss so other firms can make greater profits.

We saw this in Foz do Iguacu, where the city council provided the infrastructure, but not the organizational arrangements, for a Curitiba-style network. The city's bus firms have stuck to serving profitable corridors, and shown little enthusiasm for integration of fares or services. And in Leeds, as we saw in Chapter 5, a major bus operator said it would 'not condone or support' integration with rail. The British bus industry is happy with deregulation: it delivers handsome profits from the large and growing subsidies the government provides for managing decline, all with a minimum of interference – especially from those pesky passengers who are always bothering public operators in London and Europe with demands for high-quality services.

Creating a network is a classic example of a 'collective action problem', a situation in which individuals acting rationally produces a collectively irrational outcome. Another name for this phenomenon is market failure.

NETWORKS AND NATURAL MONOPOLY

Public transport in dispersed cities is a natural monopoly, because only a single organization can carry out the tactical planning necessary to provide an integrated network of routes and services. Without network planning, adding services is likely to reduce efficiency. In an environment like Hong Kong or Manila, wasteful competition of this kind can be sustained financially, but it cannot be afforded where demand is thin. And thinly spread demand is precisely the transport pattern that is growing rapidly as cities in virtually all developed nations disperse. In other words, it is the demand public transport needs to meet if we are to move beyond the automobile age.

Now we have the answer to the contradiction between orthodox transport economic theory and the real world. The theory is wrong, at least in the case of urban public transport. The network effect produces economies of scope that make public transport a natural monopoly, and the more dispersed demand is, the stronger the effect is.

This in turn explains why only public transport systems in which tactical planning is handled by a central public agency are succeeding in competing with the car. Deregulation and franchising, which leave tactical planning to the market, are not able to create the network effect, and are only sustainable in markets where there is no serious competition from private transport: large, dense cities, or places where low incomes still limit car ownership.

The lesson is being learned by more and more cities, generally as a result of the work of practising transport planners rather than academically trained transport economists. The *Verkehrsverbund* can now be found in most German and Austrian urban regions; Madrid has had an equivalent regional organization since 1986, and has seen a sustained increase in ridership; the other Swiss cantons have adopted different organizational forms and terminologies from Zurich, but regional and national network planning now covers the entire country. Hourly pulse-timetabled rail and bus services reach into remote corners of the sparsely populated canton of Graubunden, enabling the Swiss National Park – which has a population density of zero – to promote public transport as the preferred form of access.[6]

And the lessons are spreading beyond Europe. Singapore's Land Transport Authority observes that while the rail system is popular with locals and visitors, buses are a constant source of public dissatisfaction, because they are 'planned by the [private] operators based largely on commercial considerations'. To create an integrated system, 'LTA will take over central planning of the bus network'. Buses will be reoriented to feed, rather than duplicate, the rail system and multi-modal fares will be introduced. This will require a change from the current monopoly franchise system to one in which bus firms tender to become sub-contractors on the London model.[7]

Singapore has discovered the lesson behind public transport success in Toronto, Vancouver, Ottawa, Curitiba, Zurich, Schaffhausen and other cities

– and corresponding failure in places like Melbourne and English cities. To operate effectively and avoid market failure, a natural monopoly like urban public transport must be planned by a single public agency.

MEANWHILE, IN THE BUNKER

This trend has barely registered in much of the anglosphere, and other places where the influence of free-market ideology remains strong. The failure of deregulation is eloquently attested by the British experience, but also by the success of developing-world cities like Bogota, which have abolished it. Now that New Zealand, the World Bank and the European Commission have abandoned free-market public transport, the notion remains the sole preserve of a small cell of British fundamentalists holed up in Whitehall and free-market think-tanks. Unfortunately, the British government still takes its advice on transport policy from within this ideological bunker.

Britain's oldest free-market think-tank, the Institute for Economic Affairs (IEA), was still lauding Manila's jeepneys as recently as 2005, in a booklet celebrating both the 20th anniversary of deregulation and the work of the economist John Hibbs, a driving force behind the original policy.[8] After two decades, there is ample evidence available on trends in patronage and subsidies in the deregulated systems and London, but not one of the booklet's 117 pages refers to any of this evidence. The argument is purely rhetorical – but it worked, as the UK Department for Transport backed a continuation of deregulation the following year (see Chapter 5).

Hibbs' IEA essay did cite a single piece of data: apparently, bus usage in Cambridge increased by 45 per cent in only three years.[9] Hibbs did not specify the years in question or provide a source for the claim, but Cambridgeshire County Council, the organization responsible for public transport in the region, did record a 14 per cent increase in bus patronage over the three years to 2005.[10] In that year, the county's 570,000 residents made 17.3 million bus trips between them, around 4 million more than were made by the 44,000 residents of Schaffhausen. This represents 30 bus trips per person per year, a tenth the rate of Schaffhausen and lower even than Los Angeles or Auckland. At the 2001 census, just under 7 per cent of county residents travelled to work by public transport, with 3.8 per cent using buses and 2.9 per cent travelling by train (mainly to London): 73 per cent went by car. The bus, train and car shares for Cambridge City were 5.7, 3.4 and 45 per cent, the lower car figure resulting from high cycling rates.[11] If these figures represent success for deregulated public transport, then the case for planning is conclusively established!

The University of Sydney's David Hensher was until recently the most prominent service integration sceptic, reluctant to concede even the need for multi-modal fares. Since only 2 per cent of bus trips in Sydney involve transfers, he argued, the absence of multi-modal tickets will not concern the great majority of passengers. But this puts the cart before the horse: the low transfer rate in Sydney is caused by the lack of service integration, including the absence of integrated fares. Hensher's proposed alternative of 'cross-regional services ... in which a passenger can travel on a single mode/operator service without transfers'[12] is a chimera. In dispersed cities, travel patterns are too diffuse to allow such low-demand services to be provided economically, even if operators were able to guess the right origins and destinations to connect. In our hypothetical city of Squaresville, at least 160 routes would be needed to directly link all origins and destinations, compared with 20 using the network effect.

But even Hensher may be changing his views. His most recent paper advocating busways, published in late 2008, attributes the success of Curitiba and Bogota to integration and networking, including 'a hierarchy of feeder and trunk routes, with almost seamless transfer points.'[13] Interestingly, Hensher's paper appeared in a volume published by Singapore's Land Transport Authority (LTA), which as we have seen, is also moving towards network planning.

The concession or franchise system retains more supporters than deregulation. It was envisaged as a compromise between the free market and central planning and, like so many compromises, has combined the worst features of both alternatives. John Hibbs is right when he says that franchising requires just as much 'top-down public control' as a system actually run by a public agency.[14] But (and this is my observation, not Hibbs') public control under the concession system is exercised without the traditional safeguards needed to keep public officials efficient and even honest. Officials must judge 'beauty contests' involving packages of heterogeneous and often intangible issues, ranging from cost to the slippery concept of innovation. There is no obviously correct answer, and franchisees have a strong incentive to engage in tactical behaviour like 'low-balling', distracting attention from the real story with attractive-sounding innovations like wind-powered trams and buses that run on canola oil (don't laugh: Melbourne proudly boasts both of these).

Over time, multinational firms that specialize in bidding for franchises will become experts at manipulating beauty contests, since they have wider experience and stronger incentives to win than the government officials acting as judges. And worse still, the beauty contest judges are insulated from the consequences of their mistakes – by legal complexity, secrecy, 'commercial-in-confidence' provisions, but also by an ability to blame the franchisees for any problems. Such a system creates a strong likelihood that bad decisions will be made, and then covered up rather than openly acknowledged.

The result is a textbook case of an environment in which problems ranging from poor performance to 'regulatory capture' to outright corruption can flourish.

The British rail system seems to be an example of poor performance. The Office of Rail Regulation, which succeeded previous bodies such as the Strategic Rail Authority, is a unit of the Department for Transport. The office and its predecessors have maintained more independence from the franchisees they regulate than their counterparts in Melbourne. Independent assessments of UK rail franchising have delivered verdicts ranging from total disaster through to the proverbial curate's egg, one of the more optimistic concluding that it has avoided the worst results of bus deregulation and even produced modest innovations in fare discounting schemes.[15] But nobody can name a genuine innovation in service of the kind seen in Zurich's suburban network and across the Swiss national rail and Postbus systems. At a time when the inhabitants of Switzerland's cities – which would only count as towns in the UK – are looking forward to 15-minute all-day service frequencies across a nation-wide integrated network, residents of big British cities pay much higher fares for less frequent, poorly coordinated services.

Trips across different British rail operators' territory involve a bewildering array of timetables and fare types, with even the amount of time one must leave for connections varying according to the operator involved. Here is part of the valiant attempt by National Rail, the marketing umbrella group established by the British rail firms, to explain:

> Example. *At Barnham a different minimum connectional allowance applies for Train Operator SN. This means that if your journey involves changing between two trains both of which are operated by SN, you need only allow 2 minutes. If, however, one or both trains are provided by any other Operator then the minimum of 5 minutes (as shown after the station name) applies.*[16]

Multi-modal journeys involving rail and bus are even more trying, and are only attempted by intrepid souls in whom the spirit of British explorers from bygone centuries still lives. An indication of the dismal state of affairs is unwittingly provided by the radical journalist George Monbiot in his best-selling, and otherwise excellent, climate change manifesto, *Heat*. Rather than recommend the multi-modal solution which has proven effective in Switzerland, Monbiot champions a 'visionary' proposal by an economist to cater for inter-city travel with swarms of buses operating on motorways, based at terminals on the outskirts of urban areas. Inter-city public transport in Britain is so dysfunctional that even radicals apparently can't envisage practical solutions.[17]

As the 2009 recession began to adversely affect the demand for travel, British franchisees – who were happy to take the credit for patronage rises during the economic boom – signalled that they would require large increases in previously agreed subsidy levels.

At the other end of the spectrum, corruption of city officials by tramway franchisees produced a cavalcade of scandals that led to the US reform movement of the early 20th century (and also, as we have seen, an industry that was bankrupt even before the car began to offer serious competition). Melbourne since 1999 and Curitiba before the mid-1980s provide examples that are part-way along the spectrum, with Melbourne offering a striking instance of regulatory capture so complete that the operators and regulator actually boast about being 'partners'.[18]

CREATING AN EFFECTIVE PUBLIC TRANSPORT AGENCY

The market cannot deliver effective urban public transport, especially in dispersed cities, but it does not follow that the mere existence of a public agency will solve the problem. We saw in Chapter 5 that support for privatization in the 1980s was influenced by the poor performance of many public authorities in the US and the UK. As Mark Twain discovered on his 1895 visit to Victoria, public operators are perfectly capable of replicating the lack of integration found in market-based systems.

Regional public transport agencies must be dynamic and efficient if they are to succeed in dispersed environments where the car offers real competition. This is partly a question of organizational structure, but culture and history are equally important.

Why were government subsidies for public transport in US cities followed in so many cases by declining operating efficiency rather than radically improved services? Why did the introduction of similar subsidies in Canada only a few years later produce better results?[19] An important part of the answer lies in organizational history. Public transport in Canadian cities was taken into public hands earlier than in the US, and in response to disputes about service, rather than bankruptcy. Managers of public systems inherited enterprises that were financially sound and well managed. Most US systems were taken over only after decades of decline in the quality of both management and service. In Canada, government subsidies allowed these efficient public operators to expand into low-density suburbs, replacing private firms, as we have seen in the cases of Toronto, Vancouver and Ottawa. Many US transit systems never had the opportunity to acquire efficient operating cultures, as they were rapidly transformed from failing private firms confined to inner cities to region-wide public agencies charged with serving difficult suburban terrain.

Organizational history also helps explain why buses and rail in London remain poorly integrated, more than seven decades after the establishment of the London Passenger Transport Board (LPTB). The Toronto Transit Commission (TTC) may well be the world leader in rail–bus and rail–tram integration, with 'free-body' transfers at most stations, where buses, and even trams, arrive and depart from terminals inside the fare gates. One reason for this high level of integration is that the TTC expressly designed its rail system to replace the busiest tram lines and link with the remaining routes. The *Zürcher Verkehrsverbund* comes from a different history to the TTC, being an umbrella body like the LPTB; however, it was established with the express objective of integrating services and fares.

The London changes of 1933 merged a dozen pre-existing tram, bus and underground operators, who had begun life as competitors. The different entities were rationalized into road transport and railway divisions, unintentionally perpetuating the rivalry. The lack of integration was exacerbated by the decision to keep most surface railways outside the LPTB's remit.[20] Despite the introduction of multi-modal daily and periodical Travelcards in 1981, during Ken Livingstone's first term as Mayor of Greater London, single, off-peak and some longer-term tickets remain single-mode, while route connectivity and timetable integration remain patchy. The recent 'London Overground' initiative to bring some surface railways closer to the service standards found on the Underground is the first big step towards integration in almost three decades.

Public transport organizations in many cities developed inward-looking cultures in the days when low car ownership meant most residents were 'captive' to public transport. They concentrated on the relatively simple task of carrying large passenger flows on radial routes, and paid little attention to providing a total service for all needs. With the advent of the car, many such organizations lacked the dynamism to pursue anything more ambitious than the 'easy option' of managing decline. A culture developed that Vuchic calls the 'self-defence of incompetence'.[21] He notes that 'the less competent employees are, the more they resist any changes', an observation that applies with equal force to public transport agencies as a whole. This problem seems to have been particularly serious in the UK and Australasia before deregulation and franchising, but has not been cured by these measures.

Efficient, passenger-focused agency cultures can evolve from fortunate organizational histories, but usually have to be created. This issue has been poorly understood in many institutional reform exercises, which have assumed that setting up appropriate bureaucratic structures is sufficient. Bad organizational cultures have to be tackled directly, rather than by simply rearranging the same people in different public or private administrative units. This may require new staff at senior levels, the involvement of advisers from outside the organization, and strong leadership from local communities and politicians. This kind of work is difficult but necessary, even if it is more arduous and boring than a constant rearrangement of organizational flow-charts.

One important lesson from all our success stories, even Curitiba, is that transparency and public participation increase the effectiveness of a public transit agency, provided the agency's staff have enough confidence in their own expertise to engage in genuine public debate. Zurich's transport planners now agree that the 1960s and 1970s proposals to replace trams with a metro were mistaken: their defeat forced planners to come up with proposals that achieved better outcomes at lower cost. And the same is true of the nation-wide pulse-timetable system that replaced the Swiss Federal Railways' earlier plans for 'bullet trains'. Stefan Bratzel's study of sustainable urban transport success stories in Europe confirms the critical importance of public debate and even conflict in reviving public transport.[22]

A related success factor in a number of the cities studied by Bratzel has been a productive, although not always harmonious, relationship between 'town' and 'gown' – one that reached its apogee in Zurich with Professor Kunzi's move from the operations research programme to the transport ministry (see Chapter 8). The coalition which blocked the city's 1973 metro proposal was based at the University of Zurich and the adjacent Federal Institute of Technology (*Eidgenössische Technische Hochschule*, or ETH). Researchers at ETH, in particular, have played important roles in operational innovations on the local and national rail systems, including the current 'Puls-90' project, which seeks to increase national rail capacity without substantial new infrastructure by lowering headways to 90 seconds (by contrast, British rail headways are actually widening, as operating practices become steadily more conservative).[23]

The same phenomenon can be seen on a less intimate level in other successful cities: the 'freeway revolts' in Toronto and Vancouver were based at the Universities of Toronto and British Columbia, while UBC staff and students have lobbied for service innovations like B-Line express buses and the U-Pass periodical ticket for tertiary students (see Chapter 12). Unfortunately, this level of positive interaction is quite rare. Most transport researchers concentrate on collation and modelling of aggregate data rather than direct attacks on specific management and planning problems. And in the UK, Canada and Australasia, declining government support has encouraged academics to seek funding from outside sources, making many researchers reluctant to offend potential 'industry partners' by criticizing existing practices. The head of the Institute of Transport at ETH Zurich laments the absence of direct financial support from the federal railways, since it restricts the amount of research the institute can conduct. But 'there are also advantages, because we can focus on "total public transport systems" as a whole.'[24]

Related to the question of participation is the notion of subsidiarity, or allowing problems to be solved at the lowest level of government consistent with efficiency. Some of the most damaging urban transport decisions, such as British bus deregulation, Melbourne rail franchising and the European Commission's abortive bid to make franchising compulsory, have been top-down measures imposed by higher-level governments. A strong say for local and regional governments has been critical to all our success stories, even those like Toronto that have relied on higher levels of government for intervention at critical stages. Bus patronage in London took off rapidly once the British government surrendered control to Transport for London (TfL), while the absence of interference from national and state governments allowed Jaime Lerner to revamp Curitiba's bus system.

Subsidiarity was originally justified as promoting participation, but also efficiency, by preventing the state being 'overwhelmed and crushed by almost infinite tasks and duties.'[25] The benefits of subsidiarity – which is actually listed as a guiding principle in the Swiss and Zurich Cantonal constitutions – can be most clearly seen in the lean, simple organizational structure of the *Zürcher Verkehrsverbund* (Figure 8.1). The ZVV can focus its energies on the critical tasks of tactical planning and cost-control because it delegates operations to skilled, reliable sub-contractors.

The value of simple organizational structures suggests a cautious approach to a popular recipe for coordination, namely to have the same body in charge of roads and public transport, and possibly even land-use planning. There are examples of agencies that successfully manage roads and public transport – TfL and Vancouver's Translink are two – but there is a risk of loss of focus. Interestingly, these two bodies both sub-contract much of their service delivery: to private firms in London, and to subsidiary companies in Vancouver. And it is by no means clear that having a single agency responsible for roads and public transport will prevent roads policy undermining sustainable modes: it is more likely to result in a 'balanced transport' compromise, in which each section of the agency gets its share of the cake. When the car competes for funds with sustainable modes in a fair, public contest it usually loses, as even Auckland's transport planners of the 1950s understood.

WHO SHOULD BE IN CHARGE?

Agency structures are also important, however, and there is a range of viable options once the failed choices of deregulation and franchising are eliminated. These are strategies 1 to 4 on the continuum discussed in Chapter 5. All of them involve the transit agency taking responsibility for tactical planning, but each deals with operational and strategic issues differently.

Every successful agency must have some common features that seem to be non-negotiable. The agency must have jurisdiction over the entire functional urban area rather than just the central municipality (the lack of this element is probably the key factor holding public transport in Greater Toronto back). It must control overall finances, allowing the pooling of revenue to avoid endless disputes and permit the cross-subsidy that is essential to network planning. Finally, it must be allowed to operate independently of the day-to-day political and media cycle, while being publicly accountable for its performance. This combination is necessary to guard against capture by vested interests (ranging from trade unions to private contractors), encourage efficiency and customer focus, and enable the agency to advocate for adequate funding in the public arena.

The concern for independence is one reason why most contemporary analysts are sceptical about the first option on the continuum, of a government or municipal department. Political interference and bureaucratic remoteness from the consequences of decisions can inhibit efficient and innovative tactical planning. British rail timetables are now planned mainly by the Department for Transport's Office of Rail Regulation. Franchisees bid to operate services within the constraints of this bureaucratically planned timetable. It is difficult to envisage an environment in which those responsible for timetabling are more remote from the consequences of their decisions – and the results, predictably, are stagnation and even decline in efficiency and innovation.

By way of contrast, the transformation of OC Transpo into a department of the new City of Ottawa appears not to have adversely affected efficiency or innovation. This seems to be due to two key differences with the British experience: first, OC Transpo is a 'hands-on' agency that must bear the consequences of its operational decisions; secondly, the Ottawa bus system is much smaller than the UK rail network, and therefore a more manageable size.

The most popular transit agency model is the semi-autonomous public authority: examples include the Toronto Transit Commission, Translink, the *Zürcher Verkehrsverbund* and Transport for London. Some of these organizations have strong political control: the TTC's board is made up entirely of elected councillors, while the the Cantonal minister for transport chairs the ZVV board, which also includes local government representatives. Others rely on professional directors of the kind one might expect on the board of a private company: the government of British Columbia recently introduced this system for the Translink board, while TfL's board, although chaired by the Mayor of London, is mainly made up of professionals.[26]

The real difference among agencies of this kind is the extent to which they operate services themselves or delegate operations to other bodies, including private firms. Although there is a clear tendency to separate tactical and operational functions, through the 'federation' approach of the ZVV or through private contracting, as in London, there remain important exceptions. The TTC serves a larger population than the ZVV and carries more passengers, but performs operations in-house to achieve efficiencies in timetabling and resource allocation that would not be possible with sub-contracting (see Chapter 5). Translink sub-contracts all its services, but mainly to subsidiary companies that it owns; some bus services are operated by the City of West Vancouver's transit department, and the private sector also has a role, mainly in para-transit. As Eliot Sclar reminds us (see Chapter 5), contracting out can save money and simplify workloads in appropriate cases, but when used unwisely, it can increase costs and lower service standards.

One reason for using the federation model instead of a single mega-operator is to simplify the task of unifying different transit systems across an urban region. This is the way the *Verkehrsverbund* concept developed in Germany, and it may well be the appropriate solution to integrating the efficient operations of the Toronto Transit Commission with the remaining public transport providers across the Greater Toronto Area.

The rule on operations seems to be horses for courses. There is no single correct answer, and the best solution will depend on local conditions, preferably chosen on the basis of a dispassionate comparison of the alternatives, rather than through top-down impositions like compulsory competitive tendering. The only universal principle is that the public body must control tactical planning, which rules out full privatization, whether through franchising or deregulation.

TAKING PUBLIC TRANSPORT SERIOUSLY

The other critical factor for public transport agency success is the transport policy environment. If public transport is treated as merely an adjunct to a car-dominated environment, for city commuters and the disadvantaged, or if inadequate funding is provided, or if public transport improvements are constantly undermined by expansion of the competing road system, then no amount of internal effectiveness and innovation will develop an optimal outcome. Effective public transport agencies are most likely to prosper when incentives for sustainable transport are complemented by disincentives for the automobile (see Chapter 3). And while this book argues that the role of urban density, in particular, has been overemphasized, it remains true that land-use planners can help or hinder public transport, particularly through their influence over the location and design of trip attractors such as employment, retailing and services.

If all these elements are in place, the next challenge is to actually design a public transport network that will provide anywhere-to-anywhere travel and reap the benefits of the network effect. Gregory Thompson noted in 2003 that the importance of transfer-based networks is not widely appreciated in the transport planning literature, with the result that little guidance is publicly available on planning such networks. When Gustav Nielsen wrote his HiTrans manuals in 2005, he also found that there was little published material to draw on. Nielsen's manuals have partly addressed this deficiency, as has Vukan Vuchic's *Urban Transit: Operations, Planning and Economics*, also published in 2005. With the exception of these two books, there is no publicly available material on the fundamentals of network planning, so the next chapter will provide a basic outline of the basic principles. Readers wanting more detailed information will find it in Nielsen's and Vuchic's books.

NOTES

1 Davison (2004, p260).
2 E.g. Ceder (2007, pp327–330); Balcombe et al (2004, chs 6 and 7).
3 Mees (2000, pp138–150); Nielsen (2005, pp84–93).
4 Thomson (1977, ch. 3, esp. p100).
5 Thompson and Matoff (2003).
6 www.nationalpark.ch/snp.html (accessed 30 August 2009); Sorupia (2007, ch. 5).
7 Yam (2008, p7); see also LTA (2008a, pp28–32, 38–40).
8 Hibbs (2005, p72).
9 Hibbs (2005, p65).
10 Cambridgeshire County Council (2005, p25).
11 ONS (2003, p288, table KS15), excluding 'working from home'.
12 Hensher (2007, p58).
13 Hensher (2008, p27).
14 Hibbs (2005, pp64–65).
15 Nash and Smith (2007), but see also Kain (2007) and Wolmar (2005).
16 National Rail (2008, p6).
17 Monbiot (2007, pp147–154). Monbiot justifies his preference for buses with a table showing that a nearly full coach produces 83% as much greenhouse gas per passenger as a 70% full train. The same figures suggest that if both vehicles were full the

emissions per train passenger would be lower. Monboit then suggests adding train-like on-board facilities to buses (2007, p151), lowering occupancies and increasing emissions per passenger to a level even further ahead of that for trains. But the real weakness with the analysis is that it compares present UK practice on a single-mode basis, rather than assessing the potential of an efficient multi-modal system.

18 Hensher (2007, p36) thinks Melbourne's regulator was 'quite possibly' captured.
19 Frankena (1982).
20 Barker and Robbins (1974, vol. II, ch. XVI).
21 Vuchic (2005, pp316–317).
22 Bratzel (1999).
23 Leuthi et al (2007); see also 'Padding prevents service improvements', *Modern Railways* October 2008, p3.
24 Brändli (1996, p15).
25 Pius XI (1931, par. 78).
26 Vuchic discusses selection of board members at (2005, pp300–301).

10

Planning a Network

Our customer wishes to set off from a place of his own choosing, travel quickly, comfortably, cheaply and in safety to his destination, and arrive there at a time set by himself; nothing else will do.

Professor Heinrich Brandli, Institute of Transport, ETH Zurich[1]

ENTHUSIASTS AND ECONOMISTS

Many books and reports dealing with public transport start from the perspective of the operator, or even the enthusiast, rather than the passenger. The tell-tale sign is an emphasis on technology – preferably advanced and exciting – and infrastructure, with the task of combining the different bits of technology and infrastructure in ways that serve people's travel needs either ignored or treated as uncomplicated. Typically, texts of this kind will begin by extolling the virtues of metros, busways, smart cards or light rail, depending on the preference of the writer, discuss different public transport modes and technologies separately, and conclude by demanding increased investment in the preferred solution. Inconvenient truths, such as the fact that the large increase in tram patronage in the City of Zurich during the 1980s (see Chapter 8) occurred on a fleet of vehicles dating mainly from the 1950s and 1960s, are glossed over or ignored entirely.

Conventional transport economists dismiss technology-based enthusiasts with a knowing smile. But their theories are no more useful to policy makers seeking a way out of automobile dominance than those of the train-, tram- and busway-spotters. The pre-eminent example of this approach is the UK Transport Research Laboratory's manual *The Demand for Public Transport*, originally published in 1980, but comprehensively revised in 2004.[2] The manual is so widely used it has become known as the 'Black Book', and reading it provides insight into a question that mystifies analysts outside the UK: why are local policy makers so determined to ignore the lessons from public transport success stories across the English Channel and the Atlantic?

The 2004 version of the Black Book is based on elasticities of demand, which, as the previous chapter showed, are easily employed to convince policy makers that substantive change is too difficult. A lengthy discussion of fare elasticities is followed by separate discussions of elasticities of demand for walking, in-vehicle and waiting times. A short section on interchanges suggests that these should be avoided at all costs. The effect of income is then analysed, with the conclusion that high incomes (as, for example in Zurich?) reduce the demand for local public transport. A final chapter discusses 'new public transport modes' – light rail, busways and park-and-ride – separately, just as the enthusiasts do.

At no point in the Black Book's 237 densely typed pages is any reference made to the network effect, pulse-timetabling, discounted 'environmental tickets' or any of the other innovations that have actually produced success in the cities where public transport is gaining ground at the expense of the car.[3] The emphasis on secondary sources, elasticities and mathematical equations produces a kind of fog that makes it hard to see the real world. So the high capital cost of Edmonton's light rail system is attributed to the fact that it 'was the first modern light rail system and therefore may have had high costs because of its innovative nature',[4] when a moderately enterprising secondary school student armed with Google could uncover the real reason in minutes: the main section was built underground, to subway/metro standards.

The overall impression the Black Book creates is that current British conditions are approaching the best of all possible worlds, and that no serious change is likely or even desirable.

BEYOND THE CONVENTIONAL APPROACH

Network planning starts at the opposite end of the spectrum. While it is important to make correct decisions about fare levels and technologies, it is next to impossible to do so unless the context for these decisions has been set through a planning process based on people's needs. Ideally, this would begin with a regional transport and land-use plan that sets serious targets for mode shift to more sustainable forms of transport, and backs these targets with appropriate institutions and resources. The public transport network is then planned to serve these goals, with decisions about fares and technology coming later in the process, not at the beginning.[5]

The type of public transport network provided will depend on the decisions made about system objectives. If public transport is treated as a supplement to the car for city centre commuters and the disadvantaged, then only a limited network will be provided: peak-period expresses and basic offerings at other times. But if the objective is to provide a real alternative, for reasons that have hopefully been made clear in the early chapters of this book, then public transport needs to match the 'anywhere to anywhere' service provided by the car.

Competing with the flexibility of the private car requires something that is hardly ever discussed in conventional public transport planning texts. It has been developed mainly by practising public transport planners in Europe and parts of North America, and largely ignored by academics, especially in the anglosphere. I have called it the 'network effect', a term adopted by Gustav Nielsen in his *HiTrans Guide* (2005); Gregory Thompson independently christened it the 'whole-system or network approach'.[6] A network of routes is provided, allowing passengers to travel between all parts of a city by transferring from one route, or line, to another, just as motorists navigate a road system by turning at intersections.

The key to the whole concept is transfers, as we saw with the discussion of Squaresville in the previous chapter. Conventional transport planning treats transfers as a barrier, but in network planning they are an opportunity. Transfers are the means to link what would otherwise be a collection of individual routes (Nielsen suggests using the term 'line' for this operational element of a network, and this usage will be followed in the rest of the book).

Transferring always involves some inconvenience for passengers, so the single most important principle of network planning is to reduce the inconvenience as much as possible. Naturally, this requires that transfers should be free, which means a fully multi-modal fare system, but network and timetable design are also critical. There are two basic conceptual approaches to creating a transfer-based public transport network: timed and random transferring.

The random approach can be seen on the Paris Metro, the Toronto Transit Commission's subway, tram and bus network, and trams in the City of Zurich. Frequent services are provided all day long on all lines in a 'grid' network that covers the whole service area, as illustrated in Figure 9.1C (with necessary adaptation to real-world cities that generally don't have perfect grid street and rail systems). Convenient transfers are possible in all directions at any place where two or more lines intersect.

The timed approach is found in suburban Zurich, Schaffhausen and some North American cities, as well as across the entire Swiss national rail and Postbus system. Rather than offering high frequencies at all times, different lines are timed to meet at designated transfer points, at intervals such as every 10, 15, 30 or (generally only in rural areas) even 60 minutes. Timed transfer networks tend to be laid out on a hub-and-spoke pattern, rather than a grid. This approach is less expensive to operate than a high-frequency random-transfer network, but harder to plan. It requires careful coordination of timetables, and reliable operations, since if one service arrives late at an interchange, the others must wait for it. The more interchange stations that are provided, the more complicated the process becomes. In suburban Zurich, all-directions transferring is only possible at a limited number of stations, such as Wetzikon (see Chapter 8); Schaffhausen's much smaller public transport network has a single interchange point.

The two approaches share many common features. They both rely on cross-subsidy, since similar service levels (frequencies and hours of operation) must be provided across the whole network; this requires a pooling of revenues. This in turn means that a single organization must handle fare pooling, as well as planning routes and timetables to produce an integrated network of services.

KEEPING IT SIMPLE

In both cases, the central challenge is to provide sufficiently high occupancies to support high system-wide service levels, on cross-suburban lines as well as radial lines, and to low-density as well as high-density areas. This challenge is met by offering a sparse, but high-quality, network comprised of relatively few lines operating at high service levels. As Gustav Nielsen says in his *HiTrans Guide*: 'the number of lines should be as few as possible in order to create an efficient, high quality main line system for the majority of public transport users.'[7]

A sparse network concentrates services, allowing higher frequencies and longer operating hours. It is also simple and stable, and thus easier for passengers to understand. Ease of understanding, or legibility, is not regarded as important in traditional public transport systems designed for regular commuters or 'captive' patrons, as it is assumed people will use the same services every day and become used to any quirks or complications. But region-wide networks are for everyone: regular users, occasional travellers, people visiting unfamiliar parts of the city, hikers and tourists. They must be stable and comprehensible, just like a road system. The model is networks like the Paris Metro and Zurich tram system, rather than the bewildering tangle of low-quality lines found in cities as diverse as Auckland, Canberra and Manchester.

This means that a public transport network should be comprised of fixed lines that follow the same routes, with the same stopping patterns, at all times. Special routes that only operate at peak hours, and separate night or weekend networks, should be avoided. If services are added at peak period, or thinned out at night, this should be done without disrupting the basic line pattern. A good example is provided by the suburban rail system, or *S-Tog*, of Copenhagen. There are seven main lines, and on most a mixture of express and stopping trains operates. The stopping patterns and even the departure times are the same all day long, every day of the year. On most routes 10-minute services are provided on weekdays and during shopping hours on Saturday; frequencies drop to 20 minutes at other times by the simple process of deleting every second train. Only two lines have additional trains in peak period, and these are slotted between the regular services without breaking the basic pattern. The entire system-wide map and timetable takes up a single, letter-sized sheet of paper.[8]

As well as making the network legible for passengers, a simple structure like that in Copenhagen creates opportunities to increase system reliability. Because only a limited number of service types are operated, recovery strategies can be devised to deal with disruptions such as signal failures or train breakdowns. Instead of the chaos that occurs in such situations on rail systems in places like Australia and the UK, a pre-arranged programme for restoring services and advising passengers can be swung into action. Recovery strategies can be recorded and refined using computer systems and even integrated with signalling and train control systems, as is occurring with the Swiss Federal Railways' Puls-90 programme.[9]

The temptation to depart from the principle of simplicity is strongest for bus planners, since buses have the flexibility to go anywhere there are suitable roads. Ten years ago, the operator of Canberra's bus system restructured its network following extensive consultation. One of its busiest inner-city lines was changed from a direct route following a sub-arterial road to a circuitous, meandering pattern. One deviation required two additional right and two additional left turns, adding up to five minutes to each trip. The change enabled buses to call at the door of the Canberra Youth Hostel, saving backpackers a 250m walk. Unfortunately, the main concerns of the young, fit hostellers had not been the walk to the bus stop, but infrequent services, early finishing times and confusion created by the operation of different night and weekend networks. The route change increased operating costs and deterred passengers frustrated at the twice-daily detour past the hostel. Frequencies were cut back even further, to once an hour for off-peak services, making the actual problem that was irritating hostellers worse. Recently, the deviation has been removed, leaving passengers with a less frequent version of the same service provided a decade ago.

So bus planners should design routes as if they were operating trams or trains, with simple, direct structures and as little duplication and overlap as possible. This involves following what Nielsen calls the 'one section one line' principle. Each corridor is provided with a single service; closely spaced and overlapping lines are avoided because, as the Toronto Transit Commission (TTC) says, 'parallel routes … split the potential demand [resulting] in many routes competing for the same passengers and no route attracting enough demand to warrant a higher frequency service'.[10]

When a number of routes converge on a single corridor, the same principle can be applied. While in theory, 20 bus routes running hourly down a joint corridor means a service every three minutes, in practice it means bewildered passengers. A single line running every five minutes would use less resources but provide a better service. This approach will often mean employing the 'trunk and feeder' model used in Curitiba and many other places. The main section is operated as a single line, using higher-capacity vehicles, while the outer sections are converted to feeders and operated with smaller, cheaper-to-run vehicles. This enables the trunk section to be served economically, avoiding vehicle congestion and saving resources, which can then be redeployed to provide higher service levels on the feeder routes.

In many networks, these feeder lines are designed to double as cross-suburban links, as for example with the TTC's bus network. Instead of simply connecting residential areas to trunk corridors, feeder lines can be designed to run across two or more corridors, transforming the hub-and-spoke pattern into something like a spider-web. 'In the multidestinational approach, suburban bus routes are neither parallel routes to the CBD nor specialized "feeder routes"... Rather, they are treated as general purpose routes that interlock with each other through transfers to make intrasuburban mobility possible, while also feeding passengers onto trunk routes or dispersing passengers from trunk routes'.[11] Carrying radial and cross-suburban passengers on the same service is one way of creating occupancy rates high enough to support good service levels.

The same principles of route design also mean resisting the temptation to provide off-route deviations, such as the one to the Canberra Youth Hostel discussed above. Such deviations delay through-passengers and increase operating costs and system complexity. Off-route destinations that are beyond walking distance from stops are accessed by transferring to connecting lines.

One exception to this rule is the need to provide direct access to rail or busway stations located on separate rights of way. Here the optimal solution is provided by the Toronto model, in which station locations are selected to allow surface routes to call at their entrances without leaving arterial roads; sometimes this involves separate roadways that bring buses and trams to station entrances without negotiating side-streets or difficult intersections. The same approach can also be used to serve substantial trip generators, like universities and shopping centres, without delaying through passengers. Small, relatively inexpensive sections of bus-only roadway can save many passenger- and bus-hours.

The focus on through routes and lines can be extended to city centres, which are often dominated by large on- or off-street terminals for bus lines. As well as wasting valuable land, these terminals prevent bus routes serving people who wish to travel from one part of the city centre to another. It is often better to link surface routes across the city centre, combining the functions of radial access and central distribution on a single line. This again allows increased efficiency and higher occupancy levels, avoiding the expense of dedicated 'city shuttle' type services. Good examples are provided by trams in Zurich, Toronto and Melbourne, and buses in Curitiba and Schaffhausen.

With a simple, efficient network in place, it will be easy to identify candidates for upgrading to higher standards, through express buses like Vancouver's B-Line, busways or rail. These will be the lines with high, and growing, patronage.

TIMED TO CONNECT

Conventional public transport timetabling has been 'demand-based', meaning that service frequencies are determined by existing patronage levels. If usage rises, service is added; if it falls, services are cut. The problem with this approach is that it tends towards decline: if patronage falls because services are no longer relevant to people's travel needs, the operator will cut frequencies further, exacerbating the problem. New demands will never be served, because the operator never provides the services that allow these demands to manifest themselves.

Under network planning, service provision is 'supply-based'. Timetables are designed to provide anywhere-to-anywhere travel throughout the day, even though this means some lines will be lightly loaded at particular times. Schaffhausen provides an excellent example, with 10-minute frequencies all day long on all major routes, and differences in patronage accommodated through different-sized vehicles. Instead of providing high service levels on a few trunk routes only, consistent service standards are offered across the entire network.

In a random-transfer network, frequencies must be high enough to enable minimal waiting times, or what Nielsen calls a 'forget the timetable' service. Somewhere between six and ten minutes is generally regarded as the threshold headway for this kind of network, although some systems extend this to 12 or even 15 minutes for low-demand routes and times (e.g. late evening). Vancouver's Translink sets an upper limit of 15 minutes for 'non-timed connections' in the inner part of its network, but most routes operate more frequently than this for most of the time.[12] Conversely, in Schaffhausen, where trips are short, all local routes are timed to connect at the central interchange even though 10 minute headways are provided at most times.

Timed transfer networks rely on what the Swiss call an integrated pulse-timetable. Departure times are the same all day long, and a 'clock-face' pattern is used – meaning one that repeats every hour, such as every 10, 15 or 30 minutes, and not 25, 40 or 90 minutes. If additional services are added in peak period, these are slotted in between the regular departures to avoid disrupting the basic pattern. For example, Copenhagen *S-Tog* trains leave Farum terminus, 20km north of the city centre at 6, 16, 26, 36 and so on past each hour. After 6:26 pm on weekdays, 3:46 pm Saturdays, and all day Sundays, the departures at 6, 26 and 46 past the hour are removed to give a 20-minute headway until the last departure at 12:16 am. Additional trains run in peak hour, leaving Farum at 7:01, 7:21 and every 20 minutes until 9:01 am.

Regular-interval, clock-face departures make the timetable easy to remember, partially compensating for lower frequencies than in the 'forget the timetable' approach. But the regular pattern also enables simultaneous scheduling of different routes at key interchanges, as seen at Wetzikon in Zurich in Chapter 8. On many well-run public transport systems, feeder buses are timed to connect with trains, but timed transferring extends this approach. If all train and bus lines that serve a key interchange point operate at the same frequency, then all can be scheduled to arrive together and wait a short time, enabling transfers between all rail and bus lines, before departing on the out-bound journey. This approach is adopted for rail and bus in Edmonton and Portland, for middle and outer suburban buses in Vancouver and, as we have seen, for buses in Schaffhausen, all modes in suburban Zurich, and for trains and PostBuses across Switzerland.[13]

It will not be practical to provide all-directions transferring at every interchange point, since if schedules are synchronized at one station, it is unlikely that the same trains and buses will arrive at the very next station simultaneously. So at minor interchanges, schedules are coordinated to ease transfers in the dominant direction of travel, generally to and from major centres of activity. This means that passengers transferring in other directions at minor interchanges may have longer waits, which underlines the importance of maximizing service frequencies even on timed-transfer-based networks.

In some large urban regions, such as Zurich and Vancouver, the timed and random transfer approaches are mixed. Frequent services and random transfers operate in the inner city, clockface timetables and timed transfers in outer areas. This raises the question of what happens where the two different service types meet up: for example, where Vancouver's 'forget-the-timetable' Skytrain meets outer suburban bus routes running every 15 or 30 minutes. Transferring from the bus to the train is easy, because frequent services mean minimal waiting, but 'outward' transfers can be a problem, as we saw in Chapter 7 in the case of Ottawa. The solution, as Vuchic points out, is to coordinate timetables and let passengers know which train is the one to take to connect with the local bus.[14] Unfortunately, this information is rarely provided, even in well run systems like Vancouver's.

The goal of the various network timetabling approaches is to minimize waiting times generally, but particularly the time required for transfers. The other requirement for quick transfers is well designed interchanges.

FIVE EASY STEPS: DESIGNING INTERCHANGES

The quality of interchange facilities varies enormously across public transport systems. Poor results are often, but not always, the result of insufficient investment. In cities where generous funding has not been accompanied by careful network planning, interchanges can become architectural or engineering monuments that do not actually serve their primary function – which is to speed transfers between services.

A striking example of this syndrome is the vast underground bus terminal in central Brisbane, built at a cost of hundreds of millions of dollars. The initial stage was built before the city's first busways under the city's biggest shopping mall, but is now mainly used by services from the South-East busway; in 2008, the terminal was extended under neighbouring King George Square, in conjunction with the opening of the first stage of the northern busway. Most routes that serve the interchange terminate there, reflecting Brisbane's history of operating radial buses in competition with trains (see Chapter 7). So anyone wishing to continue their journey must change.

Because Brisbane's busways operate on the 'direct service' principle, rather than employing transfers to higher capacity vehicles as in Curitiba, the terminal must accommodate large numbers of terminating buses. The facility is so complicated it is shown on two separate maps.[15] There are 28 platforms in all, separated by four bus roadways that cannot be crossed on the level. To change from one route to another, passengers must work out which stop the second service leaves from (no easy task!), ascend to the ground level shopping mall, locate the entrance to the second platform amidst the visual cacophony, then descend again. If a mistake is made, as often occurs, the process must be repeated. By the time the second stop is finally reached, the connecting bus is likely to have left, leaving a wait of up to an hour for the next service. Grown transport planners with PhDs have been reduced to gibbering wrecks by the frustration of it all.

The goal of interchange design under network planning is to make the distance covered between connecting services as short as possible: Nielsen recommends 'a five-step distance [with] protection from the weather in a clean and nice environment'.[16] It will often be less expensive to do this than to build a monument that wins architectural or engineering awards.

Toronto is the benchmark for rail–bus and rail–tram interchanges, with 'free-body' transfers at most subway stations outside the CBD. Trams and buses are actually brought inside the ticket gates on special roadways, and stop at the top of the escalators serving the station platforms. Similar arrangements are provided at the main railway station in the German city of Freiburg,[17] and at key stations on the new Southern Railway in Perth, Western Australia (although in Perth transferring passengers must still show tickets to bus drivers).

The ideal arrangement for transferring train passengers has different services pulling in on opposite sides of the same (island) platform, as at Wetzikon. This pattern is not always easy to arrange, but some rail rapid transit system designers have gone to great trouble and expense to provide cross-platform transfers at junction stations; examples include the Montreal Metro (Lionel-Groulx station) and Hong Kong MRT (Prince Edward/Mong Kok).[18]

Interchange points for bus-to-bus (and tram-to-tram) transfers are by far the most numerous, since every intersection where two or more lines meet is an interchange. This fact is often ignored, particularly in cities without a commitment to network planning. For example, Melbourne's private tram franchisee has commenced a programme to speed services by reducing the number of stops in the CBD. This involves moving tram stops away from intersections to mid-block locations, where they provide less disruption to automobiles, and eliminating stops at cross-streets without tram lines along them. The result is that tram-to-tram interchanges now involve up to 200m extra walking, while changes to and from buses, which operate along the cross-streets where stops have been removed entirely, are even more unattractive.

By contrast, in Toronto and Vancouver buses and trolley-buses stop twice at major intersections, once on the 'approach' side and again on the 'departure' side.[19] If such stops are provided on both lines that cross at an intersection, passengers can transfer in any direction without walking more than a few steps, and without crossing roads. Providing a similar level of convenience for transferring tram passengers is more complicated, because trams usually run down the middle of streets. There are many excellent examples, in cities from Zurich to Gothenburg, of convenient, attractive tram-to-tram interchanges, generally involving total or partial pedestrianization of intersections where major routes cross.[20]

Naturally, the best networks provide clear and comprehensive information at interchange points, enabling passengers to easily ascertain the transfer options available to them, where to walk and how long they will have to wait.

THE PARK AND RIDE PROBLEM

Park and ride was an important part of the 'balanced transport' compromise dating from the 1960s. Instead of driving all the way to the centre of congested cities, suburban commuters were encouraged to drive to rail or bus stations and board express services bound for the centre. Some historic towns in the UK have used a similar approach to accommodate visitors travelling by car while keeping their centres free of parked vehicles.

Some public transport systems rely extensively on access by car, especially by residents of low-density areas. Interestingly, reliance on car access is usually inversely related to the system's overall success in creating mode shift. Melbourne's rail system has nearly 40,000 park and ride spaces, three times the 14,000 spaces on Toronto's subway, but Toronto carries nearly twice as many rail passengers.[21] When a 400-space bus park-and-ride station was opened in Melbourne in 2003 as part of a freeway extension, planners proudly pointed out that it soon filled. But a subsequent survey found that literally 98 per cent of commuters had previously walked to their local stop and taken the bus for the whole trip: in other words, park and ride had increased the number of car trips, not reduced them![22]

The problem with park and ride is the same as with the balanced transport compromise generally. It does not provide a real alternative to the car, and will not play a major role in moving us beyond the automobile age. Park and ride is popular for peak period travel to city centres, but is rarely used for off-peak and non-central journeys. If provided on a large scale, it wastes valuable land around stations that could otherwise be used for transit-oriented development, as well as adding to traffic levels in rail-oriented sub-centres. Finally, cold engine starts mean that short park and ride trips often produce almost as much pollution as would be the case if the traveller continued all the way to their destination: this is particularly so for schemes operating on the edge of city centres or small towns.

There will always be public transport patrons who use cars to access the network, because they live in very remote rural areas with limited service, or simply dislike walking to the bus stop. Some parking needs to be provided for these passengers, lest they drive all the way to their destination. But park and ride should be a supplementary access mode, with the main emphasis being on feeder services, walking and cycling (more on this in the next chapter). The best place for public transport users to leave their cars is at home.

NETWORK-FRIENDLY FARES

Transfer-based networks require transfer-friendly fares. This means a multi-modal system in which passengers pay for the distance travelled, usually through a zonal system, rather than the number of transfers they make. All tickets, with the possible exception of those for very short trips, should be multi-modal, not just special daily or periodical 'travelcards' (as they are called in the UK). Multi-modal single tickets will usually be valid across the specified number of zones for a designated time, generally between one and two hours.

Multi-modal fare systems dovetail with an emphasis on discounted periodical tickets, such as the monthly environmental passes in Swiss cities like Basle, Zurich and Schaffhausen. Most regular travellers use these tickets, which speeds boarding and encourages residents to rely on public transport for a wider range of trips than just the journey to work. The periodical ticket approach also helps deal with disruptions to service, which occasionally happen even in Switzerland. Instead of storming off to the garage to get the car, people will typically wait until their monthly ticket has expired. As long as disruptions are very rare, as they should be in well-run systems, by the time the monthly expires, most people will have forgotten that their train was cancelled weeks earlier.

Zurich and Vancouver are both renowned for extending the environmental periodical ticket to university students. Newspapers, banks and even churches target university students, because they are at a stage of life where long-lasting habits are formed. Discount schemes like the Vancouver U-Pass, which provides every student with a semester ticket as part of their student fee, are aimed at cultivating a life-long public transport riding habit. They have the added benefit of eliminating fare evasion by a population that in many cities forms the largest group of evaders.

Some commentators advocate going further than this and cutting fares to zero. There have been a few experiments with free travel, but little mode shift has been achieved. The reason free public transport will not take us beyond the automobile age is that mode choice is influenced more by service quality than by fare levels. Although, as we have seen, discounted periodical tickets can help bring about mode shift, when they do so they generate additional revenue, partly defraying the costs. That's why places like Zurich and Schaffhausen combine heavy discounts for monthly tickets with high cost-recovery and low subsidies per trip.

This kind of 'win–win' outcome is not possible with free travel: if it generates additional patronage, the result is simply a further increase in public subsidies. When governments decide to offer free travel, often to special groups like children or pensioners, they are usually signalling that they have run out of ideas for addressing the real problems. This was certainly the case when the UK government announced free nation-wide off-peak travel for people aged over 60 in 2005 – after effectively abandoning its 1998 transport White Paper, with its ambitious goals for reductions in car use. The substantial cost of the free travel scheme, which commenced in 2008, would have been better spent improving services.

Multi-modal fares must be distinguished from technologies like smart cards, which are usually introduced as an alternative to free transfers: Hong Kong and Singapore pioneered smart cards to preserve their single-mode fare systems, by making it simpler to collect separate fares from transferring passengers. Singapore is now moving to a multi-modal system, as we saw in Chapter 3, but smart card technology has little role in the move.

Indeed, some cities that are adopting smart cards are using them to make multi-modal journeys more difficult. Predictably, Melbourne is in the vanguard, with its new smartcard system requiring passengers to validate on boarding and alighting every vehicle. This means that someone who uses a bus to reach the station, then a train, then another bus or a tram, will have to validate 12 times on a return journey. Again, the rule should be that technologies are chosen after network planning, rather than as an alternative to it.

MULTI-MODAL MARKETING

When Melbourne's trams were taken over by private franchisees in 1999, the first thing the general public noticed was a change of colour scheme – from the traditional green and gold, the Australian national colours, to grey. The change was much criticized, not least because it made trams harder to see, as they now matched the colour of the roadway. One wag even quipped 'I thought that everything was going to be grey under socialism, not free enterprise'. But the real reason the change was a retrograde step is that it made the lack of integration between modes official: Melbourne's trams, trains and buses all carry different liveries, emphasizing the fact that they don't link together to form a multi-modal network.

Of course, it might be argued that Melbourne's public transport operators are at least being honest in not marketing their services as if they were a network. Marketing must be engaged at all stages of network planning: there is no point bringing marketers in at the end of the process and asking them to 'sell' a sub-standard product. When the Auckland Regional Transport Authority tried this a few years back, as we saw in Chapter 5, the authority's advisers told it the existing deregulated system, with its muddle of different companies, timetables and liveries, simply could not be marketed. The principles of network planning are designed to produce a system that 'markets itself' through simplicity and ease of use, but this does not mean that efforts should stop there.

Common liveries and 'branding' for vehicles, stops, maps and timetables help passengers appreciate that a public transport system really does work as a network, as well as aiding practical matters like distinguishing regular services from tour buses and chartered vehicles. Yet in many big cities, such as Sydney, it is not possible to even obtain a map showing all the public transport services that operate. With a single agency in charge of tactical planning, the system can, and should, look as if it was all operated by the public body, even when private firms are used as sub-contractors. The sense of coherence is enhanced by measures like carrying out timetable revisions on a planned cycle, with changes introduced simultaneously across the whole system rather than on an ad-hoc basis (a planned cycle also makes it easier to ensure that timed connections are maintained).

The concern for quality should flow across to general system ambience. Deserted, poorly maintained stations and interchanges with infrequent visits by random patrols of armed security guards do not inspire a sense of public confidence. This is why, as we saw in Chapter 8, the ZVV introduced conductors on late-evening trains, and why passengers without tickets are required to pay a 'special fare' rather than fined. Because the public transport network is intended to be used by everyone, rather than just transit captives, nothing can be allowed to appear punitive or second-rate.

PUBLIC TRANSPORT NETWORKS FOR RURAL AREAS

The network effect can even make a difference in rural areas, where it has been widely assumed that public transport has no role at all, other than providing a basic service for the disadvantaged. In this context, 'rural' does not mean outer suburban or exurban, but small towns and villages – the British government uses a threshold of 10,000 residents – that are not part of the commuter-shed of a major city.

Peter White has provided a portrait of public transport in one such area, the municipal district of East Lindsey in Lincolnshire, in successive editions of his book *Public Transport*. East Lindsey has 130,000 residents spread over 1760km^2 in a series of towns and villages. The population is growing rapidly, as the district is popular with retirees. The largest settlements are Louth, with a population of 14,000, and the seaside resort of Skegness, which has 19,000. Skegness is the only town served by rail, and the trip to London takes around three hours.

To say that public transport is marginal would be an understatement: it is used by only 3 per cent of workers, a lower share than in Los Angeles. Thanks to localized employment, a healthy 21 per cent walk or cycle, but 73 per cent travel by car. Thanks partly to the large number of elderly residents, 20 per cent of households are without cars.[23] Tripmaking rates are not available for East Lindsey, but across the whole of Lincolnshire, which has 647,000 residents, the average was 23 bus trips per person in 2004/2005.[24]

Life is not easy for people dependent on East Lindsey's public transport, even if those aged over 60 can now travel for free outside peak hours. Services have declined for decades, trapped in a classic vicious cycle with falling patronage. In the last decade, the county and municipal councils have begun restoring services, assisted by special rural transport grants from the national government. But the councils are hamstrung by deregulation: for example, as soon as a service becomes 'profitable' (with concession reimbursement), operators will register it as a commercial route, preventing it cross-subsidizing emerging or feeder routes.

At White's most recent portrait, around the time of the 2001 census, only one bus route in the whole municipality ran at all on Sundays – a council-initiated 'Interconnector' between Skegness and the county seat of Lincoln. Many did not run on Saturdays either. Smaller towns and villages often received a single trip a day, or even less, with some seeing one bus a week. Since White's report, the councils have added further Interconnect routes between major towns, with the result that Louth now has five buses on Sundays (four in winter). However, since formal network planning is illegal under Britain's deregulated regime, connections between routes are poor, and buses do not meet trains at Skegness either. People relying on public transport have a limited choice of destinations and an extremely limited choice of times.[25]

Car-less residents of East Lindsey would count themselves lucky, however, by comparison with their counterparts in Australia. In *A Very Public Solution*, I described the situation on the North Coast of New South Wales, where 213,000 people are spread over an area the size of Lincolnshire. The region borders the famous Gold Coast and draws a torrent of tourists to resorts like Byron Bay and Ballina. Most are 'backpackers' drawn by the region's natural beauty; the same qualities have attracted many residents, making the region the 'alternative lifestyle' capital of Australia. Byron (Bay) Shire is the only council in the nation with a Greens majority.

Visitors without cars, low-income, environmentally aware locals and students attending the local university in Lismore create a large potential market for region-wide public transport. But the North Coast is impossible to get around without a car. There are a couple of buses a day to Sydney and Brisbane (the daily train to Sydney was withdrawn in 2004), and a few local services used mainly by school children. There is much commuting between the region's towns, which are between 10 and 40km apart, and at the 2001 census, the share of workers walking and cycling was much lower than in East Lindsey, at 8 per cent. Less than 2 per cent used public transport, leaving 87 per cent travelling by car.[26]

The absence of public transport is graphically demonstrated every Sunday, at the community markets held in villages like Nimbin and The Channon. Thousands of locals and tourists descend on stalls selling organic food, handcrafts and 'wellbeing' products, showing their support for recycling, self-sufficiency and environmental awareness generally. As there is no public transport, everyone comes by car, creating traffic jams extending for miles, and covering every available surface with parked vehicles.

There are no serious proposals to change any of this. A decade ago, the Lismore Council sought advice from Brisbane-based transport experts, who told them not to bother with public transport: there wasn't enough demand.[27] In 2008, Byron Shire released a bike plan.

Rural public transport need not be as bad as in East Lindsey, let alone the NSW North Coast. We have already looked at rural Sternenberg, in the far corner of Canton Zurich, and the small town of Schaffhausen, but for somewhere really remote we should visit the Swiss canton of Graubunden.

Graubunden has a population of 187,000 scattered across 7105km², about the same area as Lincolnshire or the NSW North Coast. A quarter of the canton's residents live in or around the capital, Chur; the rest are scattered across villages of a few hundred or a few thousand residents, and tiny hamlets. Of the canton's 206 municipalities, 29 have fewer than 100 residents – but all of them are provided with regular public transport every day of the year.[28]

The Swiss Federal Railways (SBB) connects Chur to the rest of Switzerland, but local transport is provided by the Rhaetian Railway (*Rhatische Bahn*, or RhB), owned jointly by the canton and federation, Postbus Auto, and municipal operators in Chur and a few larger towns. The cantonal government provides the subsidies that support the system, and ensures that it operates as a network. The careful network planning is on display at the main station in Chur, where SBB and RhB trains leave from adjacent platforms, connected directly by escalator to the Postbus terminal on the next level, all adjacent to the *Stadtbus Chur* (Chur City-bus) terminal in the *bahnhofplatz* at the front door of the station.[29]

Hourly services are provided all day on RhB and Postbus corridors, with less frequent bus links to hamlets of under 100 people. For example, the village of Lu, in the Val Mustair, is like a smaller, remoter version of Sternenberg (see Chapter 1), located up a mountain path off the main valley road. The whole municipality has only 62 residents, but they receive eight minibus services a day (seven in winter, five on Sundays), each of which connects at the valley village of Fuldera (population 115) with an hourly service to the regional centre of Zernez (population 959). At Zernez, timed connections are available to hourly RhB trains that in turn connect at other interchanges to the rest of the Canton, and other parts of Switzerland.

If these arrangements sound reminiscent of Zurich, this is no coincidence. Canton Graubunden sought advice from the ZVV when, in the mid-1990s, it restructured its public transport to create a more effective network.

Annual public transport use in Graubunden equated to 146 trips per head in 2007 – higher than in any Australian city, and above the rate in any British urban area other than London and possibly Tyneside – but a third of these trips are made by tourists. Tourists provide more than a third of the revenue, because locals benefit from discounted periodical tickets like those in Zurich and Schaffhausen; however, nobody travels for free. At the 2000 census, 19 per cent of Graubunden's workforce travelled by public transport, 21 per cent walked, 9 per cent cycled and 50 per cent went by car. For travel to school, the shares were 31 per cent for public transport (about a quarter by school bus, three-quarters by regular buses and trains), 51 for walking, 13 for cycling and only 4 per cent for travel by car.[30]

Graubunden may not yet have left the automobile age behind, but public transport there provides a real alternative to the car. The integrated rail and bus network supports, and is supported by, high rates of walking and cycling, especially for shorter non-work trips. This close relationship between public transport and the only truly sustainable modes of travel is critically important if the environmental damage created by automobile dominance is to be reduced.

NOTES

1   Brandli (1990, p132).
2   Balcombe et al (2004); Webster and Bly (1980).
3   The closest is a brief, inconclusive mention of 'simplified networks' in Balcombe et al (2004, p99), sandwiched between much longer discussions of dial-a-bus and community buses.
4   Balcombe et al (2004, p140).
5   Vuchic (1999, pp82–87).
6   Thompson and Matoff (2003, p311).
7   Nielsen (2005, p106).
8   www.dsb.dk/Find-og-kob-rejse/Indland/koreplaner/ (accessed 30 August 2009).
9   Leuthi et at (2007).
10   TTC (1990, p9).
11   Thompson and Matoff (2003, p298).
12   Translink (2004, p20).
13   Vuchic (2005, pp224–234) discusses timed transfer networks in section 4.5.
14   Vuchic (2005, pp216–217).
15   www.translink.com.au/maps.php#interchange
16   Nielsen (2005, p113).
17   Illustrated at Nielsen (2005, p100).
18   See Vuchic (2005, pp220–223).
19   E.g. Translink (2004, p32).
20   See Nielsen (2005, pp100–101).
21   See also Mees (2000, pp231–233). Passenger and parking numbers in this discussion are for urban rail only.
22   Two of my students uncovered the results by telephoning the bus company; the survey report has since disappeared.
23   ONS (2003, tables KS1, 15 and 17).
24   Lincolnshire County Council (2006, p10).
25   White (2002, pp142–143); Lincolnshire County Council (2008).
26   ABS (2003, table B1; table W18 – figures compiled on the same basis as for Table 4.1 in Chapter 4).
27   Mees (2000, pp281–283).
28   Statistics from Graubunden (2008); this section draws on E. Sorupia (2007, ch. 5); Petersen (forthcoming).
29   See station plan at: http://mct.sbb.ch/mct/infra_services-uebersicht-bahnhofplaene-chur-a4.pdf (accessed 30 August 2009).

30 Trip rate from Graubunden (2008, p13); mode shares from Swiss Federal Statistical Office (SFSO), 2000 Census 'pendler' tables A2A and A2E, Graubunden, Kantone (18).

11

Every Transit User
is Also a Pedestrian

WALKING AND PUBLIC TRANSPORT: COMPETITORS OR ALLIES?

Increasing the use of public transport is not enough to make urban transport environmentally sustainable. Trains, buses and trams produce greenhouse gases and other pollutants, even if these are emitted from the power station instead of the tailpipe. Increased patronage only offers environmental benefits when it reduces car travel – provided passengers are carried at sufficiently high occupancy rates. If patronage gains come at the expense of walking or cycling, or because overall travel has risen, then environmental problems are increased, not reduced. Some free travel and park-and-ride schemes have produced increases in ridership while worsening environmental outcomes, as we saw in the previous chapter.

The only completely sustainable forms of travel are walking and cycling. Increases in cycling can impose small financial costs for infrastructure and parking, and increased risk to pedestrians (as discussed below, cyclists occasionally injure and even kill pedestrians). But more cycling will not increase pollution or the demand for oil, and will even improve overall fitness levels.

Walking produces similar benefits and no costs at all, whether it comes at the expense of the car or not. Indeed, medical practitioners and researchers have been largely responsible for the recent revival of interest in walking: transport planners have traditionally paid even less attention to walking than to public transport and cycling. Walking is now seen as an important part of the response to the declines in fitness, and associated health risks, resulting from sedentary lifestyles. Increased walking can improve health as well as the urban and global environment.

Unfortunately, in most places the trend has been to less walking, not more. The UK's National Travel Survey found that walking trip rates fell by 16 per cent in the ten years to 2005, following steady declines in previous decades.[1] Even in Zurich, as we saw in Chapter 8, walking is declining for trips to work, although it remains very high for school travel.

Precise rates and trends are difficult to estimate, because most travel surveys either ignore walking or understate it. Some explicitly exclude walking, while others omit short trips (e.g. under a kilometre), most of which are made on foot. Travel surveys that count all travel often miss short walking trips because respondents don't remember them. Careful use of travel diaries is needed to record all these trips. When this was done in Melbourne in the mid-1990s, it appeared that there was twice as much walking as in other Australian cities: in fact, the difference really showed that the other cities' surveys were missing half of all walking trips. Many surveys categorize trips on a 'main mode' basis rather than counting each stage separately: a walk to the tram stop, followed by a tram ride, then another walk to the destination will be recorded as 'tram'. Finally, many surveys combine the number and length of trips to produce 'passenger-kilometre' figures – making walking trips, which are much shorter than car, public transport and even cycle trips, appear insignificant.

The importance of walking is usually underestimated, but the level of under-statement varies from one survey to another, making it difficult to track trends over time and to compare different cities and countries. In this book, I have focused on trips to work and school, which people usually remember, and surveys usually report on a comparable basis. These figures reduce the difficulties of cross-city comparison, but need to be studied closely to reveal the true importance of walking. For example, as Chapter 8 reported, 66 per cent of people living and working in the City of Zurich travel to work by public transport; only 10 per cent walk, while another 6 per cent cycle. But virtually all the public transport users walk to the tram, train or bus stop, so the share of workers walking for at least part of their work journey is more like 76 per cent.

There has been little research into the relationship between public transport and walking, the main exception being two reports from the British-based academic and consultant Carmen Hass-Klau.[2] The two modes can interact in different ways.

The first is as competitors: high-quality public transport will attract some people who would otherwise walk, which means an increase in pollution and greenhouse emissions. Mediocre public transport and low car ownership are significant factors behind the relatively high rates of walking in many UK cities, but this is hardly the best way to promote walking. It is inequitable and unsustainable, since poor public transport will drive increases in car ownership as incomes rise, ultimately producing declines in walking.

Walking can support public transport, since as Ruedi Ott, head of traffic planning at the Zurich City Council says, 'every public transport user is also a pedestrian'. Therefore, 'if people no longer wish to leave their homes on foot, whether because of unattractive footpaths, pointless detours, pollution caused by emissions, security problems, or because they feel that, as pedestrians, they are not treated as participants in traffic in their own right, it will not be possible to promote the use of public transport instead of the car.'[3] Making life easier for pedestrians will also encourage public transport use.

Public transport can in turn support walking. Because every transit user is a pedestrian, public transport trips generate walking trips – except in systems that rely heavily on park-and-ride – as we saw above in the case of Zurich. But high quality public transport also promotes walking indirectly.

The first way it does this is by reducing car ownership. Hass-Klau's research in Europe found that even when income, family type and other factors are corrected for, high quality public transport lowered car ownership levels by about 9 per cent on average, with bigger falls in some cities. The second way public transport influences walking is more subtle, but it may be more important. As far as I am aware, it has been the subject of no systematic research at all.

WALKING AND HABIT FORMATION

A very high share of trips, even in car-dominated cities, are short enough to be made on foot. This applies especially to non-work trips such as the journey to school. But in most urban areas in English-speaking countries, only a small share of these short trips are in fact made on foot. As concern about pollution, greenhouse emissions and sedentary lifestyles has grown, a range of programmes has been developed to deal with the problem of short car trips. Social marketing campaigns with names like Travelsmart and school-based programmes such as the 'walking school bus' attack the problem by persuading urban dwellers to change their behaviour.

The assumption behind the 'behaviour change' approach is that people would stop driving short distances if only they were better informed. If this sounds a little patronizing, that may be part of the appeal: there is a long history of campaigns to encourage virtuous behaviour among the masses, dating back at least to the temperance movement of a century ago. Rather than change the reality, we should change people's attitudes. Naturally, the same approach is attractive to governments that don't want to change the substantive realities of transport policy. Is it a coincidence that behaviour change is generously funded in Australia and the UK, but plays little or no role in Scandinavia and Switzerland?

Encouraging results have been reported from behaviour change trials. Residents who have accepted Travelsmart literature, and schools with walking buses, all say that there is now much more walking and less driving than before. Unfortunately, these reports cannot be relied on as indicators that genuine, lasting change has taken place, for two reasons. First, it is rare to see follow-up surveys taken to see whether changes in behaviour outlast the original programme. One of the few cases where this was done is the British city of York. Follow-up surveys showed that 'the intervention was successful initially in inducing behavioural change but behaviour returned back to normal levels of travel 12 months later.'[4]

The second problem is that behaviour change studies are set up in ways that almost guarantee inaccurate results. It is a commonplace of the medical and social scientific literature that results obtained under such circumstances will be unreliable because of the 'good subject effect'. Participants in experiments want to help the experiment succeed, by giving the 'right' answer. If it is made clear at the outset that a particular result is not just correct but morally and environmentally so, then this result will be reported whether or not it really occurred. The participants aren't being dishonest; they are just trying to help.[5]

Sources uncontaminated by the 'good subject effect', such as censuses and national travel surveys, produce less encouraging results. The Australian and British cities that have seen the most intensive applications of behaviour change programmes are precisely those in which walking is either minimal or in decline, or both. The European cities where walking is a major travel mode are those where behaviour change programmes have not been used. Nobody in Zurich has ever seen a walking school bus, but only 3 per cent of students across the whole canton travel to school by car. In Canton Graubunden the share is only 4 per cent, one point higher than the figure for Canton Schaffhausen, where 49 per cent of students walk, 17 per cent cycle and 30 per cent use public transport. Neither canton has seen a walking school bus either.[6]

So why is car use so low, and walking and cycling so high, for education trips in these Swiss cantons? The trends apply in suburbs and rural areas, not just in inner cities, so density can't be the explanation. Nor can the extensive pedestrian priority measures found in Swiss inner cities explain the high walking rates of suburban students, although they doubtless help, as do other measures like lower speed limits. The answer lies elsewhere.

Transport planners and researchers often forget that most people are not very interested in transport. They have lives, jobs, friends and families to worry about: transport is simply a means of reaching them. So economic analyses that assume every traveller performs a cost–benefit analysis of the competing modes before setting out on each journey may be as far off the mark as behaviour change literature that wants people to think about global warming or even fitness before doing so. We are all creatures of habit.

People in car-dominated environments can lose the habit of walking. In large sections of Australian, Canadian, US and British suburbia many residents would struggle to recall the last time they left home on foot; the activities of leaving the house and getting into the car have merged. Pious exhortations to walk more for the good of one's own health or that of the globe may make some people guilty enough to change their own, or their children's, travel mode for a while, but without the reinforcement of habitual walking, change is unlikely to last. Just as the children of smokers are more likely to smoke themselves, so the children of households where all adult travel is made by car are likely to graduate quickly from the school bus to the automobile.

Recent work by Dutch medical researchers – significantly, not transport planners – confirms the critical importance of habit. A study of cycling rates found that habit was more influential than good intentions. The researchers concluded:

Health education efforts to increase physical activity levels have com-
monly used persuasive communication strategies in which the target
population is provided with information on, for instance, the health
benefits of regular activity … [these] approaches may have limited value
for strongly habitual behaviours… Any behaviour that can be performed
on a regular basis in a stable context is likely to become habitual …
[walking] may also become habitual rather than intentional.[7]

The Dutch researchers did not discuss in detail the alternative approaches that would respond to the importance of habit, but did note that 'policy changes at the macro level' are likely to be required.

Here, then, we have the key. Something needs to happen to the substantive reality of transport policy to make walking a natural, habitual activity. Provision of a comprehensive, high-quality public transport network does this, by creating large numbers of walking trips to and from stops and stations. Even in suburban and rural parts of Canton Zurich, it is rare to find a household where nobody uses public transport. Having acquired the habit of walking to the bus stop, people then walk to other local destinations such as schools and shops.

Comprehensive public transport promotes walking even in urban environments that would otherwise discourage it. The 'middle suburbs' of Toronto, the outer sections of the City of Toronto, present a hostile environment for pedestrians. Designed by developers in the 1950s and 1960s in accordance with modernist ideas derived from Le Corbusier, these suburbs feature cul-de-sac street systems, large surface car parks and no corner stores. Main roads are lined by the back fences of houses, and drive-in shopping malls.[8] Yet huge numbers of pedestrians negotiate this forbidding landscape to reach the Toronto Transit Commission's high-quality arterial bus routes. By contrast, the equivalent areas of Melbourne were largely subdivided between the 1880s and 1920s, and feature 'traditional' designs with straight streets and plenty of corner shops. But hardly anyone walks and most corner shops have closed for lack of custom. This is not an argument for continuing with pedestrian-unfriendly designs, but it does show that high-quality public transport can generate walking trips in the most unlikely places.

This is why high rates of public transport use are generally accompanied by higher rates of walking, as we saw in Chapters 4 and 8. While high-quality public transport may suppress walking by offering attractive competition for short trips, it also promotes walking by helping create a walking habit in households. It appears that the second trend greatly outweighs the first, with the happy result that walking and public transport can reinforce one another, working as allies in the move beyond the automobile age.

CYCLING AND PUBLIC TRANSPORT:
THE LEGACY OF THE WHITE BIKE

The situation with cycling is more complex. We do not see the same happy coincidence we saw with walking: higher cycling rates are usually accompanied by lower public transport use, and often reduced walking as well. In Australia, cycling is positively correlated with car use, at least for travel to work: cycling rates are highest where car use is highest. Sydney and Brisbane, which have the lowest rates of car use, also have the lowest cycling rates (see Table 4.1).

This bad news may come as a surprise, given that many commentators regard cycling as the epitome of sustainable transport. It certainly generates more excitement than walking, despite catering for fewer urban trips, even in cities hailed as cycling models (this is often overlooked because surveys understate walking). Unlike walking, cycling is a hobby as well as a mode of transport, and for some people it is more than that.

The humble bicycle played a central role in countercultural movements of the 1960s, beginning with the Provos, a surrealist-style group operating in Amsterdam. The Provos announced a series of 'white plans' covering everything from childcare to policing. The most famous was the White Bike plan, which called for the city council to provide thousands of free bikes, painted white and scattered around the city, as an alternative to cars. The Provos staged a publicity stunt to promote the idea, painting ten bikes white and leaving them unlocked on city streets. The council confiscated them and the proposal came to nothing.[9]

Despite the lack of results, the White Bike concept became a legend among countercultural movements, and it was widely believed that there had been thousands of white bikes in Amsterdam. The legend was reinforced when Ivan Illich anointed the bicycle as the ideal urban transport mode in his 1974 manifesto *Energy and Equity*. Transport problems could be solved with simple, do-it-yourself measures: like the car in the 1920s (see Chapter 2), the bicycle would avoid the need for messy collective action or planning. University of Toronto philosopher Joseph Heath argues that some forms of cycling activism are 'an individualized and basically apolitical environmentalism' that evades the fact that urban transport is a classic instance of a 'collective action problem'.[10]

Copenhagen actually installed a White-Bike-style scheme in 1995, and just as in Amsterdam the publicity has been out of all proportion to the results. Copenhagen has about 1500 'City Bikes', and surveys show that they are used 'primarily by tourists and young men', for short trips that would otherwise be made on foot. As a result, 'the City Bike adds nothing to the cycle traffic of Copenhagen.'[11] Yet, in a development that could have been scripted by surrealists, over a dozen other cities have been inspired to instal similar schemes.

The main legacy of the surrealist White Bike seems to be a preference for stunts and myth-making over collective action and planning, and a disdain for the unpleasant realities of empirical evidence. When the results of the 2006 Australian census were released, the country's three main broadsheet papers all led their coverage with the story that cycling rates had increased. And indeed they had: cycling numbers across the country's seven capital cities had jumped by nearly 13,000 since the 2001 census (to 1.1 per cent of the workforce). But nobody reported the much larger increase of 32,000 in the number who walked to work, or the 72,000 additional public transport travellers – let alone the fact that the numbers travelling by car had increased by 312,000.[12]

Tim Pharoah, a strong advocate of cycling and walking, points out that more sustainable modes can compete with each other as well as with the car. Just as there is no environmental benefit if increased public transport patronage comes at the expense of walking or cycling, there is no gain if cycling rises at the expense of walking, or because people are cycling for recreation (although there may be health benefits). He offers the example of Munster, Germany, where cycling's share of trips rose from 25 to 31 per cent between 1982 and 1990, exactly matching a fall in walking from 13 to 7 per cent. Car use remained unchanged at 55 per cent, as did public transport, with only 7 per cent of the travel market.[13] The average resident made 73 public transport trips in 1990, a lower rate than in many Canadian, Australian and US cities. The low usage rate reflected relatively poor service. Following the closure of Munster's trams in the 1950s, bus routes became less frequent and more complicated, even incorporating a separate 'night network' operating after 9:00 pm. Since then, public transport has been improved, and the trip rate has risen to 117, higher than in most Australian, US or British cities, but still less than half the rate in Schaffhausen and a seventh the rate in Zurich City.[14] Munster has attracted (and deserves) much praise for its excellent cycling facilities, and even proclaims itself a 'model city', but it is not yet a model of sustainable urban transport.[15]

So when one hears that an increase in cycling has been achieved or proposed, the question should be: was this at the expense of the car? The two cycling capitals of Britain are the cities of Oxford and Cambridge. While Oxford often wins the University Boat Race, its traditional rival wins the bike race hands down. Cycling accounts for 28 per cent of work trips in Cambridge, compared with 16 per cent in Oxford. But travel to work by car is almost identical in the two cities, at 45.7 per cent in Oxford and 45.0 in Cambridge – because Oxford has more walking (16 versus 15 per cent) and more than twice as much public transport use (20 versus 9 per cent). And since there is little cycling outside the central urban areas, car use across the whole of Cambridgeshire is actually higher than in Oxfordshire (73 per cent versus 69).[16]

There are exceptions to this depressing picture. Hass-Klau cites German data suggesting that in the cities of Munich and Freiburg, public transport and cycling have increased in tandem, leading to falls in car trip shares.[17] The small city of Troisdorf, near Cologne, apparently increased cycling from 16 to 21 per cent of trips without adversely affecting walking or public transport: instead, car use fell from 56 to 51 per cent.[18] So cycling can complement other sustainable modes in the right policy environment. The question is what is the right environment?

In a refreshingly frank discussion of the tensions that occur between pedestrians, cyclists and public transport vehicles, Pharoah points out that some kinds of cyclist mix well with pedestrians and public transport passengers, but others do not. Young children and other 'slow' cyclists can coexist with pedestrians, but commuting and racing cyclists generally do not. 'A great deal depends on cultural context of walking and cycling', he notes: in cities like Amsterdam, Freiburg and Copenhagen, most cyclists ride 'sedate' machines, while British cyclists tend to ride racing or mountain bikes.[19] Australian cyclists have an even stronger preference for expensive racing-style bicycles, as well as Olympic-style lycra uniforms. Helmets, which are rarely seen in Europe, are now compulsory throughout Australia.

These differences reflect the composition of cyclists in high- and low-cycling countries. Where cycling is widespread, it is popular with both sexes and a range of ages and classes; as cycling declines in importance, it becomes increasingly restricted to young-ish middle-class males. In Copenhagen, the majority of cyclists are women, but 75 per cent of workers cycling in Melbourne in 2006 were male, with the Sydney figure even higher at 83 per cent. The UK National Travel Survey for 2005 found that cyclists came from households with higher than average incomes, in contrast with walking, which is most important in low-income households; male cyclists outnumbered females by between two and five to one, depending on the age group.[20] This narrow profile contributes to, and is exacerbated by, the poor relationships with both motorists and pedestrians that come from the marginal status of cycling and the lack of safe bicycle paths.

Politicians have also learned from the White Bike that declaring support for cycling can create the illusion of a sustainable transport policy. This is handy when governments wish to deflect public concern over automobile-dominated substantive priorities. In Melbourne, every new freeway has its accompanying bike path, even though freeways, which bypass places people want to reach, provide unsuitable cycle routes. The state's automobile association sponsors 'Ride to Work Day', while the road agency sponsors the 'Great Victorian Bike Ride'.

Because it does not form part of a coordinated effort to reduce car use, tokenistic cycling policy is usually poorly thought through, with a focus on stunts and satisfying the demands of the small, but vocal, group of existing cyclists – whose male, middle-class demographic profile mirrors that of transport planners. So measures that appeal to 'racing' cyclists, such as showers at work and high-security storage for expensive bikes, predominate at the expense of practical issues like safe cycle paths and reduced speed limits. Where bicycle routes are provided, this is often at the expense of pedestrians, rather than motorists.

An example of this confused thinking is the curious notion of shared bicycle–bus lanes, a concept most fully developed in Auckland. The city's 'cycle network' consists mainly of bike–bus lanes, with some shared footpaths and a very small number of separate bicycle roadways.[21] It is easy to see why automobile-oriented transport planners might lump the 'sustainable modes' together on the same infrastructure, but a moment's reflection reveals problems and dangers. As Pharoah argues and illustrates with an excellent photograph, 'buses and cycles hinder one another when they share the same space'.[22] Moving buses travel faster than bicycles but then stop to pick up and set down passengers, so bus drivers and cyclists race one another between stops. This slows buses down, increases driver stress and endangers cyclists: after all, buses are much bigger than cars, and take longer to stop.

Across the Tasman Sea in Melbourne, similar problems were created in 2008 when the Melbourne City Council introduced bike lanes on the roads feeding into Swanston Street, the city's main tram artery. Swanston Street was converted to a transit mall in the 1990s, and was not designed to accommodate cyclists. Within months, a cyclist struck and seriously injured a passenger alighting from a tram, and another cyclist died after skidding on the tram tracks and falling into the path of a bus. The fact that walking, cycling and public transport are all more sustainable than car travel does not invalidate the laws of physics.

Another example of confused objectives is the widespread support for the carriage of bicycles on urban buses, trams and trains. Recreational cycling in rural areas is an environmentally benign form of tourism that is encouraged by sensible public transport providers: bicycles can be carried on RhB trains and Postbuses throughout rural Graubunden. But bikes are not carried on urban buses, or on peak-period RhB trains, because they take up too much space.

Public transport, it should be recalled, only offers environmental benefits relative to the car if high occupancy rates can be maintained. This is not possible if significant numbers of passengers bring bicycles with them, because a bike takes up as much space as three or four people, and slows boarding and alighting into the bargain. While the occasional cyclist can be accommodated, especially in off-peak periods, if all passengers took bikes with them, the environmental outcome would be no better than if they travelled by car.

The bike–rail combination is usually proposed as a remedy for problems that don't exist in genuine public transport networks. For example, Professor Frank Fisher, the long-serving director of the Graduate School of Environmental Science at Melbourne's Monash University, avoided the rail–bus shambles described in Chapter 1 for decades by bringing his bicycle on the train and cycling from Huntingdale station to the University. As a follower of Ivan Illich, Fisher was practising what he preached, but he goes further, arguing that bike–rail 'makes for the fastest, healthiest, environmentally sanest, community-oriented transport system in existence'.[23] The message is that instead of demanding that governments fix public transport, individuals should help themselves.

There are two problems with this argument. The first is that a train-load of passengers with bikes would not be environmentally sane because, as we have seen, another three or four trains would be needed just to carry the bikes. The second problem with Fisher's argument is that it places the burden of dealing with poor public transport on individuals, letting governments off the hook. The bike–rail option would not be needed if Monash University was served by buses that connected with trains: at York University in Toronto, where this is the case, even people too lazy to cycle can reach campus easily without using cars.

There is no evidence that on-board carriage of bikes actually attracts significant numbers of former motorists, especially in public transport networks that already offer convenient connections to a full range of destinations. There has been little independent evaluation of bikes-onboard programmes, but the Toronto Transit Commission did report in 2006 on a trial programme to carry bikes on 110 buses serving five TTC routes. The routes were selected in consultation with the city's cycling committee, and served the outer parts of the City of Toronto (i.e. the 'middle suburbs'), where it was expected that demand would be greatest owing to longer trip lengths and walking distances to stops. Among those selected was the TTC's busiest bus line, route 29 along Dufferin Avenue, which carries 44,000 passengers per day. The trial covered two summers and one winter, and cost around Can$200,000. Usage rates were minimal: between 9 and 15 bikes per day on route 29, and 19–32 across the five routes, many of whom were existing TTC patrons. The cost per new passenger was at least $10,000. TTC staff recommended that the project be discontinued in view of these disappointing results, but the elected councillors on the TTC board voted to extend the scheme to all TTC bus lines and investigate fitting bike racks to trams.[24] Surrealist cycling policy did not stop with the Provos.

FROM SURREALISM TO PRACTICAL POLICIES

The real area where cycling and public transport can work together is access to stops and stations. Successful bike-and-ride schemes, mainly serving rail stations, can be found in Dutch, German, Swiss and Danish cities, among others. Some larger stations offer a range of services, including bike hire and repairs. By cooperating instead of competing, public transport and cycling can deliver environmental and health benefits.[25]

Cycling offers an environmentally friendly alternative to park-and-ride, costing less to build, using much less land and creating far fewer traffic problems. Cyclists are more likely to ride to their local stop or station, rather than travelling to a city-edge parking station, as happens with less successful car park-and-ride systems. Bicycle parking can be provided at a wider range of locations, including smaller tram and bus stops where lack of space would prevent the provision of car parking. The role of bicycle access to public transport is likely to be greatest in exurban and rural areas where even the best feeder bus networks may not satisfy everyone. Bike parking will be simpler and cheaper to provide in regions where cycling is a significant mode of transport, because these are the places where cyclists are least likely to ride very expensive machines that must be stored in secure lockers.

Public transport and cycling do not show the simple and powerful positive feedback found with walking, but they can support one another if the overall policy environment is designed to promote mode shift from the car to more sustainable modes. The question of the policy environment brings us full circle, back to politics.

NOTES

1   DfT (2007/2008).
2   Hass-Klau (2003, 2007).
3   Ott (2002, pp78–79). Interestingly, he was speaking at a seminar on 'alternatives to congestion charging'.
4   Haq et al (2008, p563).
5   Morton and Mees (2005).
6   Swiss Federal Statistical Office, 2000 Census 'pendler' tables A2E, Kantons Zurich (1), Graubunden (18) and Schaffhausen (14).
7   de Bruijn et al (2009, p193).
8   Mees (2000, ch. 7).
9   'The White bike comes full circle', *Independent*, 16 July 2000.
10   Heath and Potter (2005, p294).
11   Krag (2002, p235).
12   Mees et al (2007, p6, table 1.8).
13   Apel and Pharoah (1995, p258, table 37). The low walking figures suggest that the surveys in question may have understated walking by omitting shorter trips.
14   Munster (2008, p190, table 6.5).
15   www.muenster.de/stadt/exwost/portrait_e.html (accessed 30 August 2009).
16   ONS (2003, table KS-15 – excluding 'working from home').
17   Hass-Klau (2003, p191).
18   Bohle (2002, pp212–213).
19   Pharoah (2003, p365).
20   Mees et al (2007, p13, table 2); DfT (2007/2008).
21   City of Auckland (2007, p3, fig. 1).
22   Pharoah (2003, p364).
23   Fisher (2002, p312).
24   TTC meeting 1874, 20 September 2006: 'Report – Bicycle racks on buses: results of pilot project'; minutes, item 25.
25   McClintock (2002, chs 12 and 13); Martens (2004).

12

The Politics of Public Transport

POINT GREY GOES GREEN

Students and academics from the University of British Columbia (UBC) played key roles in moving transport policy in Vancouver away from the road to autopia. From the freeway controversies of the 1960s to the Livable Region Strategic Plan of the 1990s, the UBC community was the mainstay of the coalition arguing for sustainable transport. So it was something of an embarrassment for all concerned that the university itself was so car-oriented. Established on spacious grounds at Point Grey, some 12km from the city centre, UBC offered ample parking for staff and students. A green belt of parkland separates it from the city, discouraging walking to campus, while the only public transport is buses, since the nearest Skytrain station is 10km away.

A university survey in 1997 found that 53,000 staff, students and visitors entered the campus each day, of whom 77 per cent arrived by car, 18 per cent by public transport, 3 per cent by bike and 1 per cent on foot. A decade later, staff and student numbers have grown by a third, as enrolments and research activity expand dramatically. But 20 per cent fewer cars entered the university each day in 2007 than in 1997, enabling the university to close thousands of parking stalls and use the land for more productive purposes. Public transport's share of travel has more than doubled, to 44 per cent, while trips by car have declined to 52 per cent of the total – still a majority, but now an embattled one. Public transport patronage has nearly tripled, from 19,000 trips per day to 54,000.[1]

The turnaround in transport mode share at UBC in the past decade has been one of the most dramatic recorded anywhere. It is the result of a policy agreement in 1997 by the university and the regional planning agency, the Greater Vancouver Regional District. The package was a classic combination of incentives for public transport with disincentives for the automobile (see Chapter 3). The cost of campus parking doubled, with some of the additional revenue used to support the introduction, in 2003, of U-Pass, a discounted monthly public transport ticket provided to all students through a surcharge to their student union fee.

The U-Pass scheme, which was modelled on programmes at other North American universities, has received a great deal of attention, since the results at UBC have been more dramatic than in other places. But the trend was already underway beforehand, with a 50 per cent increase in public transport use between 1997 and 2002. This was mainly the result of substantial service improvements, including the introduction of the first B-Line express bus service along Broadway, the main access route to the university. The extra services were made possible by staggering lecture start times to spread the morning peak. So the UBC U-Pass succeeded because it was introduced as part of a coordinated policy package.

The results have exceeded the expectations of the planners of the 1990s, reflecting the fact that universities are excellent places to change established transport habits, because so many new students and staff start every year. Translink has struggled to provide enough bus services to accommodate demand, with the main bus corridor along Broadway now carrying over 60,000 passengers per day, nearly half of them heading to or from UBC. Peak-period bus lanes, replacing general purpose traffic lanes, were introduced along Broadway in 2006, and Translink is accelerating plans to replace the B-Line bus route with an extension of the Skytrain.[2]

One unexpected result was a decline in walking, cycling and car-pooling to campus, confirming that 'sustainable' modes can compete with each other, as we saw in the previous chapter. Walking and cycling to campus had been relatively insignificant in 1997, but car-pooling was an important access mode. 'The bus is a big carpool that leaves every few minutes, all day long' one student explained.[3] But because public transport is more efficient than car-pooling, and because the loss of walking and cycling trips was more than matched by the shift away from the automobile, the overall result has been a big improvement in environmental outcomes. And walking is actually increasing within the campus boundary, as the university uses land formerly set aside for parking to construct thousands of on-campus residences for staff and students.

A striking feature of the transport programme at UBC, and a major contributor to its success, has been ongoing, extensive participation from across the university community. The process was overseen by an advisory committee with strong staff and student representation; UBC students and faculty carried out research that helped refine the details of the plan. The U-Pass scheme had to be approved by a student referendum, and this only occurred after three years of negotiations between the Alma Mater Society (the student union), the university and Translink. The discussions became acrimonious and often seemed to be going nowhere. The transit agency was determined to avoid a blowout in subsidies; the student body was anxious to keep costs down. The university's decision to subsidize pass costs helped break the deadlock, and the U-Pass referendum attracted a record turnout and a 69 per cent Yes vote.[4] UBC staff and students also lobbied for many of the pre- and post-U-Pass service improvements that reinforced the shift to public transport. The outcome is a triumph for public 'ownership', in both senses of the word.

While transport has changed dramatically at the University of British Columbia, things have remained much the same across the globe at Monash University in Melbourne. A few years ago, a group of concerned students decided it was time to do something about the university's own contribution to pollution and global warming. They went on a bike ride up the east coast of Australia, accompanied by a support van powered by waste vegetable oil.[5]

OPENING A WINDOW FOR CHANGE

Monash students are probably just as concerned about the environment as their counterparts at UBC. So why are they unable to take meaningful action to improve sustainable transport options, especially since there appears to be so much more room for improvement? The Monash students are constrained by politics. There is no public transport authority to lobby for improved services or discounted periodical tickets, because private franchisees provide services under secret, commercial-in-confidence agreements. And there seems to be no point demanding change anyway, because most of the city's transport experts and environmentalists dismiss the possibility of improvement, arguing that densities are too low, or that students should literally get on their bikes.

The automobile age did not come about by accident, or because the car is an irresistible force. As we saw in Chapter 2, political decisions and failures to decide played a major part in the process, from the decision to allow privately operated tram systems to fail in Los Angeles and other US cities, to the conspiracy to build motorways instead of railways in Auckland. And it's not just elected officials who engage in transport politics. Academics from Auckland's major university led the 1950s motorway campaign in that city; the experts behind the Chicago Area Transportation Study provided a convenient, scientific sounding rationale for the failure to solve the problems of local public transport; British transport bureaucrats have maintained bus deregulation in the face of overwhelming evidence that the policy has failed. And at virtually every stage of this process, the argument that population densities are too low for public transport to be viable has been a key weapon in the armoury of those advocating autopia.

Just as politics helped create the automobile age, it has also been critical in those cities that have led the way to a less car-dependent future. Political conflict changed the direction of transport policy in Toronto, Vancouver, Ottawa, Adelaide (temporarily), Perth, Zurich and to an extent, even in Curitiba. In his study of successful European cities, Stefan Bratzel found that conflict and social crisis were essential ingredients to open 'a window for change in transport policies'.[6]

This does not mean that sustainable urban transport can operate without expertise and professionalism. What is required is a productive debate between transport planners and the community, which means the planners must be sufficiently confident of their own expertise to defend themselves in public. 'Power makes you stupid', according to Nietzsche – as quoted by Bent Flyvbjerg in his influential book *Rationality and Power* (the subject of which is a long-running tussle over transport policy in the Danish city of Aalborg).[7] But democracy and participation can have the opposite effect. Bratzel speaks of 'policy learning', in which initial successes create support for more radical change. In Canton Zurich, and at the national level in Switzerland, the need to gain public support has even forced transport planners to become more technically proficient, leading to cheaper, more effective ways of improving services. And in Perth, the same officials who had tried to close the city's rail system took charge of upgrading and extending it.

The kind of politics we are talking about here does not necessarily mean party politics. The plans for the metro and underground trams in Zurich were supported by all political parties. Professor Kunzi, the father of the Zurich S-Bahn and the ZVV, was a member of the liberal party, which supports the free market – although not in public transport. Zurich's current cantonal minister for transport, and chair of the ZVV's board, Rita Fuhrer, is from the right-wing populist Swiss People's Party – but on public transport could be considered to the 'left' of Australia's Greens-controlled Byron Shire council (see Chapter 10).

Politics and conflict frighten many people, and transport debates are particularly scary, because they involve numbers and mathematics. Environmentalists who think nothing of chaining themselves to trees to stop logging shy away from debating policies like public transport privatization. Some of the excitement about peak oil seems to be based on the hope that mother nature will force policy change, avoiding all that messy analysis and activism.

In the closing chapter of *Heat*, George Monbiot laments the dearth of protest around climate change, harking back nostalgically to the British anti-motorway campaigns of the 1990s, when 'activists lay on the road and sat in the trees and on the roofs of ministers' houses and interrupted their speeches and poured fake blood on the steps of Downing Street'.[8] Monbiot thinks the internet is partly to blame, since it allows people to generate the illusion of activism while sitting in front of their computers. I think he has a point, but there is more to the problem than this.

WHAT ARE YOU IN FAVOUR OF?

One reason for the strength of the anti-motorway campaigns Monbiot remembers so fondly is the clarity provided by a common enemy (the road lobby) and objectives (stopping motorway-building). But this strength has also proven a weakness, because it enabled activists to evade the question of the alternative to continued road-building. Is the alternative self-help, in the form of white bikes, walking buses and behaviour change? Or is it collective action: new transport policies combining traffic restraint with dramatically improved public transport and better facilities for pedestrians and cyclists?

In much of Europe, as well as parts of the Americas, there would be no doubt that the collective approach is the answer. Only where there are viable alternatives to driving that don't require mass outbreaks of heroism is it possible to gain political support for policy change, let alone to change outcomes on the ground. But in the anglosphere, we are not so sure. Collective action seems too difficult, especially in places like the UK and Melbourne, where the vested interests opposing transport change are deeply entrenched in industry and bureaucracies. Changing public transport will be hard work. But we now have sufficient experience, some of it catalogued in this book, to show not just that it is possible, but also how to go about it. By contrast, there is no evidence to show that self-help can solve the problem.

Fixing public transport is not simple, but it is a much easier task than rebuilding entire cities at many times their current densities. Not only are the massive increases in density advocated by the 'ultras' of the compact city movement unachievable within realistic timeframes, but they would also be unlikely to make much difference to transport outcomes. Ottawa already has higher public transport usage rates than Greater Manchester, despite having barely a third its density; heroic measures could raise the density ratio to one-half, but it is hard to see this drawing many of Ottawa's motorists away from their cars.

The successful cities discussed in the previous chapters have adapted public transport to the existing urban form, rather than attempting the impossible task of rebuilding themselves as completely different places. Toronto, Ottawa and Vancouver have used buses to extend trunk rail or busway networks into dispersed suburbs, and to link those suburbs to one another; Zurich and Graubunden have used the 'pulse timetable' to serve sparsely populated suburban and rural regions; Schaffhausen has used frequent, integrated bus services to mimic trams in a small town. Curitiba has done most to shape to city to fit the transport system, with its dense corridors following the arterial roads that provide busway routes, but its integrated transport system could not function without the feeder and cross-suburban links that connect busway corridors to the lower density neighbourhoods where most Curitibanos live. Urban planners can make the task of adapting public transport to cities easier, by discouraging scattered fringe development, clustering higher-density housing and major travel destinations in centres along trunk transit corridors, and designing neighbourhoods in ways that foster walking, cycling and efficient bus operation. But none of these measures can substitute for a genuine public transport network that offers convenient 'anywhere to anywhere' travel.

Density is not the main barrier to providing public transport that offers a real alternative to the car; rather, it is a rationalization for inaction. While it is easy to understand why advocates of autopia, like the Auckland motorway lobby of the 1950s or the Canberra freeway planners of the 21st century, might make this argument, it is difficult to see why so many environmentalists want to link the end of the automobile age to urban planning measures that are simply never going to happen.

The cause of sustainable transport needs to be detached from the crusade against suburbia. Suburbanites, who are the great majority of the population in developed cities, perceive the crusade as being directed against themselves and their communities – and they are probably right. It's time to share the good news: the end of the automobile age need not mean the end of suburbia; Hong Kong is not the only model for environmentally sustainable transport.

Of course, providing viable public transport will be more difficult in spacious suburbs than it would be in Hong Kong, but it is not impossible. And if some of the energy that is currently devoted to browbeating suburbanites about their backyards, or their unwillingness to cycle, is redirected to providing first class public transport, it's amazing just how much could be achieved.

There is no reason why British cities could not have public transport as good, and car usage rates as low, as the City of Zurich, and no reason why their suburbs should not be doing at least as well as the rest of Canton Zurich: their densities are considerably higher, thanks to the stronger UK planning system, and incomes are lower. Similarly, there is no reason why small towns and rural areas should not be able to match and ultimately better the performance of Schaffhausen and Canton Graubunden.

Across the Atlantic, density is not a valid excuse for poor public transport either. Many US cities have higher densities than the Canadian cities that so strikingly outperform them; others are similar to their Canadian counterparts. The same applies with even more force to Australian urban areas, which have similar densities to their Canadian cousins, as well as stronger CBDs and much more extensive rail systems. Nor can places like the outer suburbs of Toronto use density as an excuse: these areas are considerably denser than Ottawa and Vancouver, and not that different from the suburbs of Zurich.

Of course, those determined to find excuses for inaction will point to other factors. Some have argued that public transport in Toronto and Zurich benefits from winter snow, which makes it difficult to drive. It hasn't snowed for a long time in Curitiba or Bogota, and while Vancouver is a rainy city, it receives little snow. Others claim that Switzerland is special and cannot be imitated, because of social and cultural homogeneity,[9] or even the legacy of the Protestant Reformation. Alas, the 2000 census revealed that Catholics now slightly outnumber Protestants in Zurich City, and that other religions, particularly Islam, are growing rapidly, as immigrants top 30 per cent of the population.[10] It's time to stop making excuses for inadequate public transport.

Providing public transport that will take us beyond the automobile age is going to be a lot of work. It will require changes to public transport 'governance' and organization, especially in cities where provision has been left to the market, through deregulation or franchising. It will also require changes to the way public transport is planned and operated, with a move away from 'tailor-made' services aimed at small sub-markets like city centre commuters and those without cars, towards an all-purpose network intended for everyone. These changes will require a new kind of transport professional, which in turn will mean changes to academic study and research. Most urban planning courses ignore public transport or treat it as something that magically happens when the right urban form is in place; transport planning scholarship is currently dominated by the conventional economics that has been proven wrong by the public transport success stories examined in this book. Change will also be needed in transport policy, with 'balanced transport' giving way to active discrimination in favour of public transport and the genuinely sustainable modes of walking and cycling.

Transport politics will have to change as well, but there is ample evidence that, when given a genuine choice, communities will not only vote for radically improved public transport, they will even use it. But the easiest change of all is the most necessary of all. Before we can provide public transport solutions for suburbia, we must stop telling ourselves that the task is impossible.

NOTES

1 UBC (2005, 2008).
2 Translink (2005, p6-53).
3 Quoted in G. Price (2005) 'U-Pass Success', at www.pricetags.ca/writings.html (accessed 30 August 2009).
4 G. Senft (2005) 'U-Pass at the University of British Columbia'.
5 Naunton (2005).
6 Bratzel (1999).
7 Flyvbjerg (1998, pp228–229).
8 Monbiot (2007, p21).
9 Cervero (1998, p306).
10 www.statistik.zh.ch (accessed 30 August 2009).

References

ABS (Australian Bureau of Statistics) (1995) *Travel to Work, School and Shops, Victoria, October 1994*, Cat. 9201.2, Canberra

ABS (2003) *2001 Census Working Community Profile Tea Tree Gully (City) LGA*, Canberra

ABS (2007) *Survey of Motor Vehicle Use: 12 months ended 31 October 2006*, Cat. 9208.0, Canberra (and previous editions)

Al-Dubikhi, S. (2007) 'Exploring the Potential for Successful Public Transport in Riyadh', PhD thesis, Faculty of Architecture, Building & Planning, University of Melbourne

AMPO (Auckland Metropolitan Planning Organisation) (1951) *Outline Development Plan for Auckland*, AMPO, Auckland

Apel, D. and Pharoah, T. (1995) *Transport Concepts in European Cities*, Avebury, Aldershot, UK

ARA (Auckland Regional Authority) (1967) *Auckland Regional Master Plan, Vol. 1: Survey Data*, ARA, Auckland

ARA (1976) *Auckland Comprehensive Transportation Study Review: Final Report*, ARA, Auckland

ARA (1983) *The Future of Auckland Suburban Rail Services*, ARA, Auckland

ARC (Auckland Regional Council) (2005) *Auckland Regional Land Transport Strategy*, ARC, Auckland

ARPA (Auckland Regional Planning Authority) (1956) *Master Transportation Plan for Metropolitan Auckland*, ARPA, Auckland

ARTA (Auckland Regional Transport Authority) (2008) *Annual Report 2008*, ARTA, Auckland

Audit Review of Government Contracts (2000) *Contracting, Privatisation, Probity & Disclosure in Victoria, 1992–1999*, 2 vols plus Appendices, State Government of Victoria, Melbourne

Auditor General, Victoria (1998) *Public Transport Reforms*, Special Report No. 57, Government Printer, Melbourne

Balcombe, R., Mackett, R., Paulley, N., Preston, J., Shires, J., Titteridge, H., Wardman, M. and White, P. (2005) *The Demand for Public Transport: A practical guide*, Report TRL593, TRL Limited, Crowthorne, UK

Banham, R. (1971) *Los Angeles: The architecture of four ecologies*, Allen Lane, London

Banister, D. (2004) 'Implementing the possible?', *Planning Theory and Practice*, vol. 5, no. 4, pp499–501

Banister, D. (2005) *Unsustainable Transport: City transport in the new century*, Routledge, London

Barker, T. and Robbins, M. (1974) *A History of London Transport*, 2 Vols, Allen & Unwin, London

Barton, H., Davis, G. and Guise, R. (1995) *Sustainable Settlements: A guide for planners, designers and developers*, University of the West of England and Local Government Management Board, Luton, Bedfordshire

Batchelor, R. (1994) *Henry Ford: Mass production, modernism and design*, Manchester University Press, Manchester

Black, E. (2006) *Internal Combustion: How corporations and governments addicted the world to oil and derailed the alternatives*, St. Martin's Press, New York

Bohle, W. (2002) 'German cycling policy experience', in H. McClintock (ed.), *Planning for Cycling*, Woodhead, Cambridge, pp209–222

Bottles, S. (1987) *Los Angeles and the Automobile: The making of the modern city*, University of California Press, Berkeley

Bouf, D. and Hensher, D. (2007) 'The dark side of making transit irresistible: The example of France', *Transport Policy*, vol. 14, pp523–532

Brändli, H. (1990) 'Measures to increase the demand for public transport: The case of Zurich', in Council of Europe (ed.), Conference on improving traffic and quality of life in metropolitan areas: Working documents and conclusions, CoE, Strasbourg, pp130–146

Brändli, H. (1996) 'Relations between railways and universities in Switzerland', *Japan Railway and Transport Review*, vol. 7, pp12–15.

Bratzel, S. (1999) 'Conditions of success in sustainable urban transport policy – Policy change in "relatively successful" European cities', *Transport Reviews*, vol. 12, no. 2, pp177–190

Brisbane City Council (2008) *Annual Report, 2007–08*, City Council, Brisbane

Bruegmann, R. (2005) *Sprawl: A compact history*, University of Chicago Press, Chicago

Bush, G. W. A. (1971) *Decently and In Order: The government of the city of Auckland 1840–1971*, Collins, Auckland

CABE (Commission on Architecture and the Built Environment) (2005) *Better Neighbourhoods: Making higher densities work*, CABE, London

Cambridgeshire County Council (2005) *Cambridgeshire LTP Annual Progress Report 2005*, Cambridgeshire County Council, Cambridge

CATS (Chicago Area Transportation Study) (1959, 1960, 1962) *Chicago Area Transportation Study: Final Report*, 3 vols, Chicago

CEC (Commission of the European Communities) (1995) *The Citizens' Network: Fulfilling the potential of public passenger transport in Europe, European Commission Green Paper*, COM(95)601, Office for Official Publications of the European Communities, Luxembourg

CEC (1998) *Developing the Citizens' Network: Communication from the Commission to the Council and the European Parliament*, COM(1998)431final, Office for Official Publications of the European Communities, Luxembourg

CEC (2007a) *Opinion of the European Economic and Social Committee on the Green paper: Towards a new culture for urban mobility* COM(2007)551final, Official Journal – European Union Information And Notices C. 51 (224), pp39–45

CEC (2007b) *Towards a new culture for urban mobility: Country sheets – Urban Mobility*, Green Paper, EU-27_En, Brussels

Ceder, A. (2007) *Public Transport Planning and Operation: Theory, Modelling and Practice*, Butterworth-Heinemann, Oxford

Cervero, R. (1998) *The Transit Metropolis: A global inquiry*, Island Press, Washington DC

Chesterton, G. K. (1929) *The Thing*, Sheed & Ward, London

City of Auckland (2007) *Cycling Action Plan 2007-2012* City of Auckland, Auckland

Clark, C. (1967) *Population Growth and Land Use*, Macmillan, London

Commission on Oil Independence (2006) *Making Sweden an Oil-Free Society* (English version), www.sweden.gov.se/sb/d/574/a/67096, accessed April 2009

Cox, W. (2008) 'Demographia World Urban Areas: Population & Density', 4th edn, www.demigraphia.com, accessed April, 2009

Creighton, R. L. (1970) *Urban Transportation Planning*, University of Illinois Press, Urbana

Cumberland, K. (1971) *Auckland in Ferment*, New Zealand Geographical Society, Auckland

Davis, D. (1978) 'Mass transit and private ownership: An alternative perspective on the case of Toronto', *Urban History Review* no. 3–78, pp103–122

Davison, G. (2004) *Car Wars: How the car won our hearts and conquered our cities*, Allen & Unwin, Sydney

de Bruijn, G., Kremers, S., Singh, A., van den Putte, B. and van Melchelen, W. (2009) 'Adult active transportation: Adding habit strength to the theory of planned behaviour', *American Journal of Preventive Medicine*, vol. 36, no. 3, pp189–194

DfT (Department for Transport, UK) (2003) *A Bulletin of Public Transport Statistics: Great Britain*, DfT, London

DfT (2006) *Putting Passengers First: The Government's proposals for a modernised national framework for bus services*, DfT, London

DfT (2007/8) *Personal Travel Factsheets: Travel to school, walking, cycling*, DfT, London

DfT (2008) *Public Transport Statistics Bulletin GB*, DfT, London

Downs, A. (1992) *Stuck in Traffic: Coping with peak-hour traffic congestion*, Brookings, Washington DC

Downs, A. (2004) *Still Stuck in Traffic*, Brookings, Washington DC

Eddington, R. (2006) *The Eddington Transport Study*, The Stationery Office, London

EEA (European Environmental Agency) (2006) *Urban Sprawl in Europe: The ignored challenge*, EEA Report No. 10/2006, Copenhagen

Filion, P., McSpurren, K. and Appleby, B. (2006) 'Wasted density? The impact of Toronto's residential-density-distribution policies on public transit use and walking', *Environment and Planning A* 28, pp1367–1392

Fischer, K. (1984) *Canberra, Myths and Models: Forces at work in the formation of the Australian capital*, Institute of Asian Affairs, Hamburg

Fisher, F. (2002) 'Widening the definition of environment for responsible urban commuters', *Urban Policy & Research*, vol. 20, no. 3, pp309–312

FitzRoy, F. and Smith, I. (1992) 'Priority over pricing: Lessons from Zurich on the redundancy of road pricing', *Journal of Transport Economics and Policy*, vol. 27, no. 2, pp209–214

Flink, J. (1970) *America Adopts the Automobile*, MIT Press, Cambridge, MA

Flink, J. (1988) *The Automobile Age*, MIT Press, Cambridge, MA

Flyvbjerg, B. (1998) *Rationality and Power: Democracy in practice*, University of Chicago Press, Chicago

Flyvbjerg, B., Holm, M. S. and Buhl, S. (2002) 'Underestimating costs in public works projects: Error or lie?', *Journal of the American Planning Association*, vol. 68, no. 3, pp279–295

Fogelson, R. M. (1993) *The Fragmented Metropolis: Los Angeles, 1850–1930* (1st edn 1967), University of California Press, Berkeley

Fooks, E. (1946) *X-Ray the City! The density diagram: Basis for urban planning*, Ruskin Press, Melbourne

Frankena, M. (1982) *Urban Transportation Financing: Theory and policy in Ontario*, University of Toronto Press, Toronto

Frisken, F. (1984) 'A triumph for public ownership: The Toronto Transportation Commission 1921–1953', in V. Russell (ed.), *Forging a Consensus: Historical Essays on Toronto*, University of Toronto Press, Toronto, pp238–271

Fullerton, C. (2005) 'A changing of the guard: Regional planning in Ottawa, 1945–1974', *Urban History Review*, vol. XXXIV, pp100–112

Garnaut R. (2008) *Garnaut Climate Change Review: Final Report*, Cambridge University Press, Cambridge

Giampetro, M. and Mayumi, K. (2009) *The Biofuel Delusion: The fallacy of large scale agro-biofuels production*, Earthscan, London

Gilbert, R. and Perl, A. (2008) *Transport Revolutions: Moving people and freight without oil*, Earthscan, London

Gleeson, B. (2008) 'Waking from the dream', *Griffith Review*, vol. 20, pp13–49

Goldberg, J. (2006) 'Draft EU regulation on public service requirements: What consequences for local public transport?', European Metropolitan Transport Authorities, Association for European Transport conference, Strasbourg, September 2006, http://www.etcproceedings.org/paper/draft-eu-regulation-on-public-service-requirements-what-are-the-consequences-f, accessed August 2009

Gomez-Ibanez, J. (2003) *Regulating Infrastructure: Monopoly, contracts, and discretion*, Harvard University Press, Cambridge, MA

Gordon, P. and Richardson, H. (2004) 'Travel trends in US Cities', http://www-rcf.usc.edu/~pgordon/pdf/commuting.pdf, accessed April 2009

Graubunden (2008) *Durchblick 2008: Graubunden in Zahlen*, http://www.gr.ch/DE/institutionen/verwaltung/dvs/awt/dokumentation/Dokumente%20Volkswirtschaftliche%20Grundlagen/Graub%C3%BCnden%20in%20Zahlen_2008.pdf (accessed 30 August 2009)

GVRD (Greater Vancouver Regional District) (1993) *A Long-Range Transportation Plan for Greater Vancouver*, GVRD, Vancouver

Hall, P. (1998) *Cities in Civilization*, Pantheon Books, New York

Haq, G., Whitelegg, J., Cinderby, S. and Owen, A. (2008) 'The use of personalised social marketing to foster voluntary behavioural change for sustainable travel and lifestyles', *Local Environment* 13(7), pp549–569

Harris, C. (2005) 'Slow train coming: The New Zealand State changes its mind about Auckland Transit, 1949–56', *Urban Policy & Research*, vol. 23, no. 1, pp37–55

Harris, C. (2007) '"Buses" last stand? Recent urban transit reform in New Zealand', *Urban Policy & Research*, vol. 25, no. 1, pp151–159

Hass-Klau, C. (2003) 'Walking and its relationship to public transport', in R. Tolley (ed.), *Sustainable Transport: Planning for walking and cycling in urban environments*, Woodhead Publishing, Cambridge, pp189–199

Hass-Klau, C. (2007) *The Effect of Public Transport Investment of Car Ownership*, Environmental and Transport Planning, Brighton, UK

Heath, J. and Potter, A. (2005) *The Rebel Sell*, Capstone, Chichester, UK

Hensher, D. (2007) *Bus Transport: Economics, Policy and Planning*, Elsevier, San Diego

Hensher, D. (2008) 'Frequency and connectivity: Key drivers of reform in urban public transport provision', *Journeys*, vol. 1, pp25–33

Hensher, D., Gwilliam, K., Burton, M., Smith, N., Van de Velde, D. and Fridstrom, L. (2008) 'The ideal contract roundtable', *Research in Transportation Economics*, vol. 22, pp188–194

Hibbs, J. (2005) *The Dangers of Bus Re-regulation and Other Perspectives on Markets in Transport*, Institute of Economic Affairs, London

Hoffman, A. (2008) *Advanced Network Planning for Bus Rapid Transit*, US Dept. of Transportation, Federal Transit Administration (report FL-26-7104-4), Washington, DC

Howard, E. (1966) *Garden Cities of Tomorrow* (1st edn, 1902), Faber & Faber, London

Hürlimann, G. (2004) 'Electronics instead of concrete and tracks! The Swiss Federal Railways 1970–2000', 8th European Business History Association conference, 16–18 September 2004, Barcelona, http://www.econ.upf.edu/ebha2004/papers/3B1.pdf

Hürlimann, G. (2005) 'The Swiss path to the "Railway of the Future" (1960s to 2000): Contributions towards a history of technology of the Swiss Federal Railways', Swiss Transport Research Conference, Ascona, Italy, www.strc.ch/conferences/2005/Huerlimann.pdf

IEA (International Energy Agency) (2008) *World Energy Outlook 2008*, OECD/IEA, Paris

Illich, I. (1974) *Energy and Equity*, Calder & Boyars, London

Inno-V, KCW, RebelGroup, TOI, SDG and TIS (2008) *Contracting in Urban Public Transport*, Report for European Commission, Amsterdam

IPCC (Intergovernmental Panel on Climate Change) (2007) *Fourth Assessment Report*, Geneva, IPCC

Irazabal, C. (2005) *City Making and Urban Governance in the Americas: Curitiba and Portland*, Ashgate, Aldershot, UK

Jane's Publishing (1988) *Jane's Urban Transport Systems 1988*, Jane's Publishing, Bracknell, Berkshire, UK

Kahn-Ribeiro, S. and Kobayashi, S. (eds) (2007) 'Transport and its infrastructure', in B. Metz et al (eds), *Climate Change 2007: Mitigation of Climate Change – Contribution of Working Group III to the Fourth Assessment Report of the Intergovernmental Panel on Climate Change*, Cambridge University Press, Cambridge

Kain, P. (2007) 'The pitfalls in competitive tendering: Addressing the risks revealed by experience in Australia and Britain', in ECMT (European Conference of Ministers of Transport) *Competitive Tendering of Rail Services*, ECMT/OECD, Paris, pp43–125

Kaufmann, V. (2004) 'Social and political segregation of urban transportation: The merits and limitations of the Swiss cities model', *Built Environment*, vol. 30, no. 2, pp146–152

Kenworthy, J. and Laube, F. (1999) *An International Sourcebook of Automobile Dependence in Cities, 1960–1990*, University Press of Colorado, Boulder, CO

Kenworthy, J. and Laube, F. (2001) *The Millennium Cities Database for Sustainable Transport*, UITP, Brussels (CD)

Krag, T. (2002) 'Urban cycling in Denmark', in H. McClintock (ed.), *Planning for Cycling*, Woodhead, Cambridge, pp223–236

Laird, P., Newman, P., Bachels, M. and Kenworthy, J. (2001) *Back on Track: Rethinking transport policy in Australia and New Zealand*, UNSW Press, Sydney

Lash, H. (1976) *Planning in a Human Way*, Macmillan, Ottawa

Le Corbusier (1971) *Urbanisme*, 3rd edn (1st edn, 1924; English translation, 1929 as *The City of To-morrow and Its Planning*), The Architectural Press, London

Leuthi, M., Laube, F. and Medossi, G. (2007) 'Rescheduling and train control: A new framework for traffic control in heavily used networks', paper for 86th Transportation Research Board Annual Meeting 2007, Washington, DC

Lincolnshire County Council (2006) *2nd Local Transport Plan*, Lincolnshire County Council, Lincoln

Lincolnshire County Council (2008) *Interconnect Network Guide: January 2008* (brochure), Lincolnshire County Council, Lincoln

Livingstone, K. (2004) 'The challenge of driving through change: Introducing congestion charging in Central London', *Planning Theory and Practice*, vol. 5, no. 4, pp490–498

Lowe, I. (1994) 'Transport and sustainable cities', in K. Ogden and E. Russell (eds), *Australian Transport Policy '94*, Montech Publishing, Melbourne, pp30–37

Lowe, I. (2005) *Living in the Hothouse*, Scribe Publications, Melbourne

LTA (Land Transport Authority, Singapore) (1995) *A World Class Land Transport System*, White Paper Cmd. 1 of 1996, Singapore

LTA (2008a) *Land Transport Master Plan: A People-Centred Land Transport System*, LTA, Singapore

LTA (2008b) *Singapore Land Transport Statistics in Brief*, LTA, Singapore (and previous editions)

Lubow, A. (2007) 'Recycle city: The road to Curitiba', *The New York Times* magazine, 20 May, p3

McClintock, H. (2002) *Planning for Cycling*, Woodhead Publishing, Abington, Cambridge

McCormick Rankin (1995) 'A Busway Strategy for Brisbane City', unpublished report, Brisbane

McLoughlin, J. B. (1991) 'Urban consolidation and urban sprawl: A question of density', *Urban Policy & Research*, vol. 9, no. 3, pp148–156

Maddock, J. (1992) *People Movers: A History of Victoria's Private Bus Industry*, Kangaroo Press, Sydney

Martens, K. (2004) 'The bicycle as a feedering mode: Experiences from three European countries', *Transportation Research D*, vol. 9, pp281–294

Mayor of London (2001) *The Mayor's Transport Strategy*, London

Mees, P. (2000) *A Very Public Solution: Transport in the Dispersed City*, Melbourne University Press, Melbourne

Mees, P. (2002) *Competitive Tendering of Bus Services: International experience and lessons for Toronto*, report to Toronto Transit Commission, Melbourne

Mees, P. (2005) 'Privatization of rail and tram services in Melbourne: What went wrong?', *Transport Reviews*, vol. 25, no. 4, pp433–449

Mees, P. (2008) *Does Melbourne need another central city rail tunnel?*, RMIT University, Melbourne

Mees, P. and Dodson, J. (2002) 'The American Heresy: Half a Century of Transport Planning in Auckland', *2001 Geography – A Spatial Odyssey: Proceedings of the Third Joint Conference of the New Zealand Geographical Society and the Institute of Australian Geographers, Dunedin*, pp279–286.

Mees, P. and Dodson, J. (2007) 'Backtracking Auckland? Technical and Communicative Reason in Metropolitan Transport Planning', *International Planning Studies* 12(1), 35–53.

Mees, P., Sorupia, E. and Stone, J. (2007) *Travel to Work in Australian Capital Cities, 1976–2006*, GAMUT Centre, Melbourne

Merz, C. (1929) *And Then Came Ford*, Doubleday, New York

Metrolinx (2008) *Green Paper #7: Transit*, Greater Toronto Transportation Authority, Toronto

Meyer, J. R., Kain, J. and Wohl, M. (1966) *The Urban Transportation Problem*, Harvard University Press, Cambridge, MA

Mindali, O., Raveh, A., Salomon, I. et al (2004) 'Urban density and energy consumption: A new look at old statistics', *Transportation Research A*, vol. 38, no. 2, pp143–162

Ministry of Transport (Victoria) (1982) *Future Context for Transport: Metropolitan Transit Authority*, Melbourne

Mitchell, J. and Rapkin, C. (1954) *Urban Traffic: A function of land use*, Columbia, New York

MMBW (Melbourne & Metropolitan Board of Works) (1953) *Melbourne Metropolitan Planning Scheme 1954*, Government Printer, Melbourne

MMBW (1971) *Planning Policies for the Melbourne Metropolitan Region*, Government Printer, Melbourne

Monbiot, G. (2007) *Heat: How to stop the planet burning*, Penguin, London

Moran, A. (2006) *The Tragedy of Planning*, Institute of Public Affairs, Melbourne

Morton, A. and Mees, P. (2005) 'Too good to be true? An assessment of the Melbourne travel behaviour modification pilot', *Papers of the 28th Australasian Transport Research Forum*, Sydney (CD-ROM)

Moser, P. (2008) *Offentliche oder private Mobilitat?* [analysis of 2005 travel microcensus], 'statistik.info' paper 15/08, Statistisches amt des Kantons Zurich, Zurich

Munster (2008) *Jahres-Statistik 2007 Stadt Munster*, Munster

Nash, A. and Sylvia, R. (2001) *Implementation of Zurich's Transit Priority Program*, report 01-13, Mineta Transportation Institute, San Jose State University, San Jose, CA

Nash, C. and Smith, A. (2007) 'Rail franchising: British experience', in ECMT (European Conference of Ministers of Transport) *Competitive Tendering of Rail Services*, ECMT/OECD, Paris, pp7–34

National Rail (2008) *National Rail Timetable, Dec. 2008 to May 2009*, National Rail, London

Naunton, A. (2005) 'Pedalling Australia for Clean Energy', *Germinate*, vol. 2, pp20–21

Neutze, M. (1981) *Urban Development in Australia*, 2nd edn, Allen & Unwin, Sydney

Newman, P. and Kenworthy, J. (1989) *Cities and Automobile Dependence: An International Sourcebook*, Gower, Aldershot, UK

Newman, P. and Kenworthy, J. (1999) *Sustainability and Cities: Overcoming automobile dependence*, Island Press, Washington DC

Nielsen, G. (2005) *HiTrans Best Practice Guide 2: Public Transport – Planning the networks*, EU North Sea Region/Rogaland County Council, Oslo

Olszewski, K. and Skeates, R. (1971) 'Singapore's long-range planning', *Royal Australian Planning Institute Journal*, vol. 9, no. 2, pp57–70

ONS (Office for National Statistics, UK) (2003) *Census 2001: Key Statistics for Local Authorities in England and Wales*, The Stationery Office, London

ONS (2005) *Focus on People and Migration 2005*, Palgrave Macmillan, Basingstoke, UK

Ott, R. (2002) 'The Zurich Experience', in London Assembly (ed.), *Alternatives to Congestion Charging: Proceedings of a seminar held by the Transport Policy Committee*, Greater London Authority, London, pp73–81

Parkin, A. and Pugh, C. (1981) 'Urban Policy and Metropolitan Adelaide', in A. Parkin and A. Patience (eds) *The Dunstan Decade: Social Democracy at the State Level*, Longman Cheshire, Melbourne, pp91–114.

Petersen, T. (forthcoming) 'Public Transport for Dispersed Urban Settlements', PhD thesis, Faculty of Architecture, Building & Planning, University of Melbourne

Pharoah, T. (2003) 'Walking and cycling: What to promote where', in R. Tolley (ed.), *Sustainable transport: Planning for walking and cycling in urban environments*, Woodhead Publishing, Cambridge, pp358–374

Pius XI (Pope) (1931) *Quadragesimo Anno*, encyclical letter, www.vatican.va/holy_father/pius_xi/encyclicals/documents/hf_p-xi_enc_19310515_quadragesimo-anno_en.html, accessed April 2009

PWC (Public Works Committee) (1997a) *The South East Transit Project*, Report no. 39, Legislative Assembly of Queensland, Brisbane

PWC (1997b) *A Re-evaluation of the South East Transit Project*, Report no 42, Brisbane

Pucher, J. (1996) 'Verkehrsverbund: The success of regional public transport in Germany, Austria and Switzerland', *Transport Policy*, vol. 2, no. 4, pp279–291

Pucher, J. (2005) 'Cycling trends and policies in Canadian cities', *World Transport Policy & Practice*, vol. 11, no. 1, pp43–61

Queensland Government (1997) *Integrated Regional Transport Plan for SE Queensland*, Brisbane

Queensland Transport (2007) *Annual Report 2006–07*, Brisbane

RCEP (Royal Commission on Environmental Pollution) (1994) *Eighteenth Report: Transport and the Environment*, Cm 3572, HMSO, London

Remak, J. (1993) *A Very Civil War: the Swiss Sonderbund War of 1847*, Westview Press, Boulder, CO

Roth. G. and Wynne, G. (1982) *Free Enterprise Urban Transportation*, Transaction, New Brunswick, US

Rudlin, D. and Falk, N. (1999) *Building the 21st Century Home*, Architectural Press, Oxford

Schaeffer, K. and Sclar, E. (1975) *Access for All: Transportation and urban growth*, Penguin, Harmondsworth, Middlesex

Schepers, N. (2008) 'Downtown Transit Solution & Rapid Transit Network – Recommendations', report to Joint Transportation and Transit Committee, City of Ottawa, 15 April

Sclar, E. (2000) *You Don't Always Get What You Pay For: The economics of privatization*, Cornell University Press, Ithaca, NY

Scrafton, D. & Skene, P. (1998) 'On the right track: railway development in South Australia 1968 – 1998', *Papers of the Australasian Transport Research Forum*, vol 22, Part 1, pp259–275

Senft, G. (2005) 'U-Pass at the University of British Columbia: Lessons for Effective Demand Management in the Campus Context', *Proceedings of the 2005 Annual Conference of the Transportation Association of Canada* (CD-ROM)

Skidmore, T. (1993) *Black into White: Race and nationality in Brazilian thought* (1st edn, 1974), Duke University Press, Durham, NC

Slater. C. (1997) 'General Motors and the demise of streetcars', *Transportation Quarterly*, vol. 51, no. 3, pp45–66

Smerk, G. (ed.) (1968) *Readings in Urban Transportation*, Indiana University Press, Bloomington, IN

Smith, N. and D. Hensher (1998) 'The future of exclusive busways: The Brazilian experience', *Transport Reviews*, vol. 18, no. 2, pp131–152

Snell, B. (1974) *American Ground Transport*, Appendix to Part 4 of Committee on the Judiciary Hearings S. 1167, US Government Printing Office, Washington, DC

Soberman, R. (1997) *The Track Ahead: Organization of the TTC under the new amalgamated City of Toronto*, report for the TTC, Toronto

Soberman, R. (2002) '"Smart" transportation for sustainable development: A case study of Toronto', *Urban Public Transport 2002: 2nd International Conference*, ACSE, Alexandria, Virginia, pp385–401

Sorupia, E. (2007) 'Transport Networks and Ecotourism Destinations: The Aim for Sustainability', PhD thesis, Faculty of Architecture, Building & Planning, University of Melbourne

STA (State Transit Authority) (2001) *State Transit Annual Report 2000–2001*, STA, Sydney

Standing Committee on Planning and Urban Services, ACT (2001) *Proposals for the Gungahlin Drive Extension*, Report No. 67, Canberra

Stanley, R. (2003) *Emerging New Paradigms: A guide to fundamental change in local public transportation organizations*, TCRP Report 97, Transportation Research Board, Washington, DC

State of Victoria (2008) *The Victorian Transport Plan*, Department of Transport, Melbourne

Statistics Canada (2003) *Spending Patterns in Canada 2001*, Cat. 62-202-XIE, Statistics Canada, Ottawa

Statistics Canada (2006) *The Time it Takes to Get to Work and Back*, Cat. 89-622-XIE, Statistics Canada, Ottawa

Statistics Canada (2008a) *Community Profile 2006: Toronto (City)*. www12.statcan.gc.ca/census-recensement/2006/dp-pd/prof/92-591/details/page.cfm?Lang=E&Geo1=CSD&Code1=3520005&Geo2=PR&Code2=35&Data=Count&SearchText=toronto&SearchType=Begins&SearchPR=01&B1=All&Custom= (accessed 30 August 2009)

Statistics Canada (2008b) 'Place of Work Highlight Tables, 2006 Census', www.statcan. ca, accessed April 2009

Statistisches Amt des Kantons Zurich (2004) *Faltblatt Hauptergebnisse der Volkszählung 2000* – Zurich, Winterthur

Stern, N. (2007) *The Economics of Climate Change: The Stern Review*, Cambridge University Press, Cambridge

Stone, J. (2008) 'Political Factors in the Rebuilding of Mass Transit', PhD thesis, Institute for Social Research, Swinburne University, Melbourne

Stretton, H. (1975) *Ideas for Australian Cities* 2nd edn, Georgian House, Melbourne

Stretton, H. (1993) 'Transport and the structure of Australian cities', *Australian Planner*, vol. 31, no. 3, pp131–136

TfL (Transport for London) (2001) *Transport Statistics for London 2001*, TfL, London

TfL (2004) *Congestion Charging Central London: Impacts Monitoring, Second Annual Report*, TfL, London

TfL (2005) *Congestion Charging Central London: Impacts Monitoring, Third Annual Report*, TfL, London

Thompson. G. (1993) 'Planning beats the market: The case of Pacific Greyhound lines in the 1930s', *Journal of Planning Education and Research*, vol. 13, pp33–49

Thompson. G. and T. Matoff (2003) 'Keeping up with the Joneses: Radial vs. multidestinational transit in decentralizing regions', *Journal of the American Planning Association*, vol. 69, no. 3, pp296–312

Thomson, J. M. (1977) *Great Cities and Their Traffic*, Victor Gollancz, London

Toner, J. (2001) 'The London Bus Tendering Regime: Principles and Practice', Thredbo 7, International Conference on Competition and Ownership in Land Passenger Transport, Molde, Norway, 25–28 June, http://lodde.himolde.no/arrang/THREDBO7/ (accessed 30 August, 2009)

Townsend, C. (1998) 'Architects, exiles, "new" Australians', in *Firmness, Commodity and Delight: Proceedings of the 15th Conference of the Society of Architectural Historians in Australia and New Zealand*, SAHANZ, Melbourne, pp379–387

Translink (2004) *Transit Service Guidelines: Technical Report*, Translink, Vancouver

Translink (2005) *Vancouver/UBC Transit Plan*, Translink, Vancouver

Translink (2008) *The Road Less Travelled: Translink's Improbable Journey from 1999 to 2008*, Translink, Vancouver

Troy, P. (1996) *The Perils of Urban Consolidation*, Federation Press, Sydney

TTC (Toronto Transit Commission) (1990) *Service Standards Process*, TTC, Toronto

TTC (2008) *Service Summary, Nov. 23, 2008 to Jan. 3, 2009*, TTC, Toronto

TTS 2001 Transportation Tomorrow Survey Summary: City of Toronto. www.dmg. utoronto.ca/transportationtomorrowsurvey/index.html (accessed 30 August 2009)

Twain, M. (1899) *Following the Equator: A Journey Around the World*, (1st edn, 1897), Harper & Brothers, New York

Twopeny, R. (1973) *Town Life in Australia* (1st edn, 1883), Penguin, Melbourne

University of British Columbia (UBC) (2005) *2005 Strategic Transport Plan*, University of British Columbia, Vancouver

University of British Columbia (UBC) (2008) *Fall 2007 Transportation Status Report*, University of British Columbia, Vancouver

UN (United Nations) (1993) *Agenda 21: Programme of Action for Sustainable Development*, New York

US Census Bureau (2004) *Journey to Work: 2000*, Census 2000 Brief C2KBR-33, Washington, DC

Vehkehrsbetreibe Schaffhausen (2008) *Geschaftsbereicht [Annual Report] 2007*, Schaffhausen

Victoria (2002) *Melbourne 2030: Planning for Sustainable Growth*, State of Victoria, Melbourne

Victorian Government (2008) *Budget Paper C: Service Delivery 2008–09*, Melbourne

Vuchic, V. (1999) *Transportation for Livable Cities*, Rutgers, New Brunswick

Vuchic, V. (2005) *Urban Transit: Operations, planning and economics*, John Wiley & Sons, Hoboken, NJ

Vuchic, V. (2007) *Urban Transit: Systems and technology*, John Wiley & Sons, Hoboken, NJ

Wang, W. (2005) 'The Singapore Model and its Capacity to Promote Sustainable Transport', Urban Planning Honours Thesis, Faculty of Architecture, Building & Planning, University of Melbourne

Webster, F. and Bly, P. (1980) *The Demand for Public Transport*, Transport and Road Research Laboratory, Crowthorne, UK

West Yorkshire PTE (2002) *The West Yorkshire Bus Strategy 2006–2011*, Leeds

White, P. (1976) *Planning for Public Ttransport*, Hutchinson, London

White, P. (2002) *Public Transport: Its planning, management and operation*, 4th edn, Spon, London

White, P. (2008) *Factors Affecting the Decline of Bus Use in the Metropolitan Areas*, Project Report, University of Westminster, London

Whitelegg, J. (1993) *Transport for a Sustainable Future: The case for Europe*, Belhaven Press, London

Wilbur Smith & Associates (1970) *Summary of the SE Queensland–Brisbane Region Public Transport Study*, Department of Transport, Brisbane

Wolmar, C. (2005) *On the Wrong Line: How ideology and incompetence wrecked Britain's railways*, Aurum Press, London

World Bank (2002) *Cities on the Move: A World Bank urban transport strategy review*, World Bank, Washington, DC

Yago, G. (1984) *The Decline of Transit: Urban transportation in German and U.S. cities, 1900–1970*, Cambridge University Press, Cambridge

Yam, A. (2008) 'Shaping urban journeys', in A. Tan et al (eds), *Journeys: Sharing urban transport solutions*, LTA Academy, Singapore, pp5–14

ZVV (Zürcher Verkehrsverbund) (2006) *The ZVV: A portrait*, ZVV, Zurich

ZVV (2008a) *Mehr Passagiere, mehr Kapazität: Geschäftsbericht 2007* [Annual Report 2007], ZVV, Zurich

ZVV (2008b) *Strategie 2011–2014*, ZVV, Zurich

Index